STREET FIGHT IN NAPLES

PETER ROBB's first book, *Midnight in Sicily* (1996), was an international bestseller. It won the Victorian Premier's Prize for Non-fiction in 1997. His book *M* (1998), about the painter Michelangelo Merisi from Caravaggio, won the same prize, and the National Biography Award, two years later. It was a bestseller in the US and a *New York Times* Notable Book for 2000. *A Death in Brazil* (2003) was the *Age* Non-fiction Book of the Year and won the Queensland Premier's Award for Non-fiction in 2004. Peter Robb has also published a book of pulp novellas called *Pig's Blood and Other Fluids* (1999), which won nothing.

STREET FIGHT IN NAPLES
PETER ROBB

A CITY'S UNSEEN HISTORY

B L O O M S B U R Y

LONDON • NEW DELHI • NEW YORK • SYDNEY

First published in Great Britain 2011
This paperback edition published 2012

Copyright © 2010 by Peter Robb

First published in 2010 in Australia by Allen & Unwin,
83 Alexander Street, Crows Nest NSW 2065, Australia

The moral right of the author has been asserted

Bloomsbury Publishing Plc
50 Bedford Square
London WC1B 3DP

www.bloomsbury.com

Bloomsbury is a trademark of Bloomsbury Publishing Plc

Bloomsbury Publishing, London, New Delhi, New York and Sydney

A CIP catalogue record for this book is available from the British Library

ISBN 978 1 4088 2232 6

10 9 8 7 6 5

Printed in Great Britain by CPI Group (UK) Ltd, Croydon CR0 4YY

IM

FRANCO BELGIORNO-NETTIS

PUER APULIAE

MENDICUS EXUL IN DEVERSORIO GRAECAE URBIS
IACEREM DESERTUS

Vvuie che facite
'Mmiezz' a la via?

Contents

Illustrations

MARKET MAN

Aniello Falcone, *Portrait of Masaniello: Ritratto di Masaniello*, circa 1647. 22.5cm × 17cm. New York, Pierpont Morgan Library. Image Graham Haber 2010.

VISITORS

Giovan Battista Caracciolo: Battistello, *Earthly Trinity: Trinità terrestre*, 1617. Naples, Pietà dei Turchini. 340cm × 250cm. Image Luciano Pedicini.

DAUGHTERS

Giovan Battista Caracciolo: Battistello, *Lot and His Daughters: Lot e le figlie*, 1625. 125cm × 184cm. Urbino, Galleria Nazionale delle Marche. Image Electa.

PARENTS

Bartolomeo Passante, *Prodigal Son's Return: Ritorno del figluol prodigo*, circa 1645. 100cm × 126cm. Naples, Capodimonte. Image Luciano Pedicini.

DROVERS

Bartolomeo Passante, *Announcement to the Shepherds: Annuncio ai pastori*, circa 1645. 180cm × 261.5cm. Naples, Capodimonte. Image Luciano Pedicini.

Preface

I owe too many people in Naples too many things, and over too long a time, to feel easy about making formal acknowledgements. Sometimes the names themselves have receded from mind over more than thirty years, unlike faces, voices, ways of being. The book itself is the residue of a passion. It took a long time to write—an even longer time to start—and nearly didn't get written at all, from out of an accumulated mass of thoughts and memories. The journey from desire to a very partial fulfilment changed direction more than once.

Anyone looking—however casually—into the long, long past of Naples owes incommensurably much to the historians, archivists and chroniclers who over the years and the millennia have set it down. Nearly all of them are Neapolitans themselves and their work is informed by a shared love of place. From the happily living—I'm thinking of Francesco Barbagallo, Carlo De Frede, Romeo De Maio, Antonio Ghirelli and Aurelio Musi among many—constellated around the great opposed figures of Giuseppe Galasso and Rosario Villari—and Ferdinando Bologna if we add a third from art history—the names go back in time over the last hundred years or so from Coniglio and Doria to Schipa, Spampanato, Capasso and the overbearing and lovable Benedetto Croce, who was never more happily himself than when laying out new findings from the archives of Naples.

Beyond these the list goes back forever, past the great writers of the Neapolitan enlightenment, past the chroniclers of the seventeenth century's upheavals, past Camillo Porzio and the unknown author of the *Chronicle of Parthenope*, back to Tacitus and Suetonius and Strabo and ultimately to Homer. Many years ago I was honoured to translate a paper for Giuseppe Galasso to be delivered at the Castel dell'Ovo: it was a miniature history of Naples *ab ovo* for the use of outsiders and maybe it planted the seed for the present production.

The ancillary figures to this reading are the booksellers of Naples, new, used and antiquarian, too vastly numerous and variously helpful over the decades to be summoned in parade now. They are booksellers who would share their coffee with an unknown client buying nothing, or hand the unknown client a rare edition on trust, with directions to a bookseller friend several streets away who knew how to handle payment by credit card. Two names stand here for the innumerable, Tullio Pironti and Rosario Würzburger, whom I also thank for gifts. Tullio's was his own memoirs of life as a champion boxer and publisher, Rosario's a rare pamphlet on Tommaso Campanella's revolution in Calabria.

Some way through work on this book I found in amazement and delight that all the extant entries in the *Dizionario Biografico degli Italiani*, now after fifty years at its seventy-third volume and a good halfway through the alphabet, are now freely accessible online at www.treccani.it, an extraordinary gift from the publisher to anyone with an interest in the Italian past. For this reason, some of the notes on *Dizionario* sources give only the website and not an entry's individual volume reference. The purpose of these and other notes at the end of an unacademic and eclectic book is to give minimally the sources of the phrases and passages I've quoted—with a few gaps—and the locations of the paintings mentioned—and occasionally, where it wasn't obvious in the text, the translation of a word or phrase. Unattributed translations in the book are my own.

In Australia the friends of the Kings Cross Library have over a long time been unfailingly courteous and helpful, even and especially when I didn't deserve it. From their unlikely present location on the main drag between Striperama (*sic*) and the heroin injecting room and directly across from the adult lingerie showroom, whose wares are viewable on lifesize models from the children's section on the first floor, they have retrieved books and articles from the collections of libraries all over Australia. Once they invited me to a champagne party. Others who have helped with getting and preserving words and putting my own into material form are Tricia Dearborn, Clara Finlay, Jane Palfreyman, Andrea Rejante, Jaclyn Richardson and Roberta Trapè and I thank all of them.

Art history is a more recent practice than life history. The writings of Neapolitan art scholars over the last few decades have driven that larger rediscovery of the extraordinary images painted in Naples in the first half of the seventeenth century. It was a flowering that began when Michelangelo Merisi from Caravaggio arrived in Naples in 1606 for two short and transforming stays. The incomparable Roberto Longhi, who brought Merisi's work to modern attention, was also the scholar and critic who first revealed the marvellous work of Merisi's contemporaries and followers that was still mostly hidden in the dim churches, dusty little museums and crumbling homes of Naples.

Among those now in Naples writing on art, I've had pleasure and instruction from conversations with Vincenzo Pacelli, Renato Ruotolo and Nicola Spinosa. Their writings, along with those of Ferdinando Bologna, the late Raffaello Causa and Stefano Causa—and from an earlier time Ulisse Prota-Giurleo's—and studies by Jonathan Brown, James Clifton, Brigitte Daprà, Giuseppe De Vito, Gabriele Finaldi, Mary D. Garrard, Pierluigi Leone de Castris, Christopher Marshall, Alfonso E. Pérez Sánchez, Wolfgang Prohaska, John Spike, Michael Stoughton and Thomas Willette have always shed light, though seeing what follows, these authors might wonder. Mina Gregori and the late

Francis Haskell gave time to conversation some years ago and I'm grateful to them. Everyone must be grateful to Raffaello Causa and Nicola Spinosa for making Capodimonte in Naples one of the great art galleries in Italy, in Europe and the world.

Percy Allum, Francesco Barbagallo and Michelangelo Cocco shared some bleak and hard-won insights into the way things are evolving now in Naples. So did Raffaele Morino and Franco Roberti of the Procura di Napoli. And I wish I could have had more than a couple of short telephone conversations with Roberto Saviano before he was blasted by fame.

I have a very specific acknowledgement to make to John Spike. His article 'The Case of the Master' conceals under its Jamesian title a succinct resolution of the uncertainties about the identity of the great Neapolitan painter who represents the culmination of what follows in this book. John Spike's article on Bartolomeo Passante seems to me—an art-historical outsider who can nevertheless recognize a tightly argued case—to be definitive until any new discoveries are made in the archives. It was published nearly twenty years ago and remains unanswerable, though as its author has remarked more recently, *academic debates, once entrenched, often take on a life of their own.* I'm very grateful to him for sending me a copy.

A book that circles the objects of its attention rather than heading directly toward a conclusion is going to exasperate a lot of readers. I hope to persuade mine that time in Naples is not linear, that the past is more present in Naples than in other cities, that some things in Naples have been happening for thousands of years and that only by indirection can you arrive at their connexions. For moments of greater confusion the chronology at the end of the book lays out some of the events mentioned in the order in which they happened.

For splendid hospitality on my last visit to Naples I thank Maria Teresa Chialant, Maria Rosaria Cocco and Ovidio Butti, Francesco and Oletta Lauro and Vincenzo and Paola Pacelli, these last especially for the several local varieties of *mozzarella di bufala*. For several decades of nourishment I thank Mario Silvestri, a child of Ponza in the sea beyond the bay, who grew up among the political opponents of Mussolini confined on that island and is now paterfamilias in Amalfi. Over the greater part of half a century Mario has provided—among much else—a *pignatta maritata* I'm sure as good as any made in Naples four hundred years ago. I have known him as long as I've known anyone in Naples—first flanked by Michele and Ciro and Natale and Gennaro in the times of don Antonio Casillo's now-vanished Dante e Beatrice, and now a few meters away among a more refractory clientèle al 53—and he's always the first friend I see when I return.

From a long time ago, and always remembered with intense feeling, is the kindness of the grand old man of the sea Pippo Dalla Vecchia and his late wife Anna Maria, of his sisters Adriana Dotoli and her husband Mario and Rosetta Nitti and her husband Francesco. And of Luigi and Teresa De Prisco. And of the late Giusto Barbini. More recent, and on another side of the world, is the hospitality of Dick and Maggie Denton at Pittaedie, looking out at the Pacific and down on a small curve of sand, a rocky promontory breaking the surf and a hillside of fragrant bird-filled Australian bush. Sometimes a boat at anchor below reminds me of the *Canopus*.

Peter Robb

I

Canopus

A light breeze. The gayest street. From the bay. Up the
Mulberries. A small revolution in Calabria

A light breeze

A brisk wind in the gulf of Salerno came out of a summer
morning and wrenched the helm under my grip. We had left
the coast and cut across the wide concavity of water on the
homeward run. Being asked to take the helm was a small sign
of confidence from the owner and master of the *Canopus*. It
had taken more than a week to earn this, and even now the
master hovered and grabbed the wheel if I deviated from
the course he had set. He was an old racer of yachts and a
perfectionist for whom sailing was about precision and control.
The canvas was taut, the boat inclined and each new surge of
the sea put new pressure on the wheel. Undeviating steadiness

meant a constant tussle under the sun-reddened glare of the master, thinking ahead of the wind and the waves, braced for the coming surge and ready to relax again as it passed.

Our yacht was compact outside and roomy below deck. She was fast, sprightly, wonderfully manoeuvrable. It was the summer of 1979 and the *Canopus* might easily have taken several people around the world under sail in comfort and safety. She had taken us no further than some way south from her home berth in Naples, down along the coast of Calabria with a ragged escort, in boating terms, of a couple of converted fishing boats.

Before this cut across the gulf we had stayed close enough to the shore to connect the pale stone dots of the *Saracen towers* strung along the cliffs and promontories of Campania and Calabria. Resting a couple of fingers on the wheel, the master held forth on the coastal people who had manned the towers hundreds of summers before. These were summers when Islam's raiders from Turkey and North Africa would hit the little beaches in lightning raids on Christendom. The eyes in the towers watched to warn their people in the villages down at the sea's edge when to take to the steep hills behind them. Landing parties burnt houses, slaughtered men, women and animals, carried off the younger and fitter to slavery. To be *grabbed by the Turks* was to be taken utterly and horribly by surprise. In the coastal South of Italy the phrase still awakens a distant tremor of fear.

The towers were hard to see from land. Only from the sea below could you see how they were linked along the coast as an integrated line of defence. They were solid, purpose-built, irregular, tapering, almost windowless and when the threat receded they were not much good for anything else than temporary shelter or farm storage. They were mostly abandoned now. After four centuries of winter storms and earthquakes they were slowly reverting to nature as piles of whitish local stone on the stony cliffs. Even in the days of the long war they crumbled fast and needed constant rebuilding.

Muslim corsairs had been raiding the coasts of Christendom for a long time. Everyone on the Mediterranean went in for a little opportunistic privateering, as Islam pushed into Sicily and Spain, and Christianity pushed back. There had been a deal of mingling among the peoples of the Mediterranean, and its Christian, Islamic and Jewish cultures were nothing if not porous. It was in the sixteenth century that things changed for everyone, including the people of Naples. Islam was bleeding the Catholic Mediterranean. Young men snatched from Italy's South found a chance in the more open Ottoman society. They took Turkish names and a few renegades became Islam's fiercest raiders on Christendom.

The master relieved me of command and brought the *Canopus* in closer to the shore. We passed Amalfi and Positano, running close to shore below the high ribbon road and the terraced lemon groves and cascades of purple bougainvillea. We rounded Punto Campanella at the final extremity of the Sorrento peninsula. We entered a rather smaller concavity whose coast now swept in an unbroken swoosh from the edge of the water to the looming grey cone of Vesuvius. We were in the bay of Naples.

Ancient Roman Naples had been a privileged and lazily loyal enclave of Greekness and the arts of living. When Rome at last fell, the unfortunate youth who had been its last western

3

emperor was dispatched to die in Naples at the end of the fifth century. As the cynosure of the Mediterranean, strategic, beautiful and rich, Naples was then fought over interminably by Goths and Byzantines, by Lombards and Saracens and later challenged by the upstart maritime republic of Amalfi. For five hundred years of the middle ages the city state of Naples mustered enough purposeful autonomy to flourish on sea trade and good governance as an independent power in the Mediterranean. Five hundred years was a long time, but for Naples it was a parenthesis and an anomaly.

The free dukedom of Naples was overtaken in the end by the region's larger powers, first drawn into the Norman kingdom of Sicily, and thence into the Swabian empire of the Hohenstaufen Frederick II. Frederick died in 1250 and the end of his line soon followed. The western French from Anjou, after the ugly episode of the Sicilian vespers, made Naples, not Palermo, the capital of the southern kingdom. In the fourteenth century, Angevin Naples was an enormous and cosmopolitan medieval city of nearly fifty thousand people, the city of Giotto and Simone Martini, of Boccaccio and Petrarch, and even at the time it seemed marvellous.

Fifteenth century Naples remained the metropolis of southern Italy and the middle Mediterranean. The huge castles and the great churches built in Naples by the Aragonese and the Angevins before them rise over the detritus of the city today like relics from an age of giants. *Don Ferrante*, or Ferdinand I, bastard son of the first Aragonese king of Naples and his father's successor, was a wholly assimilated Neapolitan and something of a portent. He was a major figure in the Italian politics of the later fifteenth century and his *Realpolitik* was much admired by Machiavelli. His sculpted likenesses, thickening and coarsening over the years, showed the beady intelligent eyes, the sensual and stubborn little mouth, the full cheeks and the thick neck of a recognizably modern southern Italian power broker.

When Ferrante died in 1494 the mesh of Aragonese power in Naples and Italy unravelled overnight. The great power rivalry of France and Spain for control of Naples—and so of the central Mediterranean—was already in place and would continue for hundreds of years. Now France wanted the Angevins back in power and in the summer of 1495 French armies invaded Italy.

Ferrante's eldest son and successor Alfonso, a brutally successful army man in his father's service, broke down under pressure as king. Tormented by bad dreams, he abdicated in favour of his own son *Little Ferrante*, retired to a Sicilian monastery and died within months. The feudal landowners of the South were already defecting to the French. People in Naples, sensing the power shift, remembered they had liked the Angevins of France. Ferrantino and his family retreated to the island of Ischia in the bay as Charles VIII of France rode into Naples at the head of his troops. The people were ecstatic. Neapolitans were good at welcoming foreign armies. Autonomy was long forgotten. They had been dealing with dominant outsiders for the last four hundred years.

The French armies, uninhibited looters and fuckers, had *the French disease*. The French called it the Neapolitan disease. Things turned ugly fast. The other Italian states joined forces against the French invaders and after three months in Naples Charles prudently returned to France. Ferrantino received a delirious welcome home. Normality returned. Ferrantino married his teenage aunt and the newlyweds were enjoying the cooler air on the slopes of Vesuvius in summer when the young king abruptly sickened. A few days later he was dead at twenty-eight and chaos was come again.

France and Spain signed a secret agreement in 1500 to carve up southern Italy between them. Naples would go to France. The pact broke down and France and Spain were fighting again in Italy. The Turks, having lately helped drive out the French, landed in the South and looked like taking Naples for themselves. The Neapolitans, open as ever to interesting proposals, saw Turkish rule as one of their options. People said *they serve the master of the moment, sighing for the one just gone and waiting for the one to come.*

A major Islamic enclave close to home on the European mainland was unthinkable to Spain. A short sharp autumn campaign ended when Spanish infantry with pikes defeated French cavalry at the Garigliano River between Rome and Naples. At the end of 1503 Gonzalo Fernández de Córdoba rode into Naples and secured, for the present, Spanish interests in the Mediterranean. The Spanish army was met in the streets with wild applause and flowers. *Those people were a kind of solution.*

Not the solution Naples imagined for itself. Neapolitans had no idea how long *those people* were going to stay. Two hundred years later they were still there. Naples realized too late the cost of joining an empire. The earlier kings of Naples, French or Spanish, had been foreigners who became Neapolitan and identified their interests with those of the place they lived in. Now the kingdom was a *vicerealm* and Naples a vassal city governed by a viceroy taking orders from Madrid.

Neither the barefoot crowds nor the plumed nobility on their best mounts imagined, at the end of 1503, that they would be seen from Madrid as a military staging post, a source of revenue and manpower to fight Spain's foreign wars. Spain had locked Naples into a global empire which soon showed signs of being seriously overstretched.

The sixteenth was the century of the sea war between Islam and Catholic Christendom for control of the Mediterranean. The white stone towers we saw from the *Canopus* were reminders that in those years southern Italy and Sicily—not for the first time in their history or the last—were the theatre of a major power conflict. They were the Spanish homeland's bulwark in the middle Mediterranean against the naval threat from an Ottoman empire that was reaching its apogee just as Spain's lurched into bankruptcy.

The bulwark badly needed shoring up and the Spanish worked hard and fast to fortify a long and vulnerable coastline. In Sicily they began building along the specially vulnerable southern and eastern coasts in the fifteen thirties and soon they had a chain of nearly a hundred and fifty watchtowers. In 1567, along the coasts of Campania, Calabria and Apulia, they built more than three hundred towers in a single year. The republic of Genoa and papal Rome joined Spain in assembling rapid deployment forces able to respond fast to signals from the towers, marines who moved fast by water from one exposed place on the coast to another. Islamic corsairs pouncing on a coastal settlement sometimes found the Christian galleys waiting.

Not everyone shared Spain's intransigence about Islam, not to mention its intolerance of the Jews, Moors, heretics and sexual irregulars who were progressively driven from a homeland obsessed with purity on all fronts. The front against Islam in the Mediterranean was never united. The most serene republic of Venice pursued its own agenda of trade relations with the Islamic nations and was a very desultory participant in the crusades whipped up in Rome and Madrid. France, tussling with Spain for power in Europe, often found it convenient to side with the Ottoman empire. The Ottomans had their own problems: enemies on their eastern borders, setbacks in their overland push into Europe through Hungary, Austria and the Balkans, and endless trouble with North Africa's Islamic rulers, who sided with Christian Spain and Malta whenever it served their interests. Republican Genoa was loyal to Madrid only because it was Spain's banker, the channel through which the gold and silver of the Americas passed, and republican Venice's rival.

The coasts of southern Italy took a great battering from Islam after the Spanish occupied Naples in 1503. The Barbarossa brothers, who began their working lives as seamen in the Aegean islands and finished in command of the Ottoman fleet, entered the major phase of their fearsome careers in 1504, when they took a Sicilian warship and the four hundred Spanish knights and soldiers it was carrying from Spain to Naples. In the next ten years they raided the coasts of Calabria, Sicily and Sardinia again and again, made incursions into Spain itself and its islands, and attacked the coastal towns of Liguria and Provence.

•

The Sorrento ridge asserts itself once again just off the mainland point, and rounding Punto Campanella the *Canopus* cut inside a last fierce rocky peak jutting from the water. This was the island of Capri. Its sheer stone cliffs and its miniscule landing places did not save Capri from Hayreddin Barbarossa, last and most formidable of the brothers, who was admiral of the Ottoman fleet in the Mediterranean and viceroy in Algiers when he took Capri in 1534 and destroyed its castle. The Capresi had been living with attacks like this for a long time. It was the Islamic raids of the tenth century that forced the islanders to move their main town from the little beachfront to a citadel high above and build the defensive network of narrow roads and ramparts that defined Capri's infrastructure ever after.

Barbarossa went on to sack the island of Procida and bombard the port towns in the bay of Naples. Then he headed up the coast and when he landed at Ostia on the mouth of the Tiber the church bells in Rome rang the alarm. He was back in full violence on Capri the next summer and nine years later, on the verge of retirement, he returned to raid the coast of Campania and threaten Rome again. In his swan song raids the following summer he seized towns on Ischia, threatened the port of Pozzuoli and made landings all down the coast to Sicily. The next year Barbarossa retired to Istanbul where he dictated five volumes of memoirs and died in sight of the Bosphorus.

We sailed past the little town of Massa Lubrense, and the master passed me his binoculars so I could pick out the white cube of his summer house among a cluster on the hillside above the jetty and the fishing boats. Everything was still and silent, shimmering in the summer heat. The occasional dot moved across the still water, leaving a thin wake which spread and vanished from the hazy surface. A hand reached up some cold beers from the galley and the master tossed me a can.

Summertime was wartime in those days. In winter the Islamic and the Christian navies retired to their arsenals to repair and rebuild their fleets for the next season. The sea closed down to galleys in winter. The battle for the Mediterranean was fought at sea, not on land, and the ships themselves were a major part of the prize. Whoever controlled the sea controlled communications and transport, controlled the Mediterranean economy.

Barbarossa's death brought no relief to the southern Italians. Dragut followed, a peasant farmer's son who had joined Barbarossa in 1520. By the thirties he was a veteran of innumerable raids on Spanish Naples and Sicily, and had won battles against the papal and Venetian fleets. In 1540 he terrorized the Spanish Mediterranean, raiding the coasts of Malta, Sicily and Spain with a fleet of over eighty galleys. Surprised off Corsica while repairing his ships, he was captured by the Genoese and freed from slavery four years later when the Turkish ships blockaded Genoa. In 1547 he sacked Malta and raided Sicily, Apulia, Calabria.

The next summer Dragut took Castellammare di Stabia, the port town below Vesuvius a little ahead of us along the coast the *Canopus* was cruising. Then he took Pozzuoli and seized a Spanish galley and a Maltese galley in the bay right outside Naples. Both ships were carrying troops and the Maltese galley was loaded with gold, seventy thousand ducats in funds raised in France by the knights of Malta for the war effort against Islam. In the summer of 1552 Dragut took both Sorrento and Massa Lubrense. His depredations gave the Islamic forces control of most of the coast between Naples and Rome. Forty galleys under Andrea Doria sailed south from Genoa to counterattack. In the first clash off Naples Dragut captured seven galleys and their German troops and in August he defeated Andrea Doria's forces off the island of Ponza. Dragut became the Ottoman viceroy of the Mediterranean Sea.

The following spring he was back in the bay after making deep and devastating incursions into Calabria and Sicily. He landed on Capri and burnt its church and convent. Five years later he sacked Reggio Calabria, landed at Amalfi and Torre del Greco, took Sorrento and Massa. And in the high summer of 1561 he blockaded Naples itself with thirty-five galleys. A couple of summers later he took half a dozen ships off Capri, all loaded with Spanish troops and merchandise, and went on to land at Chiaia, the fishing community outside Naples's defensive wall. These were a small part of his activities in the Mediterranean.

Four years later Dragut was dead, killed by cannon fire during the long siege of Malta. And at the end of the summer of 1571 the massed Islamic fleet was smashed by the Christian navies at Lepanto. Within a year Turkey had rearmed, but almost imperceptibly the Ottoman naval threat receded. As it did, Spain found itself facing even worse trouble on land.

We were gliding due north now, through a pearly and viscid summer twilight to the boat harbour at Santa Lucia, following the drift of Parthenope, whose siren song had failed to lure Odysseus on to the fatal rocks and whose drowned corpse had floated from the deep water off Capri until it washed ashore in the little hook in the coastline that was now Santa Lucia. The water, with its white plastic bags floating just below the surface like jellyfish, seemed inert and gelatinous, but there were hidden currents in the bay which could change it from foul to limpid overnight, from warm and fecal to a kind of deep upwelling freshness that reminded you how deep and nearly inexhaustible the little Mediterranean still was.

The gayest street

Walking one day in Naples and not long in the city, I found myself at a crossroads. There were two streets going steeply uphill and two heading down. I chose downhill and headed down an urban ravine, narrow enough and bent enough never to quite show where it was headed. At one point it opened out on the left on to a semicircular space noisily crowded with people, a statue in the middle and an elegantly curved red and grey façade at its back. Below the handsome piazza the canyon narrowed again then widened a few yards further downhill.

A monument, cars parked everywhere, kiosks festooned with lemons or newspapers or boiled lungs and tripes, several bars and icecream shops, oddly angled roads, narrow, dark, dirty and uphill on the right, newer, wider, cleaner and downhill on the left. People everywhere, moving randomly as they licked dripping cones, or picking over the little stalls manned by women in black selling indeterminate small objects. Boys perched on the saddles of parked Vespas, older women in shawls sitting behind cardboard cartons or small folding tables on which lay several neatly aligned packets of American cigarettes. Pairs of older men in cashmere jackets, deep in solemn conversation, pulling on dark narrow cheroots and making their way serenely through the tangle of people and debris.

A man with a sun-blackened face squatted by a basket of bright green figs holding a small set of scales, the brass weights rubbed and gleaming from use. Diagonally opposite a cluster of meditative youths stood at the edge of the roadway. They were mostly silent and looking hard at something indefinable or else not looking at anything at all. A Vespa would roar up to a knot of these standers-around for a brief, urgent conversation. Everyone in this slowly seething crowd seemed wearily familiar with everyone else. To walk into that space on that morning at the end of a long summer was to be caught in its frantic dreamlike lethargy. The scene was rich and strange in the dusty air. It was late morning by now, hot and getting sticky.

The elaborate indolence of this place abruptly broke up into hoarsely shouted obscenities and a fight over stall space. Two of the women in black mourning dresses, each built like a sumo wrestler, were punching and kicking, yanking out hanks of hair, hennaed and glossy black, and rolling in the dirt. If this had been a confrontation of men, there would have been two allies holding each arm, much ferocious theatre and no body contact. But these were women, and trying to do serious injury.

This was Piazza Carità and a lulling calm above the rapids. Below it, down into the dark-walled canyon, a tide of channelled bodies swept on past great banks housed in art nouveau or art deco and intersected once or twice by a sliver of cobalt sea. The sleek grey Fascist granite of the *Banco di Napoli 1539–1939* went on forever. An older and more resistant Naples loomed almost out of sight. Dark and narrow alleys ran steeply uphill on the right, obscured by swags of laundry, little cracks bleeding into the human torrent, almost unnoticeable though the openings were marked by watchful figures, each standing over three packs of cigarettes—Marlboro, Camel and the local killer MS—on an upended box. On the left past the banks was a huge and echoing birdcage whose marble floor and high-vaulted steel-ribbed glass roof hundreds of feet above made the scurrying and stationary figures look like tiny wind-up automata. A shoeshine throne and more cigarettes and elderly men in conversation clustered at the opening.

A few yards more and the torrent debouched into a silent sunny space filled with cars and orange buses, a couple of equestrian bronze statues rising above them. A low semi-circular colonnade enclosed the buses under a promontory's steep ridge of yellow and red buildings. The descent was walled on the left by the red and grey façade of a vast palace, with giant imperial statues set into niches. Beyond it a smear of grass, some palm trees, the emperor Augustus in bronze, arm raised toward Africa—another Fascist touch—a shore that swept to the hazy purple hump of Vesuvius, Capri jutting from the sea like a distant thorn as the road dropped to a foul and glittering sea.

Later I descended Toledo—which was the street's name—at all hours, in all seasons, in all weathers and this arrival, spilling out of the urban hive on to the open spread of the Mediterranean, never failed to take my breath away. Toledo ran down a vanished river's course to the sea with the gathered rush of its tributaries, narrow, deep, precipitous, irresistible, the only course to follow on your way down to the bay.

In its day the street changed the look of Naples and the dynamic of the city's life. Via Toledo began in the sixteenth century not as a force of human gravity but as part of an imperial planner's military scheme. It was built and named after himself by the viceroy Pedro de Toledo in 1536, charged by Madrid with bringing Naples up to scratch as Spain's Mediterranean power base. Toledo conceived it as a link in his enlarged and strengthened system of city defence. It let troops move swiftly between the Castel Sant'Elmo on the hill and the Castelnuovo down by the water. The splendid and scary Sant'Elmo fortress loomed over the city, visible from its every part and never out of mind. On the sea front stood the Castelnuovo, massive, buttressed, turretted, moated, symmetrical, and a mile away, thrust out over the water, the seriously military brutalism of the Castel dell'Ovo flanked it in readiness to repel navies, garrison troops and incarcerate enemies of the state. The Castel Capuano by the city's eastern gate had once housed the rulers of Naples, but after the Angevins built their *new castle* in the fourteenth century it housed the law courts and the common prison. The four castles defined the image of power in Naples.

Via Toledo was also for show. Spain had found its new Mediterranean capital a very rundown city whose whole infrastructure badly needed making over. It was desperately crowded. Water supply, sewerage, traffic flow, housing were no longer adequate to the pressures of daily use. Naples could no longer accommodate its own inhabitants, let alone represent

Spanish power in the Mediterranean. The considerations were more than practical, and from a higher point of view the glories of nature were not enough. Spanish imperial magnificence required a man-made pomp and a political scenography which only buildings of great size and splendour and roads and piazzas could provide. Ottoman Istanbul was a formidable rival. In that sense Toledo's road led not to the sea or the waterfront forts but to the royal palace. The sea was a scenic extra.

Toledo was teeming and deafening from the word go, the place where you saw and were seen in Naples for the next four hundred years. For Stendhal arriving in 1817 it was an incomparable delight, *the most crowded and the gayest street in the universe*. For the occupying Allied armies in 1943, Toledo was where, under a birdcage dome bombed glassless, the starving people of Naples got to know their most recent foreign armies of occupation. Some of the new invaders were the sons of the belle epoque's hungry emigrants, and now they heard *the patter of sandals, the click of hobnails, the squunch of children's bare soles as they begged, pimped, screamed, tugged, cried and offered.*

In the seventies Toledo at the end of summer was busy all day. Toward the end of the afternoon and on until well after dark its pedestrian movement might have made you think a football stadium was emptying around the corner. The crowd thinned out after eight, when people withdrew to eat, and surged back later as a leisurely and almost stately foot traffic that kept up until after midnight, as people of all ages sauntered home, licked gelati, bought contraband cigarettes, conferred intensely. The great gallery, thunderous with trafficking at dusk, began to echo emptily as night deepened. Piazza Carità at the top of the run was busy with idleness more or less around the clock.

Hot fuggy nights at summer's end and people never off the streets. Around the castle Vespas and baby Fiats swirled in the dark. You could see the haze of vapour like dandelion heads around the street lights. Knots of people and others strolling singly ranged the steep lawns and the terraces planted with rows of oleanders. On the grass by the bus stop they bought nuts or nougat or cold crescents of coconut or paper cones of pumpkin seeds from an emaciated seller with a thin moustache and a face like polished wood, who had laid out his treats alongside beer and soft drinks in tubs of melting ice.

These pleasures were for people on foot, or boys on a Vespa. Cars would pull up by a lighted bar for gelati, iced coffees, iced teas, *amari*. From the sloping lawns and the oleander terraces around the castle you didn't need a car or a scooter to reach Piazza Vittoria, Piazza San Ferdinando, the Litoranea—a tiny garden on an inlet of the sea between the old customs house and the wall below the royal palace—and Santa Lucia. Santa Lucia and its waterfront and the packed warren behind it were their own maritime territory, distinct and apart. Beyond, the gardens of the Villa Comunale were announced by mythological nudes from the eighteenth century. They enclosed an elegant wrought-iron band rotunda and the marine research station and stretched along the bay toward Mergellina and Posillipo. During the day children of the bourgeoisie bought balloons, rode miniature trains and played there on the gravel under supervision, and at night husbands rented out their wives.

In the daytime couples posed against the castle walls for wedding photographs, the bridal image's clouds of vaporous white tulle framed by stone battlements and merging into the hazy blue outline of a dormant Vesuvius floating in the distance. Then the darkest early hours of a Sunday morning were broken by what sounded like a rifle shot in the next room. Or the crack of doom. From the creaking hollow of a decrepit double bed I saw the doors of the ancient wardrobe swing open in the dark. A faint drumming began and quickly got harder. It was the first patter of a deluge that seeped into the room as palpable dampness. Rain permeated the worn sheets and raised a smell of ancient straw from the thin mattress. The wire mesh grated with new rust. The greyness lightened after a while and the drumming slowed to ordinary rain and then to a drizzle, and by the time daylight asserted itself through the clouds it had more or less stopped.

The water on the ground hadn't. The narrow downhill alleys were cascading into Toledo like waterfalls and Toledo itself was a raging filthy torrent, wooden fruit boxes and old suitcases and newspapers and broken umbrellas bouncing down it to the sea. Later in the day the weather cleared a bit, the river subsided and finally drained off altogether and Monday was fine. But it never got hot again and the staleness was gone. The streets emptied of sun-darkened faces at night and the few you encountered were white masks staring out of the darkness. As autumn cooled into winter, the nocturnal movement diminished further, but Toledo toward the end of the day always swelled into a human torrent that never dwindled until long after nightfall.

From the bay

In his family home on the hill overlooking the bay, from whose terrace the photographers from *Life* had shot the last eruption of Vesuvius in 1944, the master had several paintings by *Monsù Desiderio*. One of them showed the bay and the city imagined from the sky over the sea rather than seen from the hillside over the bay. As if seen by a high-flying bird or from an early seventeenth century aircraft.

I hadn't heard of Monsù Desiderio or seen anything like these weird black and gold gothic registerings, at once exquisitely precise and eerily unreal. Monsù Desiderio turned out to have been two people, both Frenchmen from Metz and almost exactly the same age. One had come south to Naples in the first years of the seventeenth century when he was hardly more than a boy. The other, summoned by letter or lured by curiosity and wanting to know what his younger friend was up to, followed a couple of years later. Each worked on his own and sometimes, as a topographical specialist, contributed background to another painter's work. They also worked together from time to time, and given their common nationality, age and home town and their shared expertise in the vast and minute, it was hardly surprising that after their deaths art world memories in Naples grew a little vague and that the two melded for three hundred years into a single Frenchman called Monsù Desiderio.

The elder by two years was Didier Barra, an innkeeper's son who was born in 1590 or soon after and left home in his teens. He was gone from Metz by 1608. He was drawn to vast views, which he kept sober and exact by drawing on the rapidly evolving skills of mapmakers. The younger friend, who came to Italy first, when he must have been fifteen or less, was François de Nomé. He had Didier's fascination with detail but a wilder mind that was drawn to the architectonic. The tiny human figures who peopled de Nomé's hallucinatory constructions at street level were usually done by someone else. He painted a lot of fantastical imaginary buildings of great complexity and must have seen Bruegel's *Tower of Babel* as a child. As a man he saw the Palazzo Donn'Anna on the rocks at Posillipo, commissioned from Cosimo Fanzago by the viceroy Medina for his Neapolitan wife Anna Carafa. When the viceroy was abruptly recalled in 1644, the palace was abandoned unfinished, a great spectral comb rising out of the water and open to the sky, the sea washing into its courtyard. It was no wonder both painters were drawn to Naples and the bay.

Their panoramic landscapes eerily anticipated views from planes or photographs from satellites. They had a sense of the world's curved surface, of the wispy continuities in cloud patterns seen from afar, an acute awareness of how haze overtakes any view as distance increases, a knowledge of how a sharp eye and an informed mind can on a clear day pick up the most amazing quantity of detail. Monsù Desiderio must have climbed Vesuvius many times, and the extinct crater of Epomeo in the centre of the island of Ischia, and looked directly down on the city from the promontory of Castel Sant'Elmo, and cruised inside the curve of the coastline as we had lately done, making sketches from a small open boat.

The master's painting of Naples seen looking inland from the air over the bay looked like a Didier but was in fact painted by François. The master in any case continued to talk of Monsù Desiderio as if they were one. It was a scary painting, mostly black, but flecked with tiny highlights and threaded with silver and gold. It looked like the negative of a landscape photo. Sky and sea were black, except for a dazzling slash of light, about a third of the sky, where the impenetrable clouds had rolled back to show the sun; and for an exquisite silvery streak on the black water where the sea mirrored the gash of sunlight.

A fleet of delicate warships was entering the port with miniscule pennants fluttering—each marked by a single brush hair—and the sails of the last still hoisted, made scimitars by the wind that was blowing back the covering of cloud. You could see the Castel dell'Ovo on the water at the end of its causeway and the Castelnuovo on the water's edge. Castel Capuano was just out of view on the right. The buildings receding from the waterline were picked out in white on black with maniacal autistic detail. Above the city in the centre stood the Castel Sant'Elmo on its hilltop, behind it on the right the darkened lower slopes of Vesuvius, to the left the smoking sulphur pit of Pozzuoli, caught in the blinding sun. It was François de Nomé's last known painting.

Nearly all of the buildings in this painting of 1647 were still recognizably there three hundred and more years later. In a different light—a hazy dawn—and from a lower perspective, I saw the same scene from the deck of the night ferry from Palermo. The ferry pulled into the bay around daybreak, and the land grew lighter as the boat drew nearer. The sky lightened behind the looming volcano to the east. We passed the islands, ships at anchor, began to make out the individual villas and palaces in the row along the water under the hill of Posillipo. We tracked the arm of a long and decrepit concrete breakwater with a little red lighthouse at its elbow, reaching out to sea past rusting cranes and what looked like abandoned hulks at anchor.

Palermo the afternoon before had been vivid, windswept, the sea cobalt and the peaks savage against the sky, and now in the bay of Naples everything was softened and pearly, sea, land and sky more vaguely delimited. In both cases the look was delusive. The wild beauty of Palermo and the sensual softness of Naples nursed twin horrors. It was the spring of 1982 and that summer in both cities a great killing would follow.

The vapours in the haze of moist and exquisitely polluted air softened the hard edges where sky and sea and coast all met, muted the dark looming profile of the volcano, refigured the bleak outline of the ugliest postwar buildings into a suggestive pale gold agglomeration. The silvery pinkish half-light turned rusting hulks and ugly freighters romantic as the ferry slid past and the water's foulness was unknowable below its silky surface. There were hardly any fishing boats. Inactivity on the waterfront was heavy with a pregnant stillness.

The thousands of tiny glittering panes in the windows in the royal palace looked out over the bay from the dark red walls under the roof garden, its red brick and massive granite coining above the stone walls rising from the road at sea level. This royal palace was a vast rebuilding of the smaller palace shown by Monsù Desiderio, redone to the scale and style of a golden age of absolutism, of a time when threats, internal and external, seemed to have evaporated in the Mediterranean sun. The model was Versailles, the sibling palaces were a few miles away at Capodimonte and Caserta and pleasure, beauty and *bon goût* prevailed in all of them. The palace in Naples was joined by a tunnel for royal entrances to the San Carlo theatre, an acoustic jewel of cream and gilt and red velvet which later held Stendhal and fifteen hundred others in delighted intimacy.

The ferry docked under the Castelnuovo, massive and formidable in its fifteenth century reworking, walls pocked by ancient cannon balls, and the five great round and battle-mented grey stone towers at its corners, still isolated from the city by the deep moat cut into the rising ground around its bastions. Unseen from the boat, the triumphal arch and frieze in white marble over the drawbridge celebrated the entrance into Naples of the Angevins' successors from Aragon in 1442.

Most of the great buildings in Monsù Desiderio's painting were already in place when the Aragonese arrived. You recognized everything in the *Tavola Strozzi*, the panorama of Naples from the bay done in the middle of the fifteenth century—solid, careful, exact, the water filled with small working boats, docks crowded with stevedores and busi-nessmen, a flight of large birds gliding past the promontory of the Castel Sant'Elmo, the hillside above the city still green and dotted with mulberry trees for the silkworms, water, hill and sky in interpenetrating shades and streaks of light blue and green, utterly unlike Monsù Desiderio's hallucinated darkness of two centuries later. A hundred thousand people lived in Naples when the *Tavola Strozzi* was done.

The amphitheatre city was terraced above the water. The dust and the *tufo*—the volcanic detritus compacted into a soft and porous yellow rock like Sydney sandstone and cut up into the building blocks of Naples—made a whitish gold haze when the first sun struck them from behind the shoulder of the volcano. The crumbling houses stacked in semicircles were still in shadow when Castel Sant'Elmo caught the sun first, towering gold above the rest, a great six-pointed bastion the stone of whose sheer walls was gouged from its own interior.

The Castel Sant'Elmo was what you saw of Spanish Naples from the harbour. The Spanish had massively rebuilt the fort on this highest hill. When the French were at the gates of Naples in 1528, Spain's military realized how crucial the hilltop was to Naples, because *from there you could hit the whole city*, and made Sant'Elmo the main link in the new system of defensive walls, which enclosed the city and joined Sant'Elmo with the Castelnuovo on the waterfront. Whoever controlled Sant'Elmo could cover inland approaches at the city's back and also fire with great precision into the streets of Naples below, as the Spanish artillery did when Neapolitans grew turbulent in 1547. The military garrison was bolstered spiritually and architecturally by the Carthusian monks of San Martino, whose contiguous paler walls embraced no less ground, were only infinitesimally lower than the military's and looked hardly less threatening to people huddled further down the slopes.

The ferry had already passed the Castel dell'Ovo on the left, before the breakwater intervened. It too loomed in the Strozzi panel and in Monsù Desiderio's view, jutting out to sea on the left of the little point of Santa Lucia. Its cubist oblongs of windowless raw tufo were already glowing goldish in the sun, looking like a natural growth from the tiny island of Megaris buried beneath it, where Lucullus had his villa and

24

the last Roman emperor of the West expired in 476. From the shore or from the sky the castle projected formidably and unforgettably. From the sea it seemed part of the coastline.

Behind the Castelnuovo, above surrounding roofs, to the right of the palace and theatre rose the glittering compound eye of the dome over the Galleria Umberto on Toledo, built in the Francophile eighteen nineties, when Neapolitan songs greeted the gay arrivals of early mass tourism, who shared the waterfront with the departing huddled masses of the great emigration, as southern Italy bled into the Americas.

The only decent buildings put up in Naples in the twentieth century, like the Banco di Napoli and the stupendous post office, were the work of the Fascists. Another was the *stazione marittima*, alongside which the ferry now docked. Almost alone it survived the destruction of the port by British and American bombs and the demolitions of the retreating German army in 1943. Its brilliant maritime white was lightheartedly art deco rather than Fascist neoclassical. It evoked the glamour of transatlantic crossings in the big liners of *l'entre deux guerres* and lent a touch of international drama to a day ferry trip to Capri or Ischia or Procida. Or a night ferry ride to Palermo.

The monuments of Naples failed to impose their grandeur on the people who lived among them. The buildings that looked so powerful from an approaching boat or a horse at the city gates were a part of the landscape to the locals, impersonal as rocks. Outcrops to skirt or take shelter by. They were foreign ground, occupied by foreign soldiers, foreign prelates, foreign bureaucrats, foreign judges. The great palazzi filling up the narrow rectangle of the city centre in the sixteenth century were built by the outsiders who ran

all you saw were anonymous old walls obscured by cars and washing. They were so unchanged, so unreconstructed that if you looked under the dirt you could still see *OFF LIMITS* roughly stencilled on a corner wall as a warning or a lure for the occupying troops of 1943.

In 1978 the street sellers were still locals, and in every season you saw the same person at the same corner, selling from an upturned carton or a little folding table. The merchandise during the day was the contraband cigarettes which sustained the economy of Naples in the first half century of the Italian republic. And teeshirts, toys, clocks and watches, sunglasses, handbags, newspapers and magazines.

At night everything vanished except the cigarettes, imbedded deep in the layers of the shawls worn by the women who sat on the corners. In the dark the old cigarette women wound in shawls looked even more like guerrilla sentinels, fires burning by their feet in winter, guarding the lower approaches to the encampment on the hill. Each corner had a sentry on duty, a still watcher who missed nothing in the human flow. The cigarette women were on the lookout for finance police cars on the prowl. When the cry *'a finanz'*, *'a finanz'* went up, the cigarettes—the cartons wedged in dark interstices—were gone long before the grey cars arrived. But they also kept a watch on nocturnal visits to the Quarters. At night the Quarters were off limits to the police and *carabinieri* as they had been to the Allied military a generation before.

Narrow, steep and dark, filled with watchful eyes and rocketing scooters, the alleys leading uphill off Toledo were deeply intimidating to any visitor. They discouraged casual reconnoitring. These steep gradients were intersected by long and narrow horizontal streets running along the contours of the hillside like sheep tracks. The first of these was called Vico Lungo Gelso. The hillside was green when Toledo engineered his road below it, and Long Mulberry Tree Lane ran through mulberry trees, red and white, for the silkworms that supplied one of the few productive activities in Naples.

Rising steeply to where the walls of the Castel Sant'Elmo and the San Martino charterhouse rose out of the rock, the hillside belonged to the monks of San Martino, who rented the *wild and uncultivated* slope for almost nothing to the local aristocrat who then terraced it and made money from the silkworms. The groves of mulberry trees also made the slopes a delightful resort for outdoor sex. Making love outdoors under the mulberry trees, *the Neapolitans . . . went in for a lot of wildness and grossness.* The whole thing was so very much in the open that the hillside became synonymous with shameless good times. *Are we up the Mulberries or something?* people would say when sexual behaviour in public places started getting out of hand.

The Spanish administration needed somewhere to garrison the occupying troops, and the Mulberries were right above the royal palace, the Castelnuovo and the port and close enough to the Castel dell'Ovo. And they were on Toledo's new artery built to speed the transit of troops between these places and the city's other two strategic strongholds, the Castel Sant'Elmo immediately above and the Castel Capuano at the eastern gate. The count saw there was a killing to be made up the Mulberries. He sublet the land to the Spanish, who laid out the narrower parallel streets running along the hill above and behind the new road. Steep little connecting lanes were squeezed between the palazzi and soon the whole area was built up almost to the fortress and the monastery, where the ground got too steep to level and build on.

The income from sericulture was nothing to what the count now made as a developer and entrepreneur. The Spanish administration kept building and building until the remaining orchard blocks were gone and internal courtyard gardens filled in and the inhabitants were the most densely packed in the most densely peopled city in Europe. The warren of a sixteenth century developer's housing became the *Spanish Quarters*. Europe's first urban grid plan was realized on this steep and unlikely terrain. Before the Quarters, cities just grew.

And as the pleasant greenery and amateur sex of the Mulberries metamorphosed into the darkly looming Spanish Quarters, the hillside's concentration of foreign soldiery invited an equal concentration of workers in the sexual service industries. The huge and beautiful garden vanished and the sex went indoors. Recreation became business. When the Mulberries became the Spanish Quarters, love for sale was its economic staple. Prostitution in Naples, once busiest down on the waterfront, was concentrated and industrialized in the Spanish Quarters, and there it stayed for four hundred years, long after the last Spanish troops had embarked and sailed away. A woman from the Quarters was a prostitute unless she could show reason to believe otherwise. Other sexual identities and activities weren't even discussed.

Filled with riotous foreign soldiery and the locals who serviced their needs, the Quarters were never one of the most desirable residential areas in Naples. The soldiers lodged in private houses or shacked up with their girlfriends in a neighbourhood already *full of lascivious women*. There was no military discipline and *fights . . . often broke out between [the Spanish] and the Neapolitans . . . there were a lot of killings*. The violence was private and collective and it never ended. Soldiers abused women, lived off their earnings, offended their families and were knifed in the dark by the men of Naples. Every morning bodies turned up in the alleys. After a hundred years of this the Spanish in 1651 moved their military out and quartered them in a purpose-designed barracks elsewhere. The Quarters' name and destiny stayed forever.

Beyond the soldiers, two forces converged to turn the Quarters into a ghetto. Heavy Spanish moralism was changing a socially easygoing city. The *students* and their girls themselves and the pimps and protectors ended up in the only place that would have them. The militantly counter-reformed church reinforced the Spaniards' new regime of decorum, suspicion and anonymous denunciation. The public dress and behaviour of all women was fiercely policed. Kissing in public, like carrying a weapon at night, was a major offence. Prostitutes were segregated. The civil and religious pincer grip was being felt even before the Council of Trent laid down the guidelines.

In 1547 Toledo pushed his Spanish Naples project to the point of inviting the Spanish Inquisition, which was far more fearsomely intrusive than the Roman, into the jurisdiction of Naples. After nearly fifteen years of summary justice from Toledo the people of Naples exploded. Even the aristocrats were involved. Fighting in the streets went on for months, the cannon of Sant'Elmo bombarded the city below and at the end of it there were at least a thousand dead, most of them Spanish soldiers from the Quarters. At which point Toledo, saying that he too had been against the idea all along, backed down.

A small revolution in Calabria

The streets of Spanish Naples were crowded, as the seventeenth century began and the occupation neared its first hundred years, with temporarily resident foreign entrepreneurs, diplomats, financiers, visiting clergy and military under deployment. Its stones creaked under the family coaches of newly urbanized baronial *latifundistas*, clattered under the hooves of the southern barons' and the Spanish courtiers' Arabian thoroughbreds. The narrow ways were obstructed by the barons' squads of armed enforcers and busily trodden by their servants, retainers, slaves, suppliers. Public spaces rustled with the habits and vestments of clergy of every degree and order. The ground was tramped by the boots of the occupying army and padded by the bare feet of refugees from rural poverty and brutality all over southern Italy. Naples swarmed with children, beggars and street criminals.

Peasants, fishermen, market gardeners, tavern keepers, prostitutes, idlers and *contrabbandieri* gathered in the unplanned agglomerations outside the city's fortified walls. And as the Spanish imperium lurched from bankruptcy to bankruptcy, military crisis to military crisis, in one of the dank confinements kept in the Castel Sant'Elmo for the vicerealm's most dangerous subversives, another city was taking shape inside the head of a prisoner who had no serious hope of ever seeing the real one again.

Tommaso Campanella was twenty years younger than Giordano Bruno. They were two of the most brilliant minds and resourceful men of their age in Europe. Most likely they never met, though in the autumn of 1594 the younger man joined Bruno in the Inquisition's prison labyrinth in Rome. After six months or so of interrogation and torture, Campanella was released into house arrest. Bruno continued fighting for his life for another five years, until they burnt him alive at the beginning of 1600. By then Campanella was in jail again elsewhere, now held by the Spanish in the Castelnuovo. He remained a prisoner of Spain in the various fortress dungeons of Naples, tireless, cunning, indestructible, for another twenty-six years. A month after his release from the Castelnuovo in 1626 Campanella was seized in Naples by agents of the Inquisition, kidnapped and smuggled to Rome in chains, under a false identity to get him past the Spanish authorities, back to the prison of the Inquisition he had left thirty-one years before.

Unlike Bruno, Campanella remained a convinced and devout Christian all his life. But over seven decades he was so original, inventive and so mightily prolific a writer in Latin and vernacular, prose and verse, on philosophical matters that Rome's inquisitors were at once deeply alarmed by the dangerousness of his ideas and unable to get any kind of firm grasp on quite what those ideas were. For the Spanish in the South the problem was more straightforward and no less urgent. Campanella was the leader of a failed communist revolution.

He was born on a summer evening in 1568, to an illiterate shoemaker and a mother who died too young to leave a memory, in a hovel outside Stilo in Calabria. Then as now Calabria was one of the wildest and remotest and poorest parts of the Italian peninsula. Whatever it was that produced and fed his passionate and hungry intelligence in his first years, Tommaso Campanella had the physical toughness and the mental wiliness of a poor boy from the sticks. These kept him going more than seventy years—most of them spent in vile prison cells—like the country magic which had saved his life as a sick child.

Taking orders was the only way a poor boy could get an education, and like Bruno before him Campanella chose the Dominicans for their compelling eloquence. Maybe he knew too of their unruly independence of secular and religious authority, and their incomparable library in Naples. He read books by Telesio, another Calabrian and Europe's first scientific thinker—Francis Bacon called Telesio *the first of the moderns*—and was electrified by his studies of the natural world. He went to Cosenza to meet Telesio, now almost eighty, and arrived in time to attend his funeral and fix a poem to the coffin.

Campanella was twenty-one before he got to Naples and went to San Domenico—the great church, the convent, the school, the library. After a while small troubles with religious authority began. He published a book defending Telesio. Someone accused him of *housing a familiar demon under the nail of his little finger and not taking excommunication seriously.* He was shut in the convent jail. *How come you know so much, if you've never had an education?* they asked. He answered, quoting Jerome, *I've burnt more oil reading than you've drunk wine.*

They ordered him back to Calabria immediately. He was twenty-four and it was like a death sentence. He headed north, as Bruno had. In Rome he met cardinal Del Monte, Florence's man in Rome, experimental scientist and patron of original minds, who a couple of years later discovered the unknown painter Michelangelo Merisi from Caravaggio. Del Monte was wary of the brilliant but impetuous youth from Calabria with his head full of Telesio, Neoplatonism and magic and wrote thus to Florence where Campanella was headed. When Campanella reached Florence he failed to find the position he was hoping for and moved on to Bologna, where someone stole his manuscripts and sent them to the Inquisition. Then he went to Padua. Desperately poor, he studied medicine there and made friends with Galileo. This Del Monte protégé was four years older than Campanella and starting a brilliant career. They stayed friends for life, and when the Inquisition closed in on Galileo decades later, Campanella wrote—from prison—a book defending him.

In nearby Venice in 1593, a few months after Bruno had been arrested there, he met up with Giovambattista Della Porta, whom he had known and argued with in Naples. Della Porta was a playwright, scientist, inventor, psychologist, a man of innumerable interests. A few years before in his bestselling book *Natural Magic* he had anticipated the optical principles of the telescope and set out the image projection system of the *camera obscura*. Merisi would use a camera obscura in the experiments in painting from life he made as a member of Del Monte's household over the next few years. Della Porta was temporarily in Venice because in Naples the Inquisition was looking into his work and Venice was relatively safe. Galileo in Padua was also inside the Venetian republic and under its protection.

In Rome that summer the Inquisition was going through Campanella's writings and not liking what it read. He was arrested in Padua in early 1594 and tortured on minor charges. The Inquisition, having just put Telesio's works on the *Index* of forbidden books and having read Campanella's *On the Meaning of Things*, insisted on having Campanella tried in Rome. That autumn he was in their prison in Rome and later he was tortured there. The place filled him with horror as a frightful and ineluctable trap for free minds, as *the devouring monster . . . cave of Polyphemus . . . Cretan labyrinth . . . secret tyranny's sacred fortress*. After torture he solemnly and publicly retracted the offending ideas and was released into house arrest.

In Naples a condemned criminal from his home town of Stilo, playing for time, wildly accused Campanella of heresy and Campanella was arrested again. Eventually he was acquitted but his work was banned and he was forbidden to write. He was ordered back to Calabria again and this time he went. After dragging out his time in Naples as long as he could, renewing old contacts, teaching, writing, he took a boat south and in the summer of 1598 set foot in Calabria for the first time in a decade. He was thirty years old, back in Stilo and condemned to silence. All his efforts to make a way in the greater world of the mind had come to nothing.

For a while everything was quiet. But under the placid surface of its brutalized and priest-ridden feudal poverty, Calabria was seething. The undefended coastal towns on the

Ionian Sea below Stilo were under constant attack by the Ottoman fleet, Turkish privateers and the Barbary corsairs operating out of Algiers. Inland was worse. Bandits had the run of vast tracts of wild terrain. They raided too, extorted, kidnapped and made travel a risk of life. Feudal landowners had absolute power on their estates. In the shadow of the latifundisti and far from the power in Naples, local government in the towns was paralyzed by feuding factions.

The return of Tommaso Campanella had a strange effect on the people of his home town and on himself. He was patently one of them, a powerfully built countryman who knew them all, spoke their dialect, understood their life and their nature. But to local people bound to their own narrow round he was now a man who brought news of the great world, read books, wrote them even, a man of the church. That he had come home defeated and disgraced hardly registered, not when they heard him making sense of their condition, felt how strongly he shared their anger and how vividly he imagined better things.

And Campanella felt himself drawn back into the natural magic of the country people's world, the clear consciousness of his childhood, and yet able to see things with an outsider's analytic eye. He was now a man who knew Naples, Rome, Venice, the seats of religious and secular power, the homes of money and ideas. He had lived in the homes of the powerful, spoken with cardinals, known some of the age's best minds. He had also seen the worst of the church, the ignorance and bigotry in its convents, the Inquisition's perverse and arbitrary cruelty. He had elaborated as he went along ideas for reforming the social and religious orders, in texts mostly now lost or abandoned in his travels, destroyed or suppressed by the Inquisition. Now people were listening to him and he saw a chance not just to understand the world but to change it.

Tommaso Campanella was himself under the powerful millennial influence of the coming year of 1600. Over the more recent years of the counter-reformation's crushing orthodoxy, there had been more and more vague but intense thinking among the church's freer minds about a great impending change, and the talk had become focused on the year 1600. Already the thought that a radical renewal was imminent had fatally lured Bruno back to Italy. When Campanella preached in Stilo through the spring of 1599, again and again he announced a revolutionary change about to come. He watched the stars in the night sky from the promontory over the sea where Stilo stood, believed that the conjuncture was arriving. Prophetic books confirmed what he saw in the skies and the charts, and he talked to people about what he saw and read. He knew a lot of people beside the country peasants—minor gentry, anti-Spanish landowners, dissident clerics, freethinking lawyers, frustrated provincial bureaucrats, factors and estate managers who knew what the barons were taking from the land.

Campanella's charisma put him at the centre of their vast web of discontents. He gave them a plan and a goal and more grounds for belief than they could begin to assimilate. He spent the early summer moving around the district, convincing, conferring, enrolling. Back in Stilo he held the threads together through letters in code. When the stifling dog days of summer came, communist revolution was on the agenda in Calabria. Even the marauding Turkish navy was enlisted and stood by to intervene. The aim was to overthrow Spanish rule, redistribute the land and institute a popular theocratic republic under the leadership of fra' Tommaso Campanella, who would *make new law and return every man to natural freedom*.

What happened was disaster. The web of conspirators was too loose, strung out too far. In that culture of generalized mistrust and anonymous denunciation, it was inevitable that someone would report the imminent rebellion. As happened. Two marginal conspirators in Catanzaro, losing their nerve or looking for reward, reported the plan in mid August to the Spanish administrator. Word sped to Naples and the viceroy acted with a dispatch much admired in the capital's diplomatic community. A week later two Spanish infantry battalions landed in Calabria and the revolution collapsed in defections and betrayals. Two denounced as leaders were dragged behind horses through the streets of Catanzaro, then *tortured with irons, strangled and strung up by the foot; two days later they were hacked to pieces and their heads hung in iron cages over the town gates*. Others paid out huge sums to escape arrest. Campanella himself took to the land, dressed as a peasant and sheltered by friends in houses and farm sheds until a neighbour betrayed him.

Everyone said he was the leader, so he was saved for a show of due process. After preliminary hearings in Calabria he was taken back to Naples with a hundred and fifty others. The galleys returned to port with four hanged prisoners suspended from the mast, and before the prisoners were disembarked, shackled in pairs and shuffling in file, two more were torn apart in the water by the four galleys under the eyes of the big crowd of onlookers gathered on the wharf.

Campanella was put in the Castelnuovo with the others. As the instigator and leader of the failed revolution he faced an inevitable fate. Rome and Naples squabbled viciously over rights to the prisoner. Spain refused to surrender him to the Inquisition. The lay prisoners were tried and tortured first. Campanella's interrogation began in January of 1600. After the first session he was sent for softening up for a week in the castle's underground *crocodile pit*, then brought out for several days of torture.

Under torture, he talked, and copiously, but mostly about signs, visions and prophecies of a new order. He denied leading a revolt against Spain. At the beginning of April he was found raving and nearly asphyxiated in his smoke-filled cell, his straw mattress on fire. He went on raving through torture and interrogation all that spring. The judges thought he was faking. Spies hid in the prison at night to overhear his talk with the other prisoners and write it down. Winter came and ten authoritative witnesses had declared him mad. The judges remained sceptical. He wrote a visionary account of Spain as the first Christian world power. In the early summer of 1601, after more than a year of mad behaviour, Campanella was called for a final and definitive torture session to decide whether or not he was faking. The question was crucial. If a mad person were put to death his soul would be lost and those responsible would suffer eternal torment.

For thirty-six hours he went through an alternating sequence of tortures designed to keep him conscious while feeling unspeakable physical pain. He was suspended by his dislocated limbs before the judges' bench and when he fainted the functionaries lowered him by pulleys to sit on a pointed stake. Then they slotted his joints back into place for the next session. And so on. By the end the sleepless judges were physical and nervous wrecks. Campanella was still mad. The judges gave up. Campanella was dragged to the judicial bench and his hand guided to put his mark on the document that definitively and irrevocably found him mad. He was hauled back to his cell nearly dead. When they got there he mumbled to one of the jailers holding him up, *They thought I was some fucking moron going to talk*. They dumped him on his straw.

He had lost a lot of blood and for most of the rest of the year he lay on his straw near death. Being mad, he was now an embarrassment and an irrelevance for the authorities and they let him lie there. But the tough and exuberant country boy from Calabria hadn't come through this trial to give them the quiet relief of a death in custody. He had things to do. Having defeated death, he now needed to get out of jail. He had things to write, ideas he wanted people to know about. A series of *Political Aphorisms* led the following year to the best-known thing Campanella would ever write. From his cell in 1602 he described an imaginary city governed by love and reason, whose people *had all things common . . . and distribution was made unto every man according as he had need*.

II

Quarters

The London dealer. Artemisia's way. At Pasquale's. Corner
Boy and Little Cutter. Room with view

The London dealer

A friend from Naples went to London and while he was
poking around there saw a small painting in a junk dealer's
crowded and filthy rooms. It was a grubby canvas of a seated
dark-haired woman with a crudely painted face. Her ample
body showed what might have been—under the dirt and
the overlays of varnish—creamy shoulders and breasts and
was otherwise covered by an area of darkness outlined as
a long dress. Looking up at her from the shadows in the
lower left-hand corner was a large and murky dog. Amateur
conviction told the Neapolitan that Naples was where the
seated woman belonged.

The London dealer sensed an anxiety to buy and asked for a lot of money. The tussle went on for years, over a series of ever angrier visits to London. Neither party gave way. The amiable Neapolitan was ready to throttle the dealer. Years later his fingers still flexed when he relived the frustration. *He was the only man I ever wanted to kill.* Then the dealer went mad and died and his stock was auctioned off. The small painting returned to Naples.

The seated woman was getting some attention when I saw her one afternoon, clamped upside-down to an easel in the chaotic apartments of a restorer's studio in the Spanish Quarters. Delicately applied solvents were rinsing off the dirt, the layers of varnish and the crudely applied later makeup that masked a delicate face. The restorer was a small dry man, one of those austere southerners whose gaunt features are set in their twenties and hardly change for another fifty years. He wore a paint-smeared grey dustcoat and a pair of wire-rimmed glasses and now he put the lady the right way up for the visitors.

The dog now had tusks and a snout and was a wild boar. Expert murmurs suggested this meant the lady was an allegory of *luxuria*, and the painting a portrait of a high-class courtesan. But when I went home I looked up Cesare Ripa, who codified the allegories in Italian painting at the end of the sixteenth century, and the only wild boar I could find in his *Iconologia* evoked not carnal pleasure but music, boars being famous for their fine sense of hearing. In the painting the boar did look fearsome, a savage breast being soothed. I don't recall that the woman held an instrument. She might have been a singer, and if she sat for her portrait in Naples in the early seventeenth century, I thought I knew who she might be.

The owner gazed lovingly at the finer work emerging as the crust of filth was gently washed away, the image of the woman he had sensed years before in the dirt and disorder of the English dealer's shop. The visiting expert hovered, brought his nose a few inches from the canvas, peered intently, stood back and gazed again, then turned away and did a brisk circuit of the studio staring thoughtfully at whatever was visible among the dozens of old canvases stacked in the main room or propped up to be restored.

The restorer's assistant was a thin young woman in a blue dustcoat. Her jet black hair showed up the pallor of her skin. She looked ill, but it was the normal look of a young woman of the Spanish Quarters who never got out of the dark dank maze of alleys, who ate meagrely and never saw the sun except for the few minutes of the day it cut like a blinding knife into the deep groove of her world, who never saw the sea except for the sliver of sapphire beyond the end of the other alley, the one that fell away steeply to the port, if she glanced sideways as she leant out of the balcony, lowering her basket on a cord to the vendor below. If it weren't for the young woman's gauntness, as she brought in a tray of little glasses of muddy coffee, her perfect skin might have recalled the creamy shoulders of the singer or courtesan at which the restorer was delicately dabbing again with his filthy rag.

I had seen a cluster of people like this the day before, going with a friend to his doctor's, who had rooms at the top of a six floor walk-up in the Quarters. This tubercular crowd had by the look of them barely survived the climb to the waiting room where they were now huddled, men, women, small children, ancient crones. They looked at us with burning incurious eyes when we entered the low room. My head nearly touched the ceiling. Many things were gone from Naples and the Spanish Quarters I'd once known, but the dirt, the damp, the darkness remained.

The restorer's studio was in a narrow alley on Pizzofalcone, rather than the Spanish Quarters proper. Pizzofalcone was the steep ridge looming over the little port of Santa Lucia and the Castel dell'Ovo on its tiny island. Pizzofalcone was Mount Echia, where the traders and colonists from Greece had made their settlement three thousand years earlier. On the inland side, the promontory of Pizzofalcone was separated from the hill of the Quarters by a narrow ravine, linked to the Quarters by a high arched bridge over Via Chiaia, the street of smart little shops which now ran along the bottom of the ravine.

The apartment was in a once quite handsome building that was now quietly crumbling. As we climbed the irregular stones of a long staircase whose steps, low, wide and mounting in a graceful curve, had once been designed to impress and intimidate the visitor, we caught vivid glimpses of sun on greenery, as startling as a flash of the sea in this old darkness, and through the dirty panes of the restorer's glassed-in anteroom we looked down on the jungle of a courtyard garden long ago gone wild. In that mild spring afternoon the sunlight trapped in the yard was a blinding emerald.

As we descended the broken, irregular staircase, the connoisseur said he thought the seated woman who was being restored had been painted by Artemisia Gentileschi.

Artemisia was a painter's daughter. Her father Orazio
Gentileschi was the closest friend-in-arms of Michelangelo
Merisi from Caravaggio in the Roman art battles of the very
first years of the seventeenth century, and Artemisia learnt
to paint from her father. She was thirteen when Merisi fled
Rome after killing a man in a street fight in 1606. When
she did her own first important painting four years later, her
father's turbulent younger friend had just disappeared forever
somewhere between Naples and Rome.

Artemisia's first signed painting was a spare and densely
schematic image of *Susanna and the Elders*, which owed a lot
to Michelangelo Buonarroti's Sistine ceiling and nothing
beyond the foreshortening of a hand to Michelangelo Merisi. It
showed a compactly bodied and frontally nude Susanna sitting
on a stone ledge with one foot in the water. The two male
voyeurs leant over the parapet behind her, almost touching
her. The men's heads and cloaked shoulders were over scale
and took up more space than the bathing girl's body. They
formed a looming hill, blocking the little light from the storm
clouds beyond. Susanna twisted away and raised her hands
against something closer and more dangerous than an assault
on her modesty. It portended trouble, the image of a young
girl exposed to the joined forces of older male predators,
and two years after Artemisia painted it trouble came. The
eighteen-year-old virgin Artemisia was raped by a painter
friend and associate of her father's.

Agostino Tassi was forty-five and had been in trouble
before on sexual matters involving members of both sexes,

most notably his fourteen-year-old sister-in-law, a connexion that had brought a charge of incest the year before. Tassi's relations with the younger sister came after the death of his wife, who had been stalked and murdered, an old friend claimed, after she walked out on Tassi. He was a family friend and neighbour as well as a working partner of Orazio Gentileschi's, and Orazio had made a connecting door and stairs between the Tassi and Gentileschi apartments for ease of access. One day when Artemisia was in bed and alone in the house, Tassi appeared through the door with an accomplice and in short order he raped her, despite her savage resistance.

Promises of marriage followed. Artemisia was half inclined to accept them. Rape as a courtship gambit was usual enough and Artemisia was now damaged goods. When Tassi hadn't made good on his announced intentions several months later, Orazio took him to court. The rape trial, meticulously transcribed, became notorious. Tassi was an accomplished performer in the courts of sexual crime. He smeared Artemisia with countercharges. One of them was that she had slept with her father Orazio, among various others. The rape victim was given a gynecological going-over by a couple of midwives and was cross-examined under torture. During the witness confrontation with Tassi, the screws were being tightened on Artemisia's fingers and not the accused's. *This is the ring you give me and these are your promises*, she screamed out at Tassi in one moment of pain.

Success in talking his way out of incest charges with a fourteen-year-old the previous year led Tassi to overdo it now. Not even the judges believed his claim that he'd never had sex with Artemisia at all, and they warned him against perjury when he said this. Neither did they believe him that the real rapist was the former friend who was now a prosecution witness. His own witnesses exposed and discredited, Tassi ended up in jail. Eight months later he was out again, and soon back in amicable working relations with Orazio Gentileschi. Artemisia not long after the trial married a painter brother of the witness who effectively defended her. Apart from the notoriety of the artists involved, and Artemisia's fiercely independent account of herself, there was nothing particularly unusual about these events.

The experience fed directly back into Artemisia's painting. It drove her untiring career. The same year the trial ended she began work on a canvas of *Judith and Holofernes*. Her image of female seduction and revenge owed a lot of its intimacy and violence to Orazio's dead friend Merisi from Caravaggio, who thirteen years before had painted his own *Judith and Holofernes*, another resolute young woman hacking off a bearded male head. The oppressively draped bedroom setting in Artemisia's painting, Judith's stiffly armed wielding of the severing knife, Holofernes' grotesquely upside-down face, engorged and dark from the death struggle, the partly severed head in the centre of the canvas, all came from the painting Merisi had done when Artemisia was six years old.

Revisiting and reworking this early memory, Artemisia made it almost more shocking as a women's kitchen scene of everyday domestic butchery. Her view was closer to the bodies, the room blacker. Merisi's old crone servant, stony witness in profile, became Artemisia's intent young woman much like Judith, pressing the victim's warm body against the bed to facilitate the kill, almost straddling it as if mounting him for sex. Holofernes was now helpless on his back, held down for the beheading as perhaps Artemisia had been by Tassi's accomplice in the rape. In the mesh of six powerful bared arms, under the interlocked figures of the two young women doing what had to be done, Holofernes' bare shoulders and forearms looked like raised thighs seen from below. The decapitation was also a hideous castration. The high placing of the luxuriously stacked mattresses made the ribbons of thick blood, darkening as they trickled down from mattress to mattress and slowly soaked into the stuffing, and the thinner smear of blood on the white sheet under the squirming shoulder and neck an ineradicable crime scene detail. Beside Artemisia's Holofernes, Merisi's victim seemed heroic or absurd in his desperate effort to live, his squirting arterial blood almost unreal.

She did another painting soon after of *Judith and Her Servant* just after the killing, the girl holding the head in a shallow basket on her hip like a fresh fish. This was a more usual and decorous way of handling the theme than the actual moment of bloody dismemberment. She did several restrained variant versions of the two women calmly departing with the severed head, and another more distanced reprise of the killing itself. Judith had been shown almost as often as David and Goliath among artists and their patrons for centuries—Botticelli, Mantegna, Donatello, Michelangelo, Giorgione had all done versions of her as a more or less maidenly champion of the oppressed with the tyrant's trophy head, and Rubens had lately done a flamboyant action painting of the death—but not even Merisi had charged his image with Artemisia's savagely claustrophobic sexual energy and her intimately felt detail.

She changed the almost sexless girl Judith into a vengeful contemporary woman.

Later, she was drawn more than once as a painter to the rape victim and suicide Lucretia—Shakespeare's Lucrece—not to mention Cleopatra, betrayed and defeated by men, and Susanna again, blackmailed by old lechers. But she never again did anything so savage as the masterpiece from her late teenage years. She left Rome soon after finishing *Judith and Holofernes*. She must have kept the painting through the fifteen years she worked in Florence, Genoa, Rome and Venice, because she took it with her when she moved to Naples with her five children in 1630. It was meant to be a short visit to hunt up more commissions, but in the end she spent the rest of her life in Naples. The painting is still there.

In the years when the Bourbon hunting lodge—a vast eighteenth century palace in Neapolitan red and grey on the cooler hill of Capodimonte above the city—was frequented more for what remained of the oak forest around it where the king had done his hunting than for anything contained in its echoing halls, I used to wander its corridors from time to time and look at the paintings. The hunting lodge was always meant to be a home for the great collection of art Carlo III had inherited from his mother, who was a Farnese from Parma. Royal enthusiasm for art soon flagged, though not for life in the palace and hunting in its grounds. Two hundred years later the last royal family moved out at the end of the Second World War and the last paintings looted by the Nazis were returned.

Haltingly, Capodimonte approached its intended destiny as an art gallery. Forty more years on, two and a half centuries behind schedule, the collection would reveal its glory.

At Capodimonte, silent, listless, filled with motes floating in shafts of sunlight as a handful of desultory visitors drifted along the galleries, Artemisia's piled mattresses fixed themselves in my mind. The strands of drying blood, congealed by the time they reached the lowest mattress at the bottom of the canvas, were hard and black like cooling lava, below the still-flowing red and the lighter brown smeared on the sheet by the writhing body. The violence was an anomaly in Artemisia's work. The strong and businesslike women were not. A decade later she showed *Judith and Her Servant* in the moment after cutting off the head, that instant of frozen anxiety in the dark, caught in hyper-realist lighting and *ex post facto* urgency, the severed head in the shadow almost hidden under the helper's large hand and a bundle of bloodstained towels.

It became her forte to paint women protagonists from the Bible and ancient history. Cleopatra, identified by a wiry asp, was the fleshy horizontal nude Artemisia did well. The undertones were always there, for anyone who might have wanted to hear them, in the Magdalens, Lucretias, Susannas and elders, Davids and Bathshebas, Josephs and Potiphar's wives. But even Jael driving the nail into the head of a sleeping oppressor who strangely resembled Merisi from Caravaggio had a quiet purposefulness not seen in the *Judith* paintings. She did portraits of women lightly allegorized as cultural forces. Clio, the muse of history, was one. If the dirt-encrusted London discovery was her work and if the wild boar meant what I thought it did, then Music was another. She was famous for these life portraits but not many survived.

Artemisia painted herself at work as *Painting*. Not posed and formal like the others, this was an extraordinarily angled oblique close-up, an unmediated and unadorned glimpse of a woman intently at work. The distances between subject and object, image and maker, observing and creating, intimacy and detachment were burnt away in its enactment of art-making. The symbols that identified her as an allegory of painting—the symbols listed in Ripa's *Iconology*—were so subtly present that without the guide in hand you would hardly recognize them. There was nothing like a wild boar, just a slender gold chain with a mask emblem on a pendant and the slightest disarray in a few wisps of hair to remind you of the madness of art.

Artemisia's extraordinary self-representation ended up in London. In 1638 Artemisia left Naples for England where her father was working for the king. Orazio may have piqued Charles's desire for the art of the outstanding woman painter who happened to be his daughter, and she likely took the canvas to London herself. It was in the king's collection a year or so later. Charles I was mad about paintings and the cost of his insatiable collecting was placing the exchequer under excruciating strain even as a larger political crisis put the very monarchy at risk.

Orazio Gentileschi was now seventy-five and wanted to come home. Artemisia worked with him on the vast suite of allegorical paintings for the ceiling of the queen's house in Greenwich. He died before they were finished and two years later there was civil war in England. Artemisia went back to Naples in 1642 and she never left again. Her self-portrait as

Painting was sold off after Charles was beheaded in 1649, but recovered for the royal collection when the monarchy was restored. And there it stayed, unlikely to return to Naples.

In 1636, not long before she made her journey to England, Artemisia wrote in a letter to Florence that she wanted to leave Naples on account of the hard life, high costs and *the fighting*. The Spanish empire was being bankrupted by its foreign wars, above all the irrepressible revolt of the Protestants in the Low Countries. Punitive taxes on bread, fruit and produce, even as incomes in Naples shrank and the viceroy speculated, provoked crises of hunger and desperation. It was taxation without representation, and a deep pressure of anger was building against the occupying power. Like England, Naples was moving inexorably toward a revolution.

It all got much worse after Artemisia's return, but her own failing strength and the need to keep working were the things she most mentioned in her last years. As a young woman in Florence, she had become friends with Galileo, while he lived out his last years under house arrest. They kept up their friendship by writing letters. Later she became friends with Cassiano Dal Pozzo, the first modern archeologist of Rome's buried pagan past. That friendship too was kept up over time and distance through letters. She brought up her children and married off her daughters, painting inventively and prolifically to the end. She died in 1653 after living through much greater *tumults of war* in Naples, which may have hardly registered as she got the last from her failing strength. The only record of her death was a couple of insulting sexual epigrams from Venice, which implied that she was well known for an erotic life as busy and assertive as her work as a painter. Forty years on, Tassi's mud had stuck.

Her Roman birth and her death in Naples notwithstanding, Artemisia remained by family descent and painterly affinity a Florentine, and she was buried in the church of the Florentines in Naples, just below Toledo. After a while her tomb was no longer identifiable inside the church. Around the middle of the last century the church itself was obliterated, and whatever remained of Artemisia was ground into the dense impasto of soft yellow tufo and hardened black lava and chips of brilliant white marble, of bits of Greek wall and Roman amphitheatre, of cavities and blocked water springs and unexploded bombs, of bricks and tiles and seashells and used syringes and the endless tangle of the human bones that are underfoot wherever you step in Naples today.

At Pasquale's

Pasquale's opened directly on to the street in a narrow building divided at ground level into two non-interconnecting halves. The left-hand part was in turn divided down the middle into tables on the left and a partly walled-off kitchen on the right. The right-hand part was a windowless room with several more tables and amenities at the back. This second room was connected to the kitchen by a small high serving hatch knocked through the wall, but when dishes were placed in the hatch the single waiter had to leave the other part of the restaurant and enter the second room from the street to serve them, before returning to base via the street. If you were in the second room and wanted to order, pay, ask a question or peer at food, you too had to visit the other half by first going out into the street. Likewise a customer in the left-hand part who wanted to use the amenities had to exit to the street and then enter the right-hand part of the restaurant and head for the lavatory at the back. The amenities were limited and a visit often involved some waiting. They were housed in a cupboard which left no doubt when they were in use.

A meal at Pasquale's involved a fair amount of movement for the diners in either half and a lot of movement for the waiter, whose name was Ciro and who was related to Pasquale and was badly lame. The first night Ciro followed me along the alley in the dark to thank me for a tip, swinging his useless leg behind him as he hurried to catch up. Even Pasquale moved a lot in the confinement of his kitchen, pale round face mostly hidden in clouds of steam and smoke but sometimes lit up by a sheet of yellow flame.

At lunchtime Pasquale's was almost respectable. The lower reaches of the Spanish Quarters were near enough to the banks and shops of Toledo to be invaded at lunchtime by people in jackets and ties and tailored skirts, and Pasquale did most of his trade then. Lunch was still the big meal of the day in Naples. The sawdust was on the floor and the cutlery bent and not too clean, but the food was good and at lunchtime the place was full of people who would not have been seen dead there at night. After dark everything changed. The live customers at night were all local and variously unattached. Everyone else hurried home to family.

In the densely packed uphill crisscross marked out by the seventeenth century speculators, Pasquale's pinkish building stood nakedly on the edge of a block which was strangely vacant, apart from some low sheds. The sheds gave the empty block its name, *Largo Barracche*. I imagined a bomb had fallen on it in the fatal summer of 1943 and was surprised to discover that it had always been like this. In the first days of the Spanish Quarters the sheds were occupied by ladies of the night, and of the day. As the Quarters began to realize their destiny Largo Barracche had soldiers and other people coming and going at all hours. Later the sheds were turned over to the sale of fruit and vegetables. Things had quietened down further still by 1978 and the Largo was in darkness in the evening. Pasquale's, however, was still at the epicentre of nocturnal activity, even if the activity wasn't happening in the sheds.

Titina and Rosaria used to spend time off work in the evenings at Pasquale's, sometimes before and sometimes after. They were very young and beautiful and were clearly much in demand. Titina had a mass of tawny, slightly frizzy hair and flawlessly creamy skin. Rosaria's hair was also an almost reddish blond and she had a slightly tanned skin with a saddle of delicious light freckles across her nose and cheekbones. Before she left around ten she always gave instructions to don Filippo—who had a bar around the corner and came to Pasquale's when he closed up—to send a wake-up coffee the next morning, when the espresso machine was fired up and steaming, to wherever it was she lay in bed. Later Rosaria went to Genoa, but when summer came I saw Titina on the water at Santa Lucia, flung back voluptuously in the stern of a heavy wooden fishing dinghy, basking in the misty golden light, her Titian hair trailing in the silky sea as a tiny boy struggled with heavy blue oars secured by rope and tried to keep the bow level in the water.

There were some older ladies who came less often and who may or may not have been retired. One popped in with her young grandson shortly after the new pope had descended into Naples by helicopter. *Show the gentleman how you greeted his holiness*, she told the child, heavy gold cross swinging between powdered breasts as she leant over the greasy laminex. He pressed his infant palms together and raised his eyes to heaven. Titina and Rosaria tended to sit with an older man who spoke very little and wore dark glasses all evening. One time he told me he had been a waiter all his life and was now retired. Before he was a waiter, when he was fifteen years old and the Germans had occupied Naples in the summer of 1943, he had been rounded up by the retreating Nazis and trucked off to do forced labour in Germany. But he made it back to Naples in the end and never left again.

By 1943 the Neapolitans had lived through Fascism, the Allied bombing, the German occupation. They were used to doing it tough but they also lived with narrower margins than most people, even other people in occupied Europe. When the Germans started rounding up their husbands, sons and boyfriends the women assaulted the Nazi soldiers loading the trucks. The Neapolitan housewives' assault on the Wehrmacht was spontaneous and terrifying. The German soldiers fled, the men escaped and four days of street fighting followed. After the death of hundreds of Neapolitans and a fair few of the Nazi army, the German commander colonel Scholl fled Naples at dawn, a white handkerchief of surrender fluttering from the window of his speeding Mercedes. His troops followed, pausing now and then as they fled north to kill more people. The killings were payback for Europe's first mass civilian uprising against the Nazis.

There was an ancient retired pizza-maker at Pasquale's who looked as if he had stayed starving since the war. His name was Carlo and he had hollow cheeks and a pencil moustache, a face untouched by twenty years of postwar boom times. He cleared a few tables and made himself useful in return for a scrap of food and a glass or two of wine. He disappeared silent and unnoticed some way through the evening, ignored by the paying customers and by Pasquale, whose own face was more moonlike than gaunt. He was one of the widowers who haunted the Quarters—the widows stayed at home unseen. They had no cheeks, these old men, under their cheekbones, had eye sockets rather than eyes and papery skin stretched over teeth and jaw. They were ghosts from the southern past, carefully turned out in decent threadbare clothes with a black mourning button on their lapel and living off the smell of an oiled rag, which was about as much as I ever saw Pasquale concede to the silent Carlo.

Another came for red wine and company and I don't recall him ever eating or paying, though he sat down with us, considered himself the equal of any man present and never cleared a table. He was not fading visibly like the poor *pizzaiolo*, was tall for a Neapolitan, broad-shouldered and bony, white-haired, red-faced and erect, his angry old man's eyes underlined by a pair of white handlebar moustaches. Ernesto had been a seaman and worked his way around the world, had been to Shanghai in the thirties. Singling me out as another seasoned traveller in foreign parts, he confided sometimes on the unique and unforgettable sexual expertise of Oriental women. He wore a greenish jacket of loose tweed, a white shirt with a frayed collar and a narrow black tie. He didn't talk a lot and there was something slightly remote about him. Loss or age or years at sea seemed to have left him an intense inner life and a certain alienation from the other people living up the Quarters.

Other old sailors were different. One wore a felt hat and sometimes dropped in to let the company hear a spot of unaccompanied Verdi. After which a few glasses of wine were not spurned. Another sailor was from Santa Lucia and worked the contraband boats. His hair had gone white early. It was thick and bristly, and all the whiter for his red windburnt face and dark blue seaman's jumper. In the Pallonetto in Santa Lucia, which was twenty minutes' walk away, he had a dozen children. Enzo was crossing a line in his visits. The Pallonetto at Santa Lucia was special among the Neapolitan microcommunities. When Garibaldi reached Naples in 1860 the *Barracchisti*, from the part of the Spanish Quarters where we now were, were his most militant supporters, and in the power vacuum between regimes organized crime from the Quarters controlled Naples. The Pallonetto stayed blindly loyal to the disintegrating Bourbon monarchy of *The Two Sicilies*.

If you went beyond the end of Toledo, past the royal palace and down to the right, you would see off-duty contrab-bandieri and other Luciani standing on the right-hand side of the road below the Pallonetto, staring out to sea from the beach at the bottom of their hill. Only the beach was a busy street. For a hundred years the sea and the boats and the

Sorrento peninsula and Vesuvius and Capri had been blocked from view by the heavy Umbertine palazzi built on the land reclaimed when the shoreline was pushed a kilometer further out. The Luciani were now squinting at a horizon of shops, bars, a cinema and the offices of the regional government. The contraband boats were low, light, immensely capacious, powerful, fast and wonderfully manoeuvrable. The finance boats never caught them. They went out at night and by day you could see dozens of them moored at Santa Lucia in the little port behind the office blocks, identical shapes in the same dull matte blue.

The only other singing was from Pasqualino. He sang most nights, always toward closing time, and maybe his didn't count as singing at all. Pasqualino too had seen something of the world. He had done jail time in every major country of Europe and commanded respect for this if nothing else. Back in Naples he minded cars in Forcella with a group of ex-cons. Pasqualino enjoyed wine more than the others, or enjoyed more wine more than the others, though he hardly showed it. He became a shade more loquacious, a shade less focused and did his Olga Molga cabaret dance again with a dirty tea towel flung over his head.

Umberto was younger than Pasqualino and had travelled too. Years before, another youth in the Quarters had dishonoured Umberto's sister and Umberto had shot him and fled to South America. In Buenos Aires a former neighbour betrayed him to the police and Umberto was sent home to prison. The man he shot in the alley soon recovered. One night outside, Umberto grabbed my arm and croaked, *That's him.* I couldn't see who he meant in the dark. *The guy I shot.* It seemed to be a live-and-let-live situation. I asked what Buenos Aires was like. *Terrible*, said Umberto. *Like Naples.* Umberto sold Rolex gold lookalikes down at the ferry wharf. His colleague Alfonso, who used to call in and compare notes, did the same on Vesuvius.

Mario was friendly but taciturn and dressed like a seaman in dark blue jumper and woollen beanie. I often saw him standing watch with his black pinpoint eyes at a corner of Toledo or closer to the waterfront but his purpose was never clear and he never talked about it. He played cassettes of Neapolitan songs in the evening and could recount in meticulous detail the plots of dramas by Eduardo De Filippo, which he loved. Franco the sardonic barber came late from across the alley, and Roberto, young gatherer of old metal tubes and fittings, odd job plumber, gas fitter and ultra-leftist, ate for hours.

These were some of the people who sat down to eat each evening at Pasquale's, the nightly constellation of customers whose names and orbits I'm trying to retrieve. Others came to take away, and they often came in pyjamas and dressing gown. After sundown the alleys of the Quarters reverted to their essential nature as a largely private neighbourhood space, the alleys extensions of the houses that opened on to them. A young woman came in and Roberto leapt up to peer closely at the *reinforcement salad*. It was already winter. Over lightly blanched cauliflower were green olives, salted anchovies and peppers preserved in vinegar, red and green, hot and sweet. In theory it reinforced the austere fish and seafood of Christmas eve—it was a *Christmas salad*—and in practice it was a vivid, pungent, high-contrast side dish for any of the short dark days when fresh salads and vegetables were limited and dull. *Did you see?* Roberto said when he got back to the table. *She had nothing on under that dressing gown.*

Rosario and Giacomo, who a few years before had been kids playing in the patch of steep scrub above the Quarters, the patch of no man's land between the highest point of the Quarters and the bastions supporting the Castel Sant'Elmo and San Martino, after a few more years, a brush with the law involving marijuana and American sailors on the waterfront, were both swept away in the shooting war about to break over Naples. Less often we saw a wonderfully affable elderly accountant, not part of the usual evening client spectrum at all and a throwback to the days when respectable people still lived in the old city. Or Mimmo, a country boy who had arrived in town hoping to gain a toehold in the fiercely competitive milieu of transsexual prostitution and who never lingered in the evening. A couple of thin young shipping clerks in jackets and ties worked late nights and arrived exhausted. There was a mischievous old chiropodist who did people's feet at home. These were the outer satellites of Pasquale's constellation.

Crime in the Quarters was lingering in the preindustrial phase. From time to time, even in the placid days before the double cataclysm of earthquake and heroin, there was an evening shooting in the alley outside Pasquale's. Nobody was hit when I was around. At the first crack of gunshots I stuck my head out the door to catch the drama. Pasquale sprang from the kitchen and yanked me inside by the scruff of my neck while Ciro slammed down the shutters and the wineshop opposite did the same. It had been the same centuries before when the Spanish were in control. *Serra serra*, the cry went up when the streets turned violent, and the shutters banged down all through the city in one long roll of thunder.

Pasquale himself, until the earthquake, kept going, imperturbably irascible amid bursts of steam and flashes of yellow fire and shouts of abuse at the clients or his staff, who were all family members. After the earthquake he had a nervous collapse and handed the cooking over to the next generation. His cooking was rough as bags and repetitive but with unexpected moments when he found something good at the market or in the depths of his memory. One Holy Thursday there was a soup of octopus and strange little snails I had never seen. *Where do they come from?* I asked. *'Ncopp' 'o campo santo*, Paquale said, flinging a paper-thin steak on to the griddle and raising another flame. *Up the graveyard.*

Corner Boy and Little Cutter

Umberto came to Pasquale's with a parcel under his arm, a bit later than usual and looking fed up. At some point during the day, which he had spent as usual selling his Rolex lookalikes in the waterfront area, he had got into conversation with a seaman from the US Navy who was also doing some selling. A brand-new industrial-quality boiler suit, still sealed in its factory plastic, had fallen off the back of a nuclear powered aircraft carrier—the *Nimitz* or the *Eisenhower* was sitting offshore. The sailor was in a hurry. Umberto had seized the moment and bought. He thought the overall would make a useful present for his daughter's husband, who washed cars in a little piazza near the port. The son-in-law told Umberto he wasn't interested. Relations weren't too good and I wondered whether the cold reception was because the younger man had been embarrassed by Umberto's merely turning up or whether he felt Umberto was making a comment on the level of his daughter's husband's part-time employment. Umberto himself was both offended by the response to his thoughtfulness and annoyed at having paid out good money for merchandise neither he nor anyone else seemed to want.

The overall was passed around in its plastic. Everyone had a look but no one was interested. It was too big for almost anyone in Naples. When it reached me Umberto's eye brightened. I had no need of a boiler suit but a couple of hours later as we all dispersed I had the package under my arm. A little puff of American factory air hit my face as I slashed open the sealing. It was a heavy-duty item, heavy-duty plus, in starchy thick olive green cotton drill, pockets everywhere and all triple-stitched. The US military contractor's buttons likewise would not be falling off in a hurry. It was made to measure for a lean six-footer and ideal wear for scouring out fuel tanks. I wore it once but even in the dark people kind of found it strange.

It was like another episode of someone offloading work wear in the same district a couple of thousand years before. The earlier episode was imagined but the setting was real and the events familiar. Two strangers in town wanted to get rid of a heavy and valuable recently stolen cloak. They took it to a piazza where a night market was setting up as darkness was falling.

We saw a lot of things for sale, nothing worth much, the kind of dodgy stuff that looks best in dim light . . . we decided to use this great opportunity by showing the edge of it in a corner of the market. With any luck the gorgeous cloth might pull in a buyer.

Things got complicated because the new arrivals had also lately lost a cloak of their own. It was old and cheap but it had the proceeds of a recent robbery and murder sewn into the lining. A man and a young woman were looking round the night market and recognized the high-quality cloak as theirs. They were also holding the cheap old cloak with the loot, which they had found out in the country, unaware of the money hidden in the lining.

Onlookers gathered and intervened in a rapid and noisy squall of recognitions, accusations, countercharges and efforts to retrieve property. The two pairs were exchanging cloaks when the police arrived, confiscated both garments and ordered all four to appear before a magistrate the next day to answer charges of theft. One of the market dealers, a man with a bumpy forehead, claimed authority to take custody of the cloaks pending the court hearing. The strangers realized he was counting on their not wanting to face the magistrate and absconding, which would leave him with the confiscated property. At which point the text broke off.

It probably happened in Pozzuoli, just down the road, but maybe in Naples itself in Nero's time. It might have happened nineteen hundred years later, in one of those piazza markets where second-hand clothes and brand name rip-offs were spread out on tarpaulins and stolen goods changed hands on the periphery. The street dealing, the second-guessing and the choral interventions, the obstructive bureaucracy and the man with the bumpy forehead—the dealer with connexions and influence on both sides of the law—were still constant presences in the neighbourhood in the nineteen seventies.

Something similar was happening in city crime at the start of the seventeenth century. Two knife-carrying street boys in their mid teens arrived in the city to work the piazza. First they sold some shirts filched from a saddlebag on the road, then got to work and swiftly relieved its owner of a loaded purse. They were seen, however. Not by the police but by another young worker in the same crowded space. Who made clear to the newcomers that theft in the area, and indeed all over the city, was controlled by a criminal cooperative which required a percentage of each day's takings. *The haul gets divvied up a lot of ways and every agent and contractor gets his cut.* Disconcerted—*I thought thieving was an activity exempt from taxes and excise*—but not having much choice, they went to join the system and met, along with the other workers, its boss. He was a man *about forty-five or -six, tall and dark with thick eyebrows, a heavy black beard and deepset eyes . . . a hairy chest . . . stubby hairy hands, fat fingers and long curved fingernails.*

The boss listed the system's *benefactors*, who all in various ways needed to be paid off—defence lawyers, informants in the law enforcement agencies, compassionate hangmen, people who obstructed pursuit during getaways, the girls *who sweat to help them* in jail, the families of system members and the prosecutors who mitigated charges and sentences. A police officer arrived, but the boss reassured people. *Don't worry, anyone, he's a friend and never makes trouble.* The workers themselves followed strict discipline. The boss reminded them, *Nobody fool around because breaking even the smallest thing in our order will cost him his life.*

The industry had its statutes and they were enforced by violence. The physical violence was at once what held the organization together and a dimension of its professional activity, as the morning's transactions soon showed. A well-dressed client called to discuss an imperfectly executed commission to slash someone's face open. The target had been out of reach, so a servant was slashed instead. The boss vigorously disputed the dissatisfied client's right to withhold payment, with a certain tacit reliance on the organization's professional skills to enforce a settlement. Using and controlling violence also involved the boss in arbitrating the matter of one of the girls who had been savagely beaten by her lover, who was one of the thugs. Keeping respect—self-respect and everyone else's—was a crucial part of this particular settlement.

The day went on in the organization's courtyard. Stuff happened. Eating, drinking, alarms, squabbles, adjudication. The system's army of older people spread out again through the city, on the modest but essential mission of keeping an eye on the movements of the authorities and identifying targets—the best-stocked private houses and individuals carrying large amounts of cash. Corner Boy and Little Cutter themselves, cardsharp and cutpurse, the two quickwitted but ingenuous street boys, were also given work to do even as they were effectively sidelined as mere observers of a system of which they were now formally a part. There was a faint hint of trouble to come, a sense that the boys' future would depend on the outcome of a future struggle between accepting life under the system's rules and wanting to get their autonomy back.

The city here was Seville, a great metropolitan port of Spain itself, and not the great port city of transplanted Spain in Italy. Seville held the monopoly on shipping to the Americas—the transatlantic ships came up the Guadalquivir to dock and unload—and was rich, busy, cosmopolitan and much like Naples. The social reality in its lightly fictional clothes belonged no less to Naples at the same moment in the Spanish empire's slide down to crisis. The criminal system's family values (the thieves in Seville were the boss's *adopted children*) and its Catholic piety (candles and votive offerings cementing the organization and securing real benefits) would remain intrinsic to crime in Naples, as they would to everything else in social life, for centuries.

Miguel de Cervantes, who wrote the account, had served the empire in the naval victory over Islam at Lepanto in 1571, a good thirty years before he wrote about *Corner Boy and Little Cutter.* The young Cervantes had been a Spanish marine stationed in Naples for five years and when he wrote *Don Quixote* he had a no-good in the novel dangle in front of a foolish country girl the promise of running away to *the richest and most decadent city there is in the whole wide world.* The city was Naples, as it were by definition. When the first part of *Don Quixote* came out in 1605 with this mention of Naples in its last pages, Cervantes' own memory of the city was thirty years out of date, and went back to the golden days before the crisis had bitten.

By the time Cervantes published *Don Quixote*, Naples, like the cities of metropolitan Spain, was teeming with displaced peasants, urbanized nobility, miscellaneous unemployed, motherless children, teenage delinquents, professional criminals, and orphans and street people of all ages. Along with military people of uncertain status, local and Spanish, home from one foreign campaign or about to leave on another, monastics and clergy of dubious discipline, some fugitive and others all too much at home, and girls and widows and married and single women working with what they had. Seville was fresher in the mind of Cervantes than the Naples he'd once known. He tried to get back to Naples later in life, but failed to get a job with the Spanish administration. Maybe he thought it was still the Naples of thirty years earlier. It wasn't. Spain was now drained by its imperial wars and had lately gone bankrupt again. People in Naples were paying the price.

They were even paying the price in stolen cloaks. It wasn't local criminal organizations who stole them but the Spanish military. Soldiers used to go out *caping* at night, and caping often left the garment's original owner dead in the street. Assault and robbery by the military were endemic in occupied Naples. A Neapolitan wrote in 1605 that *the Spanish have taken up caping at night and it's not safe to go around the city after dark*. The soldiers were probably no longer getting paid on time.

Room with view

A lot of the women of the Quarters looked strikingly masculine once they were past childbearing. Women who had been sylphlike girls and bountiful breastfeeding mothers hardened and thickened overnight into chunky walking armoured cars with voices like factory hooters. What followed was a long slow fade. Mediterranean normality was still free of notions of prolonging youth, or the appearance of youth, past nature's use-by date. It was economic. Why waste on clothes and cosmetics money that could feed you and your family?

These older women of the Quarters, sexually neutral and far from the public dramas of power, strong presences only to their own men and children, hardly existed outside their cramped domestic lairs. Yet they were fundamental to the Quarters' whole life, like the great blocks of tufo and the buildings that were made from them. Soft, damp, porous, indestructible, living stone under the knife. After years out in the sun and the wind and the rain, weathered to a kind of impersonal presence, simply there and never seen for themselves. Too close to have any individual being of their own and so ignored.

They were people's grandmothers, sisters, cousins, aunts and neighbours. They were always there, on street corners, steps, in doorways, in the darker recesses of home, and to children they were sometimes more present than the children's own mothers. The young mothers of small children sometimes had other things on their minds than rearing their offspring, not to speak of the offspring's fathers. The older women were the figure of the female as it fixed early in the young minds of the Spanish Quarters.

They sat in the sun plucking the tips and the tender leaves of the *friarielli* and rinsing the greens for cooking. They hung out washing, reeling great sheets from wall to wall above the alley or positioning a frame on the doorstep to catch the sun as it passed briefly overhead. They washed potatoes, trimmed artichokes, bearded mussels. They refreshed the flowers in the little shrines set into flaking walls and changed the bulbs of the electric candles. They sat bundled up on little folding chairs and sold the cigarettes secreted in the folds of their shawls. They polished skulls in crypts and kept the community in touch with the spirit world, the underworld of lightless spaces where the bones of the dead were neatly stacked. They saw who came and went. They brought out besoms and swept the worn lava blocks as clean as anyone's living room floor ought to be. They, the solid, powerful, understated androgynes, were the blocks the city was made of.

When there was no sun to sit in, the older women on street level would retreat to the windowless single-room homes they shared with the rest of their family, close the lower half of their entrances and gaze out between the open shutters of the upper half like horses from their stalls, their busts projecting directly into the alley. As social centaurs they were at once immediately present to their neighbours, tradesmen, visitors, small children playing in the street, passing outsiders, sellers of fish, vegetables, bread and items of domestic use and the buyers of anything they might themselves have for sale, for purposes of conversation, observation, transaction, information or invitation, and secure in the comfort of their own living rooms.

They could keep an eye on what their neighbours were buying, see what was being put into the baskets lowered on cords right past their noses, hear the bawled details bouncing between the street and a balcony several stories up. They were actors and audience in the theatre of their own social

70

existence, an old women's chorus allowed to comment on the action but not to intervene and without anyone's taking any notice of what they said.

Walking down any narrow footpathless alley, you were passing within inches of the intimate details of people's lives, and your glimpses had the hallucinatory precision of an old-fashioned doll's house or wartime photos of third-floor living rooms with striped wallpaper and their front wall blown off. You might see, as I did once, a lot of highly polished dark wood. Against one wall a huge ornate dresser with gleaming mirrors, a stack of plates and ornaments on its little upper shelves. Against the same wall, behind the dresser and receding into darkness, a camp stove with a gas cylinder beneath it. Well up on the wall facing the street a portrait of the Virgin with a fifteen-watt lamp glowing at its base and an ancestral portrait photo wedged into a bottom corner. A huge double bed taking up most of the floor space, with polished brass rails at head and foot, high off the floor and carefully made up. Near the door a big colour TV in matte gunmetal plastic and jammed against the bed an 11,000 cc Kawasaki motorbike, lustrous too and in that tiny domestic space more weird than monstrous, as if an enormous blue fly had settled there. The disorienting shifts of scale made the whole thing magical, a child's box for living in, lined with gleaming tiles. The Joseph Cornell box was a *basso*.

In eddies at the edges of traffic and violence, you could be walking down a little alley anywhere in Naples, nominally a public thoroughfare, and feel you were intruding into private space. The Spanish Quarters were too edgy and violent for domesticity to get much of a grip on the streets. All the same, little pergolas with vines, awnings in corrugated plastic, potplants and trellises around front doors all made their encroachments, and sometimes little picket rows fenced off parts of the alley. Sometimes it was just the setting out of clothes horses to dry jeans and shirts in the traffic fumes. A stool parked on the roadway, and someone seated on it shelling, stalking, peeling, cleaning, trimming, slicing, rinsing the things to be eaten that evening.

In the Quarters a lot of the bassi had been appropriated by ladies on the game. They were so convenient. Low rent, low maintenance, rapid entry right off the street, no *via crucis* across a tenement courtyard with tiers of spectators looking down, no endless stone staircase punctuated by children on the landings and not-quite-closed front doors. In, out, so discreet. You were being watched all the same, but it was so much easier to put the eyes out of mind and keep your client from noticing. And just above teeming promiscuous Via Toledo. Perfect.

Even more of the bassi up the Quarters were used by *femminielli* for the same purposes. If Naples was the ancient home of Mediterranean transsexualism and transvestism, the Quarters were its epicentre, and having spent their working lives in the neighbourhood the femminielli tended to hang around in retirement. As they got on, the femminielli transmuted into massive block-like figures even more dramatically than the actual women. The men who felt themselves to be women in Naples seemed impelled by the challenge of the feminine. It was the most powerfully built, the hairiest, the most gravelly voiced who seemed most strongly drawn to the other side of the gender divide. You saw them slopping around outside their bassi during daytime hours in satin camisoles and platform mules, attending to domestic tasks with hair pinned up and a ciggie in one hand, but there was no mistaking the body hair, the powerful calves or the raucous utterance.

Intimate garments were handwashed, rinsed, set out to catch the sun on a drying frame. Ashtrays emptied, a change of bed linen perhaps and a little mopping, a quick freshen-up. A spot of eyebrow plucking, leg waxing, nail painting, all done outside, weather permitting. Quite a lot of clattering around outside on the cork platforms, of leaning over the stall and exchanging hoarse shouted words about women's problems for the benefit of any passing third parties.

It was in this somewhat rackety milieu that I heard about a house up the Quarters—not a basso, but still pretty small—that might be for rent. I was directed to the *maresciallo* and we made an appointment to walk over one Saturday morning. There was, he mentioned vaguely, a tenant currently in residence who would most likely be leaving before long.

The maresciallo was a Florentine by birth. He had been posted to Naples in the nineteen thirties as a young sailor in Mussolini's navy and, surviving the war, had stayed in Naples and switched to the *carabinieri*. He was long-retired when I met him, a dapper little man in a flat cap who kept the carabiniere's ferocious moustache and kept it well blacked. Between the peak of his cap and the roll of moustache were bright black eyes, a beak of a nose and high-boned red cheeks. He lived down at Santa Lucia, in a tenement on *Crooked Alley at Santa Lucia*, which is where I went to see him some years later as he lay dying.

73

Naples had been a revelation for the brisk little Florentine. He dissolved into its sensual, passionate, complaining, shameless life, though a kernel of dry matter-of-factness had stayed intact in him from Tuscany. At some point he met a young Neapolitan and fell in love and this decided the rest of his life, though it seemed to me he would probably have stayed in any case. There was more than one Neapolitan love. The maresciallo's particular love married and had a daughter who became then herself, as she moved from infancy to adulthood, the great love of the maresciallo's later years.

As we climbed the hill from Toledo that Saturday morning, the obliquities of the maresciallo's conversation seemed to be indicating that the lady who was the current occupant had been getting behind more and more often with the rent, and was indeed in other ways not an entirely satisfactory tenant. He never said so directly but the logic of our visit seemed to be that the maresciallo might have been thinking of replacing her with me. Or maybe the lady was thinking the maresciallo was thinking of replacing her with me. If she weren't leaving, why were we calling on her? In theory we were going to admire the neat little investment he had made years ago from his tiny navy pension and savings from his carabiniere's salary.

We went through the scarred open doors of a decrepit palazzo and crossed its little courtyard. We walked up a long flight of low, irregular stone stairs and then along a covered way to a smaller courtyard further up the hill, and from the smaller courtyard along a passage which opened out into another open space far too small to be called a courtyard, a kind of light well into which the sun shone blindingly. It was almost midday and the outer squalor had abruptly given way to a zone of loving domestic adaptations which had every surface within reach painted a fresh cream.

Almost vertically above us was a wrought-iron railing edging a narrow terrace lined with red geraniums in terracotta pots. Streaks of fresh rust ran down the candy twists of the bars, and below one point where the railing was anchored to the tiny terrace a crack like forked lightning had opened in the freshly plastered wall below. The maresciallo squinted into the light and called out in a slightly peremptory voice.

There was no response and he called again more sharply. A pane of glass glinted on a sense of movement. A short, slippered and powerfully built woman was at the railing, swaddled in a dressing gown and yanking its cord tighter as she moved into view. As she loomed in front of the sun the maresciallo prepared to explain the reasons for our visit and request entry. He had no chance to give voice. Neapolitan abuse was upended over him. The lady in the dressing gown was the tenant and sensing danger she was taking the offensive. Her animadversions concerned a leaking roof the maresciallo still hadn't fixed.

In the tiny pause that followed, the maresciallo, forearm raised against the sun, covering a face now darker red above the black moustaches, peered up and drew breath for his response. He had no chance to utter it. The figure in the dressing gown got in first. More obscene invective came crashing down. Heads began to appear in unexpected places above us, around corners, in tiny windows and over unexpected ledges, outlined against the sky. Her public assembled, the lady moved from words to action. She bent down swiftly. Her arm swung over the railing. A flowerpot shattered inches from the maresciallo's feet. Red petals scattered and the smell of fresh earth filled the space. And another. And another. The maresciallo was tightly ringed by pot shards, damp clods and twisted stalks. Geranium petals clung to his trouser cuffs like splashes of fresh blood.

I'll be back, he shouted to the dumping figure, now bending for a fourth pot. *Don't you worry about that, you insolent trollop. With an eviction order.* He yanked me out of harm's way and we descended to the street. *She didn't seem to want you there*, he muttered as we retreated down the hill. It was the last I ever heard of the maresciallo's place up the Quarters.

camisole with shoestring straps slung over no less powerful shoulders. Massive forearms and fists guided the perambulator over the smooth black lava blocks. The undergarment housed a pair of abundant breasts which were emphasized less by the taut constraint of the black silk than by the opulent black beard, flecked with silver, which reached toward the cleavage.

The eyes above the beard were soft and suffering, a weary woman's. The mouth behind the moustaches was set in resignation. The dark and rather greasy hair was pulled back and fastened behind her head with a comb. If she hadn't had a beard of the kind you more often saw on a Greek Orthodox priest, she would have been any woman of the Quarters, thickened with age, subdued but undefeated by the daily struggle. Somebody stopped her and she fetched some eggs from a carton perched on the chassis underneath the bird. She was a street seller of newlaid eggs. The big red hen was her partner, her publicist and her production resource, keeping the latest batch warm in the straw.

The bearded lady with her chook and her pram of eggs were inseparable components of an obscure entity which tugged at the imagination. Naples had seen other bearded women before the egg lady with the pram, maybe often. Three hundred years or so before I saw her up the Quarters, she was not another Neapolitan struggling to arrange herself through fresh egg sales but a wonder and a portent. In the late sixteenth century Giovambattista Della Porta, the prolific playwright and boundlessly curious intellect, with one foot in the cosmos of Galilean science and the other in the world of Neapolitan magic, lived at Piazza Carità, a couple of minutes' walk away from the egg lady's beat. He published a book in

1586 on physiognomy, and in his chapter *On hair* he warned that *the bearded woman should be feared as a harbinger of great ill.* Did he have a neighbour in mind?

Forty-five years later, in early 1631, the viceroy had a woman called Magdalena Venturi brought to Naples from her village in the rocky hills of the Abruzzo. With her came her husband and the youngest of their three children, who though already robust was still at the breast. The viceroy had heard of her and wanted to see the otherwise unremarkable housewife and mother's luxuriant black beard. When she arrived in Naples the Venetian resident reported in dispatches that *she has a completely masculine face with more than a palm's length of beautiful black beard and her breast covered with hair.* To record the phenomenon and give people back in Spain a glimpse of the incidental marvels of his posting in Naples, the viceroy had his guest Magdalena painted in his rooms in the palace, standing with the baby at her breast. Her husband was included in the picture, beside and slightly behind his wife. His presence in the painting of *The Bearded Lady* might have been a courtesy to the head of the household and a way of mitigating a relentless gaze on freakishness. It also enabled people to compare and contrast male and female physiognomies and beards.

Two panels painted on the other side of Magdalena described in Latin how she had been a perfectly normal mother of three until at the age of thirty-seven she sprouted a thick beard. Her full breast and healthy third child now showed the beard had not interfered with her life as exemplary wife and mother. The painting in some ways looked ahead to the nineteenth century's pitiless photographic repertory of human types for the diseased, the racially different, the physically abnormal, the freakish, the criminal and the mad.

The painter's gaze at Magdalena Venturi might have been as unrelenting. But a painter spends a lot more time with his model than a photographer takes to expose a plate, and in the model's own direct gaze the painter registered bafflement, humiliation, exhaustion and stoicism of a complex and utterly normal kind, shown through the business of feeding a child and complicated by the hovering concern of the husband at her shoulder. There was nothing in the painting itself, beyond its explanatory caption in Latin, to distance Magdalena from the artist who *painted [her] wonderfully from life*. The hair on Magdalena's face was described as a *miracle of nature*. The painting's wide-eyed solemn stillness had something in it of an image of the Virgin and child, one that included the harried and concerned Joseph. The bearded woman had been floating through the Italian consciousness for a long time.

Siren songs

Parthenope washed up on the shore of the bay and died there. This was how Naples began. Parthenope was one of the Sirens who tried to lure Odysseus on to their rocks as he sailed toward home. The Sirens sang and promised the future and Odysseus struggled to respond to their call, but forewarned by Circe he was tied to the mast and his men had their ears blocked with bees' wax and rowed on.

A *sirena* is a mermaid, as in the little image of the mermaid on the yellow and red tin of Sirena tuna sold in Australia. It is probably a coincidence that red and yellow are the city colours of Naples, the colours that make its festive bunting flame against the blue of the sea and the sky on a clear day. *Sirena classico tuna in oil Italian style*. On the red disc under the *Sirena* and above the descriptive slogan is a *fin de siècle* mermaid, holding her hands behind her head. The golden tresses hanging down front and back of each raised arm, cascading over the otherwise bare breasts, are towy and Teutonic, with more than a touch of *Rheinmädchen*, whereas the facial features are distinctly Mediterranean and the hand that applied the lippy so heavily was clearly Neapolitan.

Her bluish silver tail, with twin flared flukes like a diving whale's, is folded back under her. Her raised left elbow reaches just outside the red disc at the top. The curved part of her lower body, which would be her shin if she were merely human, touches the lower inside of the disc directly opposite at seven o'clock. Her silvery blue scales begin, faintly, almost imperceptibly, with superb verisimilitude, on the lower side of her visible buttock, lightly caressed by the splendid forked tail. If she weren't fishtailed, the *Sirena*® would be kneeling. As it is, supported by unseen water, she seems to have picked up a few lessons in posture from her fellow marine anomaly the tiny seahorse. Columbus was disgusted when he crossed the Atlantic and in January 1493 saw three mermaids who were *Creatures . . . not so faire as they are painted* and that their faces were quite ugly, *somewhat resembling Men*. Columbus seems to have been describing dugongs or manatees and thus rather understating his disappointment. So, in a wilted and languorous posture, breasts no longer pertly uplifted, fingers no longer locked behind the golden tresses of her head, I supposed Parthenope had been when she washed up at Santa Lucia. Histories of Naples always began with Parthenope and thus I imagined her.

Parthenope got no personal mention in the *Odyssey*, where in any case the Sirens were only two. When not trying to attract the attention of a passing boat, they lounged in their meadow on an island, among the mouldering bones of the seamen they had lured to their death. Homer didn't say what they looked like. Their appeal was not their bodies and their only mentioned attraction the irresistible call of *their high, thrilling song*, which was not just seductive music but a promise of knowing the past, the future, the elsewhere. Homer didn't describe them, *leaving us to infer that they were purely human*.

It was a shock to find the Sirens shown on ancient vases as hideous and slightly absurd vulturelike birds, short and flightless, clumsy half-plucked chooks suspended in the air in most surviving images—the plucked look belonging to the human upper body, the feathers and talons showing *from the thighs*—who might have been sketched by Edward Lear. You could imagine how their unearthly music might invite thoughts of sea birds wheeling and calling above the surf and the rocks with the promise of something beyond the shore. But a seagull is beautiful and as shown on pots the Sirens were hideous fat carrion birds with stumpy wings, hardly relieved by their young girls' faces.

They had been friends of Persephone and something bad happened when they were together and she was raped and taken to the underworld by Pluto, either in Sicily or in Campania, places where a volcanically intense other life lurked under the fertile surface of the ground. Something bad happened when they tried to save their friend, or maybe because they failed to save her. Or maybe it was because they intended to remain virgins. The something bad was the carrion bird body and the great predators' talons. They might have been plucked by the muses after losing a singing contest. Sometimes they had beards as well. Physically they embodied about as many rebarbative features as a single allegorical female body could take, and it was a way of offsetting the lure of knowledge, the disembodied ecstasy of their sensuous harmonies.

As lookers and as troublemakers the Sirens were hardly different in their early days from the monstrous Harpies, to whom they seemed a kind of cousin. Harpies too were killer women with wings and talons, flying embodiments of the *vagina dentata* to the hallucinating stressed-out sailor, but they lacked the lure of song. Harpies—the *snatchers*—were attack birds, or attack women, and they came on like sudden fatal storms out of a clear day at sea. They too began as only two and became more numerous but lacking music and insight, they never won acceptance the way the Sirens did in the end. Music had a way of overcoming obstacles.

When he encountered the Sirens, warned in advance by Circe, Odysseus and his crew were making their way—in real world geography—south from the bay of Naples, sailing down along the western coast of southern Italy and heading for the treacherous water between Sicily and the mainland—Scylla and Charybdis—on the way home to Ithaca. The Sirens' island was Capri, their home the whole Sorrento peninsula, their *meadow* one of the pockets of plateau on Capri high above the sea. The bird women took off from their eyrie and wheeled over passing boats. The island offered powerful settings for their suicide when they failed to lure Odysseus to his destruction. One cliff rose sheer hundreds of meters out of the water.

Homer was silent on the Sirens' physiology and on their deaths, interested only in how Odysseus could hear their amazing music and live. He knew when not to elaborate. They threw themselves into the sea and Parthenope's body was carried ashore at the place where Naples now is, more precisely on that tiny island a few meters offshore the Greeks called Megaris, later covered by the Castel dell'Ovo. What did she look like? Were the Greek settlers who found her immediately aware she was a Siren? Did they know what they were dealing with? She would have looked like the *very old man with enormous wings* whom Gabriel García Márquez once described as brought down by torrential rains in another and later remote settlement of Mediterranean origin, on the Caribbean coast of South America. Or a large fruit bat. Bald and toothless, he was an *angel* rather than a siren, being male and arriving into a postclassical and Christian community, a tattooed seaman who spoke Norwegian. The locals put him in the hen coop with the other chooks and fed him on kitchen scraps, making money out of him while the church thought out its position on angels in the community.

Parthenope too, like the old man, was perhaps still alive and *lying face down in the mud, impeded by his enormous wings . . . huge buzzard wings, dirty and half-plucked . . . entangled in the mud . . . strewn with parasites and . . . mistreated by terrestrial winds.* Something already quite dead washed up on a beach, looking like a drowned bird with a human face, bloated and disintegrating and previously gnawed at by sea creatures in the water, was less likely to elicit intense feelings of sympathy and identification, even devotion, than a creature still palpitating with a life of its own, however faintly, a young female who might have *chosen* that particular place to come ashore. Why else would settlers have given the new place her name, and seen themselves in her?

A dead Parthenope would have been like the creature that appalled Fellini's corrupted white-suited Marcello on the beach at the end of *La Dolce Vita*. Day had just broken, he'd been up all night again, and the sea was *too calm, an enormous yellowish puddle.* Fishermen had just dragged ashore *something between a rat and a pregnant woman, nearly two meters long and bearing monstrous flippers. A few crabs are crawling up its big belly, white and obscene . . . the corpse still has something alive about it . . . a human eye with an eyelid and lashes and a hazelnut coloured pupil . . . and the eye seems to be staring at him.* Fellini's fishermen, like the Caribbean people in García Márquez, flared up in brief excitement at the commercial possibilities of their catch. One of them had seen people paying to see one of these in a sideshow at Gaeta. Only, like the angel on the other side of the Atlantic, the sideshow monster had been alive. Now, *throw it back . . . it's already dead.*

The protoNeapolitans would have done the same with an already dead Parthenope. A live Parthenope, however bedraggled, however grotesque as she neared her end, would have seemed, like the old man with enormous wings, *familiar.* In the Caribbean, the *angel*, after seeming dead of age and exhaustion, unexpectedly struggled back into the air and the housewife into whose yard he had fallen saw him disappear, *no longer an annoyance in her life but an imaginary dot on the horizon of the sea.* Parthenope, too, stayed around long enough for the locals to feel she was one of themselves, before they buried her on the high point where they'd built their central citadel, protected on nearly every side by sheer cliffs, the steep promontory now called Pizzofalcone where the city began, which dropped away to the sea and the tiny island where Parthenope came ashore.

Parthenope was eros and death. Dying at the moment of arrival, she reached orgasm and expiration at once. As a founding figure, she embodied the peculiarly Neapolitan sense of happiness glimpsed and never quite reached, of voluptuousness snatched away just as it was being realized. Love, death and the dangerous powers of music and knowledge. Mediterranean dreams frustrated the adolescent Humbert Humbert, whose murderous involutions would deprive Lolita of her childhood and her life. The defining moment of the infant Humbert with his Annabel on the Mediterranean coast of France had nothing to do with the Siren as other than human but everything to do with the maddening ecstasy of non-realization on the edge of the Mediterranean, when *(this was our very last chance, and nothing really mattered)*

we . . . found a desolate stretch of sand and there, in the violet shadow of some red rocks forming a kind of cave, had a brief session of avid caresses, with somebody's pair of lost sunglasses for only witness. I was on my knees, and on the point of possessing my darling, when two bearded bathers, the old man of the sea and his brother, came out of the sea with exclamations of ribald encouragement, and four months later she died of typhus in Corfu.

The *old man of the sea* was at once a fin de siècle athlete in long striped woollen drawers and Nereus, forerunner of Poseidon the sea god and father of the Nereids, the sea nymphs. Some ancients said the Sirens themselves were nymphs.

Somewhere in her long afterlife as the presiding spirit of the city that was called after her, Parthenope changed from being a drowned half-bird to a beautiful longhaired fishtailed woman. She survived the coming of Christianity and the long centuries before ancient learning revived. Five centuries after the founding of her city, a kneeling terracotta figure from Athens showed a siren as all woman, apart from a large and shapely pair of angel's wings and a fishtail below her ankles. Fish sirens were postclassical, Hellenistic at best, but largely medieval. Parthenope's transformation in the middle ages might have been accelerated by medieval masons' difficulties with feathers. Stone needed to be finely carved to show skin covered with feathers. The sleek tail, powerful, tapering, flexed and flaring into a bow at the end, was powerfully suggestive and less technically challenging than a pair of wings.

Siren ambiguity went back to origins and was also linguistic. In Greek, wings and flippers shared the same word, and in Latin and then in Italian, *feathers and fins* were almost identical, *penne e pinne*. Sea people of both sexes haunted the Mediterranean from the very earliest time, and the Sirens were assimilated to them, as their harmonies and the knowledge they promised became more and more intimately a part of the sensual and sexual nature of the fish women themselves. By the time she was formalized as an emblem of Naples in the early eighteenth century, Parthenope had developed a double fishtail and wore a crown suitable to a kingdom. She held her motto on a little placard. It was almost an invitation, *Non sempre nuoce*, or *Not always harmful*, and renewed her exquisite ambiguity for the age of enlightenment.

Like her city she was never quite tamed. A fish-devouring silver-tailed adolescent girl, a fresh, slender, white-toothed, carnal sixteen-year-old, otherworldly and immortal, encountered Giuseppe Tomasi de Lampedusa's handsome young classicist on the eastern coast of Sicily one summer in the last years of the nineteenth century. For her it was one of the countless sexual relations of her *millennial adolescence* with *sailors and fishermen, Greeks, Sicilians, Arabs, Capresi and a few shipwreck survivors*. For the young man in his early twenties it changed everything. Three weeks on a deserted beach were such an overwhelming erotic experience that he was unable to contemplate sex with mere women without disgust for the rest of his life.

> She only ate live food. I often saw her coming up out of the sea, her delicate torso shining in the sun while she tore into a silvery still quivering fish with her teeth, a trickle of blood running down her chin . . . she was an animal and immortal at the same time . . . in sex she showed a joyousness and delicacy quite contrary to the grim animal tale and she spoke with a powerful immediacy I've found since only in a few great poets.

The one sensual satisfaction which remained to him in his decades of solitary academic distinction was devouring the innards of fresh sea urchins. They smelt like her and their flesh recalled her sexual organs. The Siren whom the elderly professor had known as a young man was Parthenope's sister Ligeia.

Nothing material remained—no shrine, no statue, no inscription—to suggest quite what the early Parthenopeans felt about their founding Siren. Did anyone try to make a fast buck out of the creature washed up on the beach? Feelings of pity, wonder, lust, revulsion and the cash flow instinct were not likely to be much different three thousand years ago. When the geographer Strabo visited Naples at the time of Christ he found an elaborate cult around Parthenope's memory with games and guided visits to her tomb, the official rites of a city that was already a thousand years old, and a sanctuary to the Sirens on the tip of the Sorrento peninsula opposite the island where they had leapt to their death.

Everyone born into settler societies felt the same anxiety to legitimize the usurpation of someone else's ground, to give a new place dignity, lineage, meaning. At first everyone making a hardscrabble new life on the other side of the world thought only of Home, but in social adolescence a place required an identity of its own. The dying Siren they identified as Parthenope, *Virgin's Eye* herself, gave the lonely colonists' western frontier settlement a link to the figures and the stories of the life they'd left. Parthenope, dying in Naples, made them feel, on the newfound coast, beautiful but strange and scary, that it was a small world after all. Even in the far West they were still on the map of the imaginable.

In the end Parthenope was no more than picturesque local folklore and glamorous nomenclature for the classically educated tourist. The soldiers of the Wehrmacht arrived in

Naples as friends from the Third Reich and allies in the great fraternal enterprise of totalitarian empire in Europe and the world. They stayed as occupiers to reduce the city on Hitler's directive to a heap of *mud and ashes* before the British and the Americans arrived. Even before they tried to destroy Naples, the Germans had felt let down by the city and *finding [Naples] had become so much uglier than it was in the descriptions of Mozart . . . and Goethe, they changed its name to* Althénopis, *which would mean* Old Woman's Eye.

Parthenope's definitive funeral came after the Neapolitans had driven out the Germans. When the British and the Americans arrived to occupy Naples in their place, Mark Clark, the leader of a very imperfectly conceived and executed invasion, *expressed a preference for fish.* The starving Neapolitans, who were forbidden to fish in the bay among the Allied ships and the floating mines, may or may not have served him the last and most precious remaining inhabitant of the aquarium in their Zoological Station, whose collection of marine animals had been a wonder of biology. The main dish was a baby manatee, *boiled and served with a garlic sauce* according to Norman Lewis, who arrived as an intelligence officer with the British army some months later, and reported what *all Neapolitans believe.* Curzio Malaparte in 1949 added that the Siren was served cold with a mayonnaise. *A faint cry of horror escaped Mrs Flat's lips and General Cork went pale.*

A little girl, or something very like a little girl, lay on her back in the middle of the tray, on a bed of green lettuce leaves . . . her eyes were open, lips half parted . . . she was naked, but her skin, dark and shiny and the same purple colour as Mrs Flat's dress, moulded just like a tight dress the still immature yet already harmonious outline of her body, the soft curve of her waist, the slight bulge of her belly, the tiny virginal breasts, the broad shoulders. She may have been only eight or ten years old, but she was precocious and already womanly enough to look fifteen at first sight. Torn here and there, or mushed up in the cooking, the skin afforded glimpses through the splits and folds of tender silvery golden flesh . . . Her face, which the heat of the boiling water had caused to burst from its skin like an overripe fruit, was like a gleaming old porcelain mask, prominent lips, high narrow brow, round green eyes. Her arms were short, a kind of fin ending in a point like fingerless hands . . . The long slender waist ended just as Ovid described it, *in piscem*, in a fishtail . . . she gazed up at the *Triumph of Venus* painted on the ceiling, at the turquoise sea, the silver fishes, the green monsters of the deep, the white clouds floating across the horizon and smiled ecstatically. That was her sea, her lost home, the land of her dreams, the happy kingdom of the Sirens.

It was the first time I had seen a little girl boiled, and I remained silent, gripped by a holy fear. Everyone around the table was pale with horror.

Malaparte went through the American occupation of Naples in a sweat of embarrassment and humiliation and fevered imagining and was not reliable. He was even wrong about Ovid, for whom the Sirens still *weare Both feete and feathers like to Birdes* and *beare The upper parts of Maidens still*. Like all the episodes involving Parthenope and her sisters, her funeral at the banquet for Mark Clark hovered between the imagined and the merely real. Underneath Malaparte's interminable embellishments and Lewis's dry annotation of the strange things people liked to eat in Naples was a last flash of the unnamed Parthenope in Neapolitan talk. A small splash, a flick of her silver tail and she disappeared forever from the people's mind as the Americans patrolled the rubble of her city pumping out clouds of DDT.

Hungry city

Magdalena Venturi's beard, her large baby at her large breast and her ruffled, anxious husband were painted for the record by a forty-year-old Spaniard who in 1631 had been living in Naples for fifteen years.

Jusepe de Ribera had left Valencia for Italy around 1608 as a teenager, the son of a shoemaker in a town nearby. By the time he was twenty he was working for the ruling Farnese family in Parma, so brilliantly that the other painters drove him out of town. A couple of years later he was busy in Rome among the disorderly set of international painters there. He was a big spender and a roaring boy, and it may have been just ahead of his creditors that in the summer of 1616, immediately after finishing his latest Roman commission, he abruptly upped sticks and moved to Spanish Naples, which was politically secure and offered rich pickings professionally. He went back to Rome ten years later to be invested as a knight of the Order of Christ at the Vatican, but otherwise he never left Naples again, never returned to Spain.

Ribera made two smart moves when he got to Naples. The first was to marry, a couple of months after arriving, the fifteen-year-old daughter of a painter called Giovan Bernardino Azzolino. Azzolino was a Sicilian who had been working in Naples for decades. He was successful, well connected and well liked. In a single preemptive stroke, the newly arrived twenty-five-year-old integrated himself into a local painting scene that was deeply hostile to any painter from outside who might threaten local livelihoods. Twenty years later, Ribera himself would be leading campaigns against prestigious outsiders who came to work in Naples.

He also loudly asserted his Spanish identity and signed his canvases *Jusepe de Ribera español*. Neapolitans didn't call him *the little Spaniard* for nothing. His Spanishness, and his early fame in Parma and Rome, gave him entrée to the viceregal court, and within a year he was painting for both the viceroy and his wife. He was deeply attached to his own wife and stayed close to her family, and was genuinely proud of being Spanish, but these were astute positionings all the same. So was his decision never to move from Naples, which uniquely combined the advantages of Spain and Italy. After Ribera had been there nine years a fellow Spaniard asked if he thought of returning home. Ribera told him he did feel the urge, but he knew that if he went back *during the first year, I would be received there as a great painter but in the second year no one would pay attention to me because when people know you are around they lose respect for you.*

He called Spain *a loving mother to foreigners and a very cruel stepmother to her own sons*. His work had more cachet in Spain when it came from Italy in the baggage of returning viceroys, or as commissions sent to the king and aristocratic collectors. The Neapolitans, then as now the quickest people in the world to take the piss, picked up fast on Ribera's insistent identification of himself with the occupying power. The emphasis on the *little* in *little Spaniard* wiped out any compensating associations with that imperial grandeur cultivated by the representatives of Madrid. In the end, though he'd long been wholly part of the local painting scene, being Spanish would become a dangerous liability for Ribera in Naples.

How Ribera came from nowhere to dazzle the discriminating milieu of Parma with a powerfully realistic painting of saint Martin giving part of his cloak to a beggar was not recorded. How did he get such a big commission as an unknown twenty-year-old? It was his first known work and painted in early 1611. Before that he had spent some time moving around Lombardy looking at the origins of Italian realism. Anyone travelling to Italy from Valencia in the early seventeenth century would have been likely to take advantage of the intense maritime traffic, merchant and military, between metropolitan Spain's eastern port and the port of its Italian capital Naples. He might have sailed to Genoa, but there were reasons for thinking Naples was probably the first place in Italy Ribera saw, and that when he moved there from Rome nearly a decade later he already knew the place he was heading for. Ribera's first known work blazed with the dark light of Michelangelo Merisi from Caravaggio and Merisi was quite likely in Naples when Ribera reached Italy.

Merisi had arrived in Naples in the autumn of 1606 and was immediately commissioned, on account of his fame and his radical realism, to paint the main altarpiece for the church of a newly formed activist charity group. The painting had to show the *Seven Works of Mercy*. The young aristocrats of the intellectual avant-garde who founded the group

> visit the sick ... keep beds at the hospital ... bury the dead and celebrate endless masses for the dead in their church, free prisoners and serve lunch every month to a hundred and ten poor prisoners in the Vicaria ... rescue citizens in the hands of infidels, help great numbers of the city's destitute ...

They wanted this commitment shown in something really striking and different, a strong visual statement of intent, and nine days into 1607 they had it. They got more. Merisi took their seven emblematic acts of kindness—a shopping list from Matthew's *Gospel*—dramatized and made them real as a hyperrealist scene of night life in a Neapolitan alley. Painting from life, shaping his figures with light as they emerged from the darkness, Merisi radically rethought and recast his painting as he worked, just as he had at that earlier extraordinary moment in Rome, when he painted his *Matthew* suite in 1600.

No painter had ever done anything like the *Seven Works* before. Arriving in Naples at a moment of social crisis, Merisi reinvented the religious image for an urban reality that hadn't existed before, testing not just the way of representing the

Christian message but the message itself. Charity was uneasily absent from his vision of good works, with its fragmentary, overlapping and conflicting images of uncertainty and tension. The take on *I was a stranger, and ye took me in* was strictly commercial, a pilgrim being welcomed by a fleshy innkeeper with a boozer's nose. *I was naked, and ye clothed me* was saint Martin as a supremely elegant young man sadly sharing his cloak with a gauntly naked street person sitting in the dirt. *I was an hungred, and ye gave me meat . . . I was in prison, and ye came unto me* became a daughter breastfeeding her old father through the prison bars, sullen and resentful at having to do it in public. *I was thirsty, and ye gave me drink* was water in the desert from an ass's jawbone, but the image looked like someone swigging from a wineskin. The corpse being carried bare feet first through the street was so common a sight that only the awkward daughter even looked around, and then only because she was disturbed while breastfeeding her father.

The heavenly component in the upper part of Merisi's image shared that ordinariness. The angels looking down on the alley, as they wheeled tightly in the narrow street space available, were a couple of local kids, an airborne version of the idle watching youths on every street corner. Their huge wings tangled with the drying sheets doubling as angel raiment and, being real wings, cast a big shadow on the wall. The feather tips poked through the prison bars. Mary and her child Jesus were part of the neighbourhood too, looking down on the street life from an unseen window balcony, the child highly curious and interested in what he saw. If the angels looked as if they'd parked their Vespa round the corner,

Mary seemed about to lower a basket for a loaf of bread or a packet of Marlboro.

No painter before or since so caught the double valency of street life in Naples, always more than the sum of its parts, trivial and transcendent. Bruno's play *Candleman* had shown the same world a generation before, but Bruno never achieved that stillness of fully realized art which in *Seven Works* held all the egoism of the street's frantic movement in harmonious balance. For a moment. *Seven Works* was pervaded not by divine order but by an electrifying sense of imminent violence. Its immediate acclaim said a lot about the intelligence of the governors who commissioned and jealously guarded the painting—no Roman problems with *decorum* in Naples—and about the urgency of the needs they were trying to meet. Things could not go on like this. The tightly enclosed world of the streets in Naples could blow apart at any moment. The darkness was all around. Even the angel wings looked like a huge bird of prey's.

The Naples Merisi painted was a city whose own poor were being outnumbered by peasant refugees from all over southern Italy. The newcomers were camped in the streets and courtyards without work, without friends or protectors, hungry, sick and homeless. When people encountered *Seven Works* they walked in off the street and in the dancing candle-light over the altar they saw themselves acting out the Christian moral drama. The painting's ironies were pungent. Slum dwellers saw the bulky tavern host standing in his doorway to welcome the hungry poor, as in their dreams. They saw a dashing young son of the oppressor class, broadhatted and plumed, slashing off the train of his silk cloak for the benefit of a filthy naked derelict sprawled on the pavement. They saw elements of Parthenope the egg lady in the predator's wings, the milk-splashed beard, the exposed breast.

Seven Works was the shock of the real in a city where the real and the imagined were more obscurely entangled than elsewhere. The big picture and its image were labile, hallucinatory, treacherous. You had to put the glimpsed details together in your own mind. Distinctions between the seen and the imagined, earthly and unearthly, were lost in this crowded darkness where no glimpsed fragment of the world's surface seemed less memorable than any other. Any idea of beauty seemed irrelevant. The loveliest bay on earth was a couple of minutes' walk from unspeakable squalor. The nobility played out splendidly accoutred lives among the destitute in the biggest and most crowded city in Europe. They shared the same buildings and the same narrow streets. The closeness of the elegant young blood and the naked figure in the dirt in *Seven Works* was a sweaty daily reality. Personal detail, impressed close up in blinding sunlight, flickering torch flame or felt out in deep shadow, was how people perceived each other in Naples.

Every palazzo was a microcosm, with vast halls for the nobility and tiny hutches for the poor. In the streets, and in the market places and small piazzas, in the courtyards and on the waterfront, the rich and powerful had to pick their way through filthy sprawling figures, importunate beggars and sellers of produce, water, cooked food, household goods, decorative items—anything portable—swarming children, seated women, bag snatchers and pickpockets, marauding soldiery and itinerant preachers. Horses were frightened, sedan chairs were dropped and gilded coaches lost their wheels against stone walls and balusters.

A couple of months after his first encounter with the moral economy of the streets of Naples, Merisi's image of an age's crisis was ready.

Naples had exploded twenty years before. In 1585 the price of bread rose sharply, and the *people's representative* in the city government—the one member who was not an aristocrat but the viceroy's handpicked member of the higher bourgeoisie—was hated for having speculated on wheat prices and having *got rich as people's representative*. Living standards had been falling for years and the price rise came immediately after an authorization to export *over 400,000 tomoli of grain* from Naples to Spain. Southern Italy was already in deep agricultural crisis—and bad harvests would continue almost uninterrupted for twenty years or more—and others in Naples were also speculating in wine and other produce. When people protested, representative Starace said contemptuously and publicly *he would make them eat dirt*. After a public meeting, Starace was grabbed by those present and paraded through the streets in his own sedan chair, hatless and facing backwards like a common criminal.

When they saw Starace publicly humiliated, people grabbed weapons, yelled *Serra serra* and locked down the shops. Fury was unleashed, Starace was killed, and as a fairly unequivocal message to the local politicians and the occupying power, his corpse was castrated and dragged through the streets of the crowded quarters near the Market and finally dumped in front of the viceroy's palace. His family narrowly escaped being burnt alive in his house. The house itself was stripped of its immensely valuable contents, which were handed over to the city's convents. *Everyone seems happy at Starace's death*, reported the Venetian resident in his dispatch the next day, *and so far not a single person has defended him*.

The people's point was well taken by those in power.

All the rich and well off were immensely upset, less by representative Starace's misfortune than by the popular uprising, and the mob's irrational and desperate anger, which they were afraid might soon be directed against themselves.

The viceroy acted—posters were starting to appear on the walls, urging people to finish what they had begun and throw the Spanish out—and had a lot of wheat shipped in from Sicily and sold at far below cost, recovering the lost money through an extra consumption tax.

Two months later, when things were quiet again, forty galleys arrived in Naples from Spain with troops commanded by don Pedro de Toledo, the former viceroy's son. A couple of weeks later, after the administration had investigated, five hundred men were quietly taken from their homes at night. Arrest warrants were issued for another three hundred and twenty who had not been found. Thirty-one were sentenced to torture and death, seventy-one were sentenced to years on the galleys and three hundred were expelled from the vicerealm with a bounty on their heads. Twelve thousand other Neapolitans fled the city fearing arrest.

Fates were exemplary. Those sentenced to death were tortured by irons on a cart moving through the city for maximum visibility. Then their right hands were cut off at one symbolic location, and their left hands at another. They were then dragged to the Market Place, hanged and quartered. It was not about Starace. This was the old punishment for rebellion against the king. *The mob was very wrong . . . to show so little respect to its master. This was worse than killing and assassination.*

Cheaper bread brought a moment of respite in Naples, and when the men sentenced to the galleys were being marched down to the waterfront in chains, they called out bitterly to the people watching silently in the streets, *Now you've got bread and wine you don't say a word, and we're going off to die.* The physician accused of leading the revolt managed to escape to Venice with his son. Early the next year the viceroy had the man's house razed and a monument erected on the site, in which the head and hands of each man executed were displayed in little niches, and *they say a fiery cart rolls through the city, and a man on horseback with black torches who comes out of the prison and passes the place of the monument and the heads cry out.*

The price of bread went on rising. For the next few years *you couldn't walk down the streets, there were so many poor people* and the Venetian resident reported the same thing in his dispatches. This was the crisis the young nobles who commissioned Merisi's painting were trying to remedy, along with other groups inspired by the counter-reformation's call to good works and urged on by social disaster. Spain reacted so savagely to the disturbances in 1585 because it was afraid of an anti-Spanish movement in southern Italy when it was already facing revolt in the Low Countries to the north. The destruction of the Invincible Armada off the coast of England in 1588—Naples had sent four galleys and ten companies of soldiers to the invasion force—increased the sense of alarm in Madrid and brought no relief to people in Naples.

Good works were next to useless against crisis on this scale. Merisi arrived in Naples at the end of another year of famine and bread rationing. You had to be a citizen of Naples to get a ration card. *The loaves baked for foreigners . . . are tiny.* This made things worse. A couple of months after *Seven Works* was finished, the Tuscan representative in Naples reported to Florence that *the famine is so acute all through the vicerealm that entire communities are coming to Naples and going round the city calling out* Bread, bread . . . *people are dying in the streets and nothing is being done about it.*

It was no accident that most of the works of mercy in Merisi's painting had to do with providing food and drink. Or that Merisi was asked to include in his painting the additional good work of burying the dead. The population of Naples was so swollen by the influx of the starving that Spain was afraid the vicerealm's agricultural towns and territories *would be abandoned with everyone living in a single city, as happened with Cairo in Egypt,* and the administration tried again and again over the years to stop people building houses outside the city walls.

Unknown young Ribera arrived in Italy some time between 1607, when he was sixteen, and 1609. If he disembarked in Naples he might have met Merisi. In any case Merisi's paintings were there and the encounter electrified him. In Naples, Ribera could have seen not only the *Seven Works* but the monumental *Whipping* in San Domenico Maggiore, with its day-labourer torturers, and the amazing, spectral *Resurrection*, with its Christ leaving the tomb like a jailbreaker. Other, smaller paintings were in private hands, not necessarily unseen by Ribera.

Ribera went north to Lombardy, not the most obvious area of interest for a young painter new to Italian art. Did he go for sober realist art close to the evolving realism of German, Dutch, Flemish art? Or for the painterly culture of Venice, of Giorgione and Titian, the other source of Merisi's idea of what it meant to paint? Lombardy was a long way from Florentine drawing and Roman rhetoric and the mannerism of the recent past. To Rome Ribera returned and he worked there for three or four years, painting and competing with a large community of Italians and foreigners, especially from the North. Merisi's art was still the pivot on which all the new painting turned. His old associates and first followers were still around—Orazio Gentileschi, Cecco Boneri, Manfredi, Borgianni, Spada. Merisi's painting from life drew young Flemish and French painters to Rome, the exacerbated realists Ribera fell in with now—Terbrugghen, Honthorst, Valentin, Vouet. The skimpy records from Rome had him living in *the house of the Fleming*, and joined at some point by his two painter brothers from Spain, who had clearly been hearing encouraging news.

In this time Ribera did a series of five portraits showing the *Five Senses*, polemically stripped of allegorical and emblematic adornments. Ribera showed real, coarse people living real coarse lives. *The Sense of Taste* had a florid, beaky-nosed gourmand, quite like the fleshy host of *Seven Works*, with sausage fingers and shirt tightly buttoned over his gut, tucking into a bowl of pasta with a flask of rough red on the side. There were things learnt here from Annibale Carracci from Bologna and his *Bean Eater*, and things that anticipated Frans Hals, but the overwhelming presence was Merisi's. Young Ribera made his own that sense Merisi had of the unadorned and un-ideal reality of human bodies, of the play of light over surfaces and textures which gives an image substance. He was not just appropriating a style. The polemical intent further showed in the freshly halved onion being sniffed in *Smell* instead of convention's rose. *Sight* displayed the just-invented Galilean telescope. Ribera's realism gave Merisi's optical delicacy a northern and a Spanish toughness, a harder edge.

When he moved to Naples in 1616, the impulse behind the group of *Sense* paintings deepened into a vein that would run through a good fifteen years of Ribera's working life. He began doing portraits of ancient philosophers, saints and prophets. The paintings began soon after his arrival in Naples with a group of *Apostles* for a church and a series of *Saints* for the viceroy Osuña. They culminated in 1630 in more apostles and figures from the Old Testament, and an extraordinary series of *Philosophers* for the viceroy Alcalá.

Ribera's philosophers and prophets were the destitute males wandering the streets of Naples, the city's own poor and the refugees from the vicerealm's backlands. The paintings Ribera did over fifteen years are a collective portrait of the devastated but indomitable unknown and forgotten people who crowded the streets of Naples in those years, out of work or past working. Straggly bearded, ruffle-haired, sometimes toothless, their faces scored by the sun and hunger, bony shoulders covered with worn blankets, they invested the visionaries whose names they took for a moment with their own intensity of being. Their worn and weatherbeaten faces found correspondences in Ribera's technique. Impasto thickened and scored lines deepened to match the experience he was reaching for. These portraits carried none of the assertive naturalism of the *Sense* paintings. Nothing was being suggested about a moral equivalence of subject and model, still less any clever sense of ironic distance between them. The painter just linked the austerity of ancient moral grandeur and the starkness of contemporary suffering, in a reality you could see and feel.

Naples was a church town and most of Ribera's painting commissions, like nearly everyone else's, were religious. He had no trouble at all supplying images that conformed with the requirements of the counter-reformation. His paintings were often deeply disturbing, but quite where the discomfort came from was harder to identify. He specialized in martyrdoms and it would take hundreds of years for his reputation to get beyond them. Ribera's martyrdoms had a horrid fascination for nineteenth century visitors to Italy from the Protestant north. Byron had told the tourists in advance that Ribera *tainted / His brush with all the blood of all the sainted* and so they found in his paintings the frightening darkness and cruelty they associated with Spain, the Inquisition, the counter-reformation and the church of Rome. The *Spagnoletto* was the nineteenth century's byword for pain in art.

Byron was wrong. There was no blood. The early tourists peered in gloomy churches at Ribera's canvases, encrusted with varnish and candle smoke, and didn't know what was upsetting them. Painting a martyrdom for the militant counter-reformation meant confronting the mechanics of killing, and Ribera like Merisi brought a hard unblinking eye to the techniques and personnel involved in torture and death. Merisi painted these matter-of-factly. Ribera's paintings of saints dying were disturbing in their dreamy calm. The preparations for death had a monumental stillness and a kind of silence, as if the soundtrack were turned off. He nearly always showed the still, expectant moment before the killing began. Looking at the scene from Ribera's angle, you felt subliminal pain without quite knowing where it came from. The stresses of a body being pulled apart were carefully built into the structure of the Prado *Philip* and made more acute by the radiant cloud-flecked blue sky against which the old saint, his arms already stretched to breaking point, was being hoisted like a great sail by the straining crew. The sail would be the flapping skin from his flaying. In *Lawrence* the glowing wood being fanned under the grille—an economical cluster like a cooking fire's and a perfect little still life—had not yet had Lawrence's naked body placed over them.

To meet the demand for martyrdoms Ribera developed a formula as well as a humming workshop manned by highly skilled assistants, a workshop which over the years raised a lot of strong and individual painters. His own endlessly varied and briskly executed martyrdoms had a recognizable template in the *standard martyrdom composition*.

> In the foreground, the martyr's semi-nude figure . . . with difficult foreshortenings . . . wrinkled skin . . . illuminated by a powerful light . . . the executioner . . . in the guise of an anonymous laborer . . . a ragged bandana around his head . . . prepares the instruments of torture and death . . . Large human bodies occupy . . . the front plane . . . a small opening into the background, where . . . onlookers . . . witness the torment.

The paintings were all variations on a template developed not by Ribera himself but by his master Merisi. The original painting from which all of Ribera's derived was Merisi's *Peter Killed* in Rome, which showed the old man tipped backward on his cross as it was hoisted by a couple of heaving workmen. What Ribera never got—never seemed to be trying for—was the look on Peter's face, his perceptible alarm not at the slow and painful death about to come, but an old man's disorientation at his sudden backward lurch, as he peered to see where the ground was. The tragedy for an instant was brushed by the absurd. It was like the meeting of great and tiny pains in Lear's last moment in Shakespeare's play of two years later, the little detail of *Pray you, vndo this Button*, a glimpse of old age's little difficulties even as death was transforming everything.

Ribera's copious images had nothing like these details in Merisi's *Peter* or Shakespeare's *Lear*. His old faces—and he specialized in extreme old age, the wrinkles, the bones beneath the skin, the shreds of muscle and the tendons were far more of a challenge than the sleek contours of youth—were masks by comparison. The very old, the saints and philosophers who should have been dead but weren't because their thoughts and their lifetimes of physical privation had reduced them to indestructible cages of skin and bone that nursed an immortal spark, were a particular gift from Merisi. Ribera's very old men were palpably descended from Merisi's *Jeromes*, the two done in Rome a year or so before he fled and in the collections of Giustiniani and Borghese when Ribera lived there, the old man meditating and the old man writing, with only a red blanket and a white sheet twisted around his waist and a skull for company. Ribera took the sunburnt skull, the tufts of white hair around the ears, the stringy arm muscles, the slack wrinkles of the torso, the infinitely furrowed brow and the knotty old hands and reworked them powerfully and endlessly. They were often Jeromes too: Ribera liked being able to paint books, as many and as thick as possible, stacked in the hermit's desert cave, and he painted the irregular much-turned page edges and the discoloured vellum bindings with no less vigour than the old man whose skin and wrinkles they reflected.

When he slipped the religious tether Ribera's results could be startling. Ten years after setting up in Naples he did a quasi-classical and quasi-pastoral allegory of *Drunken Silenus*, a painting whose artful trappings faded into the darkness around the edges of a livid and obscene male nude who might better have been labelled *Advanced Symptoms of Precocious Alcoholic Degeneration*. The skin on display for once was not old nor the figure emaciated, and the effect was repulsive. Ribera's rare classical moments turned into Christian martyrdoms and used the same formula, the same *difficult foreshortening* of a body in pain, or about to be, the same little cluster of appalled onlookers. It was hardly surprising when the subject was *Apollo Skinning Marsyas* alive for challenging him in music. The series of punishments for *Ixion*, *Tantalus*, *Sisyphus* and other pre-Christian transgressors reduced the concepts to pure images of bodies in pain.

Ribera's eye was fearsome. Yet he seemed to have no personal stake in the cruelty he imaged. It was what he saw around him. His eyes devoured everything they saw. Their attention to the surfaces of failing bodies was so fierce it seemed to go beyond where normal vision stopped, and the savage verve of his brush to show not just the surface but a little of what lay beneath. Pablo Picasso was another Spaniard from the eastern seaboard with an eye as hungry and pitiless as Ribera's, though compared with Ribera, Picasso was a sentimentalist. Compared with Ribera, Francis Bacon was a window-dresser. The paradox of Ribera was how he brought aging, pain and death to life.

His fierce attention to the imperfections of the real eased off a little when he reached his forties. Retro prettifiers from Bologna and Rome were drawn to Naples by fat commissions and Ribera hounded them mercilessly, but despite himself he learnt from them. After fifteen years of living under it, he started noticing the luminous sky of Naples, though he used it mostly as a cyclorama to backlight the theatre of cruelty his clients kept on wanting to see. He even made some avant-garde forays into landscape painting, flights into vast horizontal stillnesses under that sky and not a human figure in sight.

This sky—Giordano Bruno, the philosopher who theorized its infinity in 1584, described himself as *a Neapolitan, born and raised under a kinder sky*, when they savaged him at Oxford—was the transforming element in the most extraordinary painting Ribera ever did. This painting was also the only work of Ribera's to leap out of its time and place and make a permanent mark on European art. But this was in another country and two hundred years later.

The *Clubfoot Boy* fell nominally into that same drear zone of documentary record whose only other instance in Ribera's work was Magdalena, the *Bearded Lady*, unless *Drunken Silenus* were counted as medical case history. It showed a beggar boy from Naples and carefully made his deformities clear, which were not only his eponymous club foot but a withered claw-like hand. Both were on his right side, the one in view in Ribera's full-length profile image. With his good left hand the boy was clutching his official permit to beg and at the same time shouldering his crutch as he turned toward the painter and bared his teeth and gums in a cheerful grin. It was one of the very few real smiles Ribera ever painted, certainly the only grin. Apart from a few marginal and unpleasant smirks and leers, the only other smiles Ribera did were on the emaciated and often toothless faces of the street people philosophers, who were the boy's older colleagues.

The boy's grin concentrated the precarious insouciance of his pose—*look, no crutch*—and transformed the picture from documentary record to incomparable truth. Unlike the *Bearded Lady*, the *Clubfoot Boy* contained no explanatory caption recording the reason and circumstances of its commission. The words on the document the boy was holding in the air were just those of the city administration's standard issue permit to beg. The painting was perhaps done for a charity like the one which had commissioned Merisi's *Seven Works*, as an incitement to good deeds, but no record survived of this. If it were, the *Clubfoot Boy* might not have been considered to have quite hit its mark. The boy in his radiant autonomy seemed to feel no need of anyone's help and the gaze that fixed the painter or the viewer was the look of a confident equal. Ribera's image was many miles from the pathos shading into kitsch of his younger contemporary Murillo's images of street children in Spain.

In his *Bearded Lady* of a decade earlier Ribera had transformed a freak show into an image of stoicism close to tragedy. In *Clubfoot Boy* from a figure of extreme poverty, of youth without hope, of crippling immobility, he made a more amazing transformation of his subject into lighthearted and joyous movement without missing a single forensic detail of the subject's dreadful clothes—an adult's and far too big—his deformities of hand and foot, his heavy crutch, shapeless satchel, crude haircut and blackened neglected teeth and the bureaucratic document that certified him as genuinely in need of help.

The radiance came in part from the luminous sky. The boy was not shown in a filthy street of Naples or, like Magdalena

him she was his sister, born during his father's time in Sicily. So no sex, but the dinner and the wine—the excellent white Greco from Irpinia—and the family talk went on so long that she wouldn't hear of his venturing out so late on the dangerous streets of Naples, a foreigner alone at night. He'd sleep at her place. She sent him upstairs with a small boy to attend to his needs. Undressed, his clothes and money belt on the bed, he asked about the amenities and was directed through a small door.

By the time Andreuccio got back to his hotel next morning—his friends had been up all night worrying—he'd lost his clothes and his money and fallen into an open sewer full of shit. He had also been stuck down a well and buried alive in the cathedral, in the massive tomb of a recently dead archbishop, expecting *to die of hunger and stench among the corpse's worms*. But he escaped, after pulling from the corpse's finger and slipping on his own a ring worth rather more than the money lost in the Sicilian girl's house. Advised to leave town fast, he went home to Perugia a little richer, though not in horseflesh, and greatly wised up on low life in Naples.

Bad Hole was a real place. In the last year of the nineteenth century, when the big clean-up of the lower city was under way and parts of Naples that had stood since the middle ages were being wiped off the map, the Neapolitan poet and archivist Salvatore Di Giacomo was writing in his deeply learned study of *Prostitution in Naples* that *Littlehole Lane* was still there, if not lately obliterated *or being so even as I write*. It was on the waterfront, between the Angevins' newly built Castelnuovo and the Market Place where Andreuccio went to buy his horses, a few minutes' walk from either. It was also right by the Naples offices of a Florentine merchant bank, the Bardi, which stood equidistant from the port, the Castelnuovo and the Market as the financial fulcrum of city and kingdom in those years of the early fourteenth century. When Andreuccio, naked and covered with shit, banged on the door and shouted for his clothes, he was menaced from an upper window by a local who *looked like he had to be a big boss*, and was urged in low voices by anxious neighbours at street level to get out quick if he knew what was good for him. He left the Bad Hole filthy, half-naked and penniless to return to his hotel, taking *a left-hand turn up a street called Rua Catalana . . . toward the high part of the city.*

In 1325 or soon after, a boy of twelve or thirteen rode down from Florence with his father to Naples. The boy was not the son of the man's wife, but his merchant banker father was determined to start him well in life nevertheless. The father was arriving to run the Bardi bank's operation in Naples and was soon a powerful figure in Naples, a *consigliere* and chamberlain whom the Angevin king Roberto called his *loyal familiar*. The boy would live there for fifteen years, and be *raised in Naples from my childhood to full maturity*. He was twenty-seven when he was forced to go back to Florence. By 1340 the Florentine connexion had soured in Naples, the Bardi bank was insolvent and so was the young man's father. But while he was growing up in Naples, northern businessmen ran the economy of Italy's biggest and richest city and controlled its international trade. *The brilliant Angevin court stayed afloat on the credit the Bardi bank brought in.* The boy, though, didn't want a life in commerce. His utilitarian schooling in Florence had been a dreary waste of time and so was work in the bank's

Naples office to an adolescent dreaming of love and art. But his job was more valuable to him than it seemed at the time.

Naples was a very different place from the small inland city of hard-faced Tuscan money makers. The boy's real life began here. Naples was the capital of a maritime kingdom and the major port city of the central Mediterranean. It was busy, crowded, cosmopolitan, and its social life revolved around the splendours of the Angevin court. It was a city of commerce and consumption, not at all of production. The provision of food, drink, fashion, sex, entertainment and religious consolation were central to its economy. Finance, shipping, construction and textiles seemed peripheral beside these. A lot of the people who crowded there had no work at all and saw little of the vast amounts of money that came into the bay, swirled around the city and flowed out again.

The boy Giovanni Boccaccio was oddly placed in all this. He was an outsider, his livelihood most comfortably assured by the Bardi merchant bank, and in Naples he had that freedom of social movement and that detachment only an outsider on a steady income can have. To Neapolitans he stood in a small way for the northern money that underwrote the southern lifestyle, and for a bourgeois culture that could aspire to mix with the aristocratic milieu of the court. At the start he was very young, darting easy and untroubled with the rest of the small fry through the port city's murkier waters. He was also a working boy, born outside marriage, lucky in the recognition and opportunity his father gave him. His very junior work at the bank interfaced with the bottom end of the financial market. He directed people to more senior colleagues or weighed tiny amounts of gold for the least important clients. When he wrote years later about Bad Hole and the Rua Catalana, Boccaccio was writing about real places he knew well, and several traces in the archives suggested that the Sicilian girl and the crime boss and Andreuccio himself might have been real people too, *living in the same place at the same time that Boccaccio was leading the life of a carefree youth in Naples*. The dead archbishop was a real one too, and buried as Boccaccio's story described.

He got out of the bank when his father let him study law instead, which was hardly better. Immersed in metropolitan high life and low life, the boy was reading intensively too, in the Latin writers of the classical past and the newer vernacular works in French and Italian. The city of endless erotic move-ment—from the traffickings of waterfront and tenements to the courtly round of dances, dinners, concerts, boating and horseback outings to the sea—was also the city where in 1224 the Hohenstaufen emperor Frederick II had founded the first lay university in Europe. Thomas Aquinas had taught in the *Studio*, and it had broken the church's grip on institu-tions of learning in Naples. Intellectuals were promoted and protected by the Angevin court the boy was already coming into contact with.

In Naples at twenty-one he met the woman he called Fiammetta. Nobody was quite sure when he wrote about her later who the *Little Flame* might have been in real life. Most believed she was Maria d'Aquino, a daughter of the king Roberto, first glimpsed in the huge austerely gothic space of San Lorenzo Maggiore. Sexually she may or may not have been fleetingly available to the banker's son from Florence. She was certainly close enough to give him ideas, though in the end she remained out of reach in the gilded otherworld of her court. The young man came tantalizingly close to sharing in the glamorous life of Fiammetta's royal round, but erotic humiliation and social rebuff followed as Fiammetta retreated into the ritual play of her world apart. She was to him what Beatrice had been to Dante, what Laura was for Petrarch, though she was less wholly assimilated into art, more carnal, more inconstant, more real.

It was a bit like the exquisite literary arts he was working so hard to attain at the same time. The young man's early work was often in Latin or in verse or in both, highly wrought and arduously attained. This was fine for the courtly world and for readers who felt they needed refined material to distract them. Boccaccio was serious too, however, and there was something strenuous in even his lightest things. The emotional intensity of his admiration for Dante and Petrarch is beyond understanding today. And although he wrote to entertain, the difficulty sometimes showed, even in his vernacular prose. Erotic play would sink under the arts of medieval rhetoric, the quick of his own experience and Fiammetta herself would drift near to being allegorized out of existence. All this had to be unlearnt, and was. Stripped, he became Europe's first great realist storyteller, the author of the book that made the work of Chaucer, Shakespeare and Cervantes possible, and the great realist novels of the nineteenth century. To reach the wonderful amused lucidity, the economy and objectivity of the stories in the *Decameron*, he had to write less about himself and in a less literary way, and he did.

The unlearning was brutally provoked. He was in his late twenties when the Bardi bank and his father's finances collapsed. After fifteen years in Naples he was suddenly back home in small, tight, middle-class mercantile Florence. The swarming low life and the courtly magic of the thrilling metropolis were a vanished dream. The Florence he went back to was economically depressed and politically racked—the Bardi was not the only major bank to go under—and its provincial grimness let him focus his mind in a way the manifold distractions of Naples never had. After three years back North he broke through the romanticizing idealism of his earliest writings in an extraordinary text, *the first modern psychological novel*—a short, intense, first-person account of love and sexual betrayal told by the woman. The woman was Fiammetta and in having her tell their story he was reliving the great erotic moment of his life as the woman, seeing it all through her eyes.

This was radical enough, but he was doing something more. He was reversing the roles further. The banker's son from Florence was reliving as a betrayed woman the agonies of humiliation and betrayal he himself had felt as the bourgeois lover of a king's daughter who was a lot less involved with him than he with her. The Neapolitan writer Domenico Rea pointed out with unassuming brilliance six hundred years later that *when he makes Fiammetta feel that anguish . . . you realize it's he himself, waiting for Maria d'Aquino to get back from holiday in the opulent countryside of the Sannio.*

I not only waited when I'd promised but in my anticipation I kept thinking he might have arrived and countless times every day I ran up to the window or ran down to the door looking down the long road in case I'd see

> him coming. I never saw a man coming in the distance
> without thinking it might be him and waiting with desire
> until he got close enough and I realized it wasn't . . . I
> spent my whole time going from the window to the door
> and the door to the window.

The intensity of the identification led Rea to suggest that *Boccaccio, in love at least, is a loser* and that this was how he attained that piercing insight into sexual relations which variously and effortlessly lit up the *Decameron*, even *Fiammetta* and the misogynistic *Crow*, and made them live. In life, in some minor sense, he lost all round. Never marrying was perhaps not a loss, and it didn't stop him fathering five children.

It had been hard at first, back in Florence. He had no work and his father could no longer support him. He was unknown in the place he came from. Florence was in economic and political crisis. There was a power struggle and the losers, a lot of them friends of Boccaccio's, were executed or exiled. Then the plague of 1348 wiped out most of Florence's inhabitants, including friends and family. Hard times toughened his imagination, made it resilient and essential but not hard, burnt off literary and romantic superfluities. His response to mass death was to put it into the background, make it the absent setting for the *Decameron*'s clear, spare and intensely various imagining of eros as the impulse of life. He got through the rocky time. He became famous and—more unusually—immensely popular as a writer, one of the few whom people read for sheer enjoyment. He was a close friend of Petrarch, admired him almost as much as he admired Dante, and saw both of these as having a depth, a seriousness, a wisdom about life that he himself could not pretend to. One of the great things about Boccaccio was that he was serious without taking himself too seriously. On the practical and professional front he was a diplomat who spoke for the Florentine state in delicate matters all around Italy.

Then he was thrown into agitation by a message from a famous and revered Carthusian who had lately died. The monk sent word that Boccaccio too would shortly die, that the time had come to abandon poetry and all profane things and think on his own end. Boccaccio was now fifty and greatly disturbed by this intimation of death, worried enough to think of getting rid of his books and burning his manuscripts. Petrarch offered some sane and realistic advice, calmed him down, and invited him to live in his own house, sharing resources and work, but Boccaccio turned down the several times repeated offer and instead he went to Naples.

Back to Naples

All the time he'd wanted to go back to Naples. He had been thinking about this for over twenty years, ever since his father had recalled him to Florence. A friend from his earliest days had become immensely powerful in Neapolitan politics and Boccaccio was quietly hoping his old friend would help him find some kind of quietly dignified position at court that would let him read and write in the city he loved. The trip was a disaster. The power player friend in Naples had dashed off an effusive letter, but now had to deal with the real presence of a touchy elderly writer from Florence, a person who added nothing to lustre at court and who seemed to feel he had some claim based on nothing more than friendship and assistance given decades earlier. Boccaccio was ignored, handed over to the servants and treated like a mendicant. He went back to Florence and fired off a furious letter to a third person, another friend who was the power player's manager, detailing his humiliations in angry, pungent prose. By the time Boccaccio signed off, the letter had grown to the length of a short book.

It was more than a personal affront, worse than contemptible ingratitude by a Florentine *arriviste* whose first steps in Naples had been taken with Boccaccio's help. Boccaccio too was a self-made man, and his angry assertion of his own worth is a statement of the dignity of letters in the world of money and power. After his long winter journey to Naples he was offered

a wretched little stretcher lined with a lumpy mattress taken a moment earlier from underneath a mule driver, with a bit of stinking blanket and no pillow in a poky little room with holes in the wall . . . an earthenware oil lamp with a flickering half-dead flame in one corner . . . in the other a little table covered with coarse and dirty oilcloth gnawed by age or dogs . . . a few filthy glasses on it and under it a stool with one leg missing . . . there was no fire in the fireplace but the room was full of smoke from the kitchen and the smell of food was everywhere.

He spent a long sleepless night *in some pain* and oppressed by *a thick fug* while daylight never came. Dinner time the next day was worse, when the hangers-on arrived to eat,

greedy and hungry and fawning, mule drivers and boys, cooks and dishwashers . . . the dogs of the court and the household rats, great chewers of kitchen scraps . . . running all over the place and bellowing like cattle, they filled the household . . . breaking the water jugs and wine flasks all over the place and turning the dirt floor into a stinking winy mud . . . I almost threw up . . . .

The chief housekeeper . . . eyes watering from the smoke, opened the battle with his stick and his hoarse voice, ordering those who were to dine to take their place at table . . . each of the filthy and disorderly mob grabbed the nearest place at the trough, wanting food . . . almost everyone had a runny nose, flushed cheeks and gummy eyes and was racked by coughing . . . they spat out foul phlegm before their own eyes and mine. It was hardly surprising. They were nearly all bare-kneed and half-dressed in wretched thin rags full of holes, abject and trembling, uncouth and hungry and they swallowed the food set before them like wild animals . . .

The food bowls . . . were cheap pottery . . . they were filthy and reminded me of the ones full of tainted blood in the barbers' shops in Naples, indeed that's where they seemed to have come from. The wooden ones were black and damp, oozing and smelling of yesterday's fat . . . [We were served] miniscule fish that even beggars would leave, cooked in rancid oil . . . sour wine . . .

It wasn't as though he claimed fancy food or special treatment.

> All I wanted was a place to stay away from the noise
> of quarrelsome thugs, a table covered with a clean and
> simple cloth, common food cleanly cooked . . . common
> wine from a clean flask . . . and a bed suited for a man
> like me in a clean room.

In middle age, the man who used to be a monied youth with
equal access to high life and low and drawn to both—

> in case you don't know, my friend, I lived in Naples and
> was brought up there from my childhood to full maturity
> and I lived among young nobles of my own age and
> however noble they might have been they were never
> ashamed of entering my house or coming to visit me

—now found himself dumped among the people at the bottom
of the heap, the cooks and grooms, the waiters, cleaners and
carriers who did the work, and the people too poor, too
old, too young, too weak, too sick, too unprepared for life
to be of any use at all. All they had was some small claim of
neighbourhood or relationship or prior employment or sheer
need, the only claim Boccaccio was now felt to have. Fiercely
defending his life of the mind against the casual arrogance
of money and power, Boccaccio now saw the magic city of
his youth drained of adventure, glamour, beauty, sex. He saw
the muddy dregs of age, hunger, discomfort, sickness and
degradation like the foul wine and the phlegm and the food
scraps ground into the dirt floor of the dining hall. He saw

the Naples of the poor, not as a privileged young outsider, but as one of the poor himself.

The clear and understated prose of the *Decameron* had never dwelt on Naples with this angry Dickensian insistence, for all that the book included *the totality of the earthly reality of his time*. The *Decameron* had celebrated individuality and shown recognizably modern people, above all women, making their own lives inside their own home, their own modest alley or town or in the courts and cities of the wider world. Boccaccio had done it in the first modern prose, laconic, fluent, understated, the words never allowed to spoil the economy of the unfolding story, charged with the delicious irony of things never quite spelled out. Readers found that the more imagination they brought to bear on these effortlessly entertaining stories, the more they enjoyed them. The more they invested, the greater the return. Giovanni Boccaccio's early training hadn't been quite the dire waste of time he'd thought it at the time.

But mostly in Naples he had learnt about life. Boccaccio looked back on Naples as the world, and in the *Decameron* he made a world of Naples. When the stories moved away from Florence and Tuscany, Naples stood behind them all. As Rea shrewdly saw, the storms at sea around the Mediterranean were all storms in the bay of Naples, the only sea Boccaccio ever knew, and when he described the busy waterfront of Palermo, the foreign sailors and visiting businessmen, the local customs officers and labourers and prostitutes, the banks and warehouses and taverns, he was talking about the working world of the Naples he grew up in. He was never in Palermo. He felt a misfit back in Florence and even before his disastrous return to the courtly world of Naples he lived reclusively out of the city in his home village of Certaldo. The diplomatic missions to Venice, Ravenna and other city states he probably seized on eagerly. Anywhere but Florence.

He knew plenty about poor people in Naples, had more than an outsider's glimpse of whores and thieves and local crime bosses. He knew how they lived. Peronella, for instance, was a young Neapolitan housewife who lived with her husband at Porta Nova, a couple of minutes' walk from Bad Hole, going away from the castle and following the shoreline a bit inland. To get there today you head down the *Rettifilo*—the wide straight road cut through in the late nineteenth century's lower city clean-up—in the direction of the railway station. Young Boccaccio knew Porta Nova well. He worked there in the Bardi bank. Peronella was *lovely and lively* and married to a builder's labourer. She supplemented his meagre and uncertain income from casual work with a bit of home spinning, but they hardly got by. Their one real asset was a very large earthenware storage jar of the kind used to store grain, oil or wine, and they were looking to realize on this.

Peronella had caught the eye of a *good-looking* young man from one of the better families in the piazza—unlike Peronella's husband he had a name, that of a real Porta Nova family—who waited until her husband left for work and then came calling. One morning while Peronella was receiving the visitor her husband came home unexpectedly. Telling her lover to hide in the storage jar, Peronella went to deal with her husband, setting him comprehensively on the back foot as husband, provider, man, in a stream of vituperation.

What's the story now, coming home at this hour of the morning? You come back with your tools in your hand and it looks to me like you don't want to work at all today. So what are we going to live on? You think I'll let you go and pawn my skirt and my other clothes while I break my fingernails spinning day and night . . . the neighbours are all laughing at me. They can't believe what I put up with. And now you come home with your hands dangling by your sides.

Peronella burst into tears and her larger and realer feelings took verbal flight. Her resentment at never having any money fed into her sense of sexual humiliation and lost opportunities. She didn't know why she didn't take a lover like all the other women. She let her husband know that *some really good-looking men* had taken a liking to her and already sent offers of money, clothes or jewellery and though she was *not that kind of woman* she was no longer sure how long her principles could hold out. Her housewife's complaint—operatic, public, intimate, erotic and economic—was still ringing through the alleys and courtyards of Naples six hundred years later. Rea heard the street cadences of his own city's Neapolitan humming under the rhythms of Boccaccio's fourteenth century Italian. And Peronella's outburst, like her whole story, came word for word from the Latin written by the North African Apuleius twelve hundred years before Boccaccio. Fernand Braudel found history's *longue durée* in the Mediterranean and it was also the long history of the imagination.

Peronella's amiable loser husband explained it was a holiday and nobody was working. He'd forgotten, and so had she.

The good news was that he'd found a buyer for the storage jar. Peronella seized her chance with a scathing attack on him for practically giving the jar away. She, a mere woman, had already had an offer of nearly half as much again from a customer who was just that very moment checking out the inside for cracks. At which point her lover climbed out and pronounced the jar sound but not entirely clean inside. Peronella's husband, *blinded by the thought of the extra money . . . loses all sense of reality and from now on doesn't notice a thing.* A hardscrabble Neapolitan like his wife, just as anxious to survive, he put down his tools, stripped to his underwear and climbed inside to scrape off any encrusted deposits that might get in the way of a quick sale.

Peronella peered over the rim to point out all the bits her husband missed. Her young lover, interrupted earlier, now took her from behind *just as in the wide open fields the stallions, unbridled and hot with lust, mount the mares*—the poetic image of the youth's coupling with Peronella was enriched rather than compromised by the reminder that with the jar taking up so much space there was hardly room to move inside the tiny basso. Her lover reached orgasm just as Peronella's husband finished scraping the dregs from the jar. His head popped up over the rim and the lovers pulled apart in perfect synchrony, the choreography of confinement matched in the precise economy of Boccaccio's words.

Once you got off the streets the whole of Naples was a place of terrible entrapment. Andreuccio's visit to Bad Hole was the beginning of a series of nocturnal entries into ever smaller and darker spaces, each more noisome and scary than the one before. His journey through the city was a kind of anal penetration of its entrails. From the crowded Market Place to the whore's little sitting room to the upper chamber, to the privy, to the open sewer in the alley, to the dark doorway, to the bottom of the well where he was lowered to wash in an unlit street and then abandoned, to the final suffocating embrace of a rotting archbishop's corpse in a closed tomb where he expected to die. The elegance or grandeur of the setting deceived, whether it was the whore's room tricked out for the occasion with some costly looking drapes to make her seem a lady, or the vast and austere marble splendour of the cathedral of Naples. Inside, everything was dark and foul confinement.

The people Andreuccio met in Naples were ambiguous and treacherous and yet quite plainly what they were, all wonderfully open and almost ingenuous in their ill intent. The long-lost sister of Bad Hole was a whore and the whole neighbourhood in league with her. The thieves who reversed Andreuccio's fortunes intended to use him and let him die. The priest was a grave robber, the only crook of his party not in awe of death, at least not until he climbed into the casket and Andreuccio grabbed his foot. The poor neighbours of the street-level hovels in Bad Hole, in the finest touch of unchanging Naples in the whole story, were at once Andreuccio's genuinely solicitous friends and the doers of the bidding of the local boss on the upper floor. Andreuccio survived—and did rather well—because in the space of a few hours of medieval inner city darkness he managed to become more Neapolitan than his hosts, as ingenuous as they were, as cunning a survivor and a faster learner.

Peronella was like that too in her absurd and banal erotic triangle with husband and lover, and the elaborate improvised theatre that fooled only her poor slow husband. If indeed it did fool him. Appearing to be fooled was a way of maintaining a precarious decorum among people who all knew far too much about each other because they lived on top of each other. When Peronella loudly told her husband, for the benefit of listening neighbours, that all the other women in the neighbourhood already had lovers, she was pre-emptively letting them know that she knew as much about them as they did about her. She was also reminding her generic *husband*, in case discovery and a confrontation turned ugly, of the local sexual norms. Nothing to get too excited about. Everyone was doing it.

Peronella's voice and her body were the only means available of controlling her social reality. As in all theatre, a kind of shimmering doubleness of the fiction and the reality gave the drama its own value. When Andreuccio visited the young whore, the same thing happened in her meticulous *mise en scène*, her pleasure in passing herself off as his sister, her mastery of the role, in matching the known details of his father's life and asking after the siblings whose names she had just learnt. Her performance rose to high art in the show of controlled hurt at her treatment by the family, that admixture of bitterness and hard-won serenity that prevented it from being maudlin, cloying, suspect. It was all manifestly in excess of the ingenuity required to get her hands on his money.

The owners of the faces appearing at the windows, one after another, when Andreuccio had crashed through into the sewer in the lane and was banging on the door—the servant woman who seemed to think he was drunk, the threatening bearded boss, the fearful whisperers at street level—were playing a well-polished choral role, at once onlookers and participants, in a way instantly recognizable to anyone who's ever been involved in a disturbance in a Neapolitan alley or courtyard. And Peronella's husband was perhaps less slow on the uptake than he let himself seem. Indifferent to whom Peronella fucked when he was out, he might have got the lover in the jar's number instantly and played along with Peronella for the sake of an improved deal on the storage jar. As always in Naples, the ambiguities floated in the air.

Don Ferrante

It had the speed and cruelty of film. It unfolded more than five hundred years ago, but the event (a dynastic wedding), its incomparable setting (a great turreted and moated castle looking out over the water at Vesuvius and Capri) and the protagonists (southern Italy's richest and most powerful men, arriving sleekly in the company of bejewelled wives, sisters, daughters and eager hot-eyed sons, each family surrounded by its tight squad of functionaries and security men) had the familiarity of a drama played out countless times before and since in the bloody Italian theatre of the *bella figura*.

The lead figures in this drama were not the young man and the teenage girl who were about to be married. The supporting lead was the count of Sarno, the richest and most formidable magnate of southern Italy, who had until not long before been merely the businessman Francesco Coppola. He was the father of the groom. The godfather figure was don Ferrante, otherwise known as Ferdinando I of Naples. The year was 1486 and the Spanish house of Aragon had ruled Naples for the last forty-five. Don Ferrante was over sixty and fleshy, but his mop of hair was still thick and his face—the imperious beak of a nose over the small mouth with a slightly projecting lower lip—a mask of power. He had six children by his first wife, two by his second and another ten by a series of lovers. He was the uncle of the bride. Neither Ferrante nor his niece had yet appeared to greet the guests.

Coppola had made a fortune in mining—silver, lead, alum—and in food, textiles and soap. He owned a fleet of ships and ran a private army notable even by baronial standards. His title and its benefits were a spin-off of his close business partnership with Ferrante, whereby he had *come from being a lightweight to being immensely rich.* What lent the marriage a certain piquancy is that Coppola, like the other most prominent guest at the wedding, had lately been deeply implicated in the *barons' plot* against Ferrante. The other prominent guest was Ferrante's royal secretary, the chief administrator of the kingdom of Naples. Antonello Petrucci was a spectacularly successful self-made lawyer, his origins in a peasant family outside Naples almost forgotten, a man who displayed *such wealth and magnificence that no trace of his low birth* appeared. He and his adult sons had also been ennobled.

The wedding's antecedents were fresh in everyone's mind, but they were part of an old story. The landowning barons of the South were amply represented at this gala wedding. Collectively, and in some cases even individually, the landed dynasties were wealthier than Ferrante's house of Aragon. The barons had been defending their interests against Ferrante's vigorous efforts to redirect baronial wealth and power toward the house of Aragon. The struggle had been going on for years, for decades. Ferrante had won the latest round.

Coppola and Petrucci had played ambiguous parts in a conspiracy that would have seen Ferrante and his son Alfonso murdered. Between the man who enabled their rise and the class they had lately joined, the king's two favourites had leant toward the latter. Ferrante, not for the first time, decisively outmanoeuvred the barons, and the treachery of his own men was obscured by Ferrante's magnanimity in victory. Spain brokered a treaty, Ferrante pardoned the conspirators and made generous concessions to baronial interests. *If only you'd asked—* he said. He went hunting with his enemies on their estates and now the match between Ferrante's very young niece and one of Coppola's sons looked to everyone like further dynastic bonding. Coppola himself, whose enormous wealth had not quite freed him from an arriviste's uncertainties, was over the moon about the wedding in the Castelnuovo.

He was so taken and enthusiastic that without thinking further he took his daughter and his young sons to Naples. And to add to the celebration he also took almost all the gold, silver and jewellery he had accumulated in the course of his life . . . the day of the wedding he was moved to tears of tenderness.

The secretary of the realm also came with a substantial family party, *his sons and their wives, who as intimates of the count had* come to the wedding in rich and gorgeous dresses . . . Everything began splendidly. Through his tears Coppola saw that *the king had embellished the Castelnuovo magnificently to match the occasion.* Minutes passed. Coppola was *waiting with his whole party in its over-elaborate pomp for the king and the bride to appear and begin the celebration.* Musicians and court functionaries set the tone for the guests as *they began in celebration with music, song and dancing.* Coppola and Petrucci, along with the other architects and executors of the recent plot and their wives and families and their entourages, waited for Ferrante to enter.

Ferrante did not appear. The keeper of the castle entered with a troop of soldiers. Exits were barred and the barons seized. Festivity turned to horror.

> Amazement gave way to fear and pain and nothing was heard but friends' moaning, relatives' weeping, servants' complaints and women's indignation, and the clamour of the soldiery, whose insolence grew as they manhandled the people who had to leave and the ones who had to stay, closing doors, raising the drawbridges, filling everything with weaponry, shouting and confusion.

Outside, the city was in shock—Naples loved a party—as *the people let out of the castle came out pale and trembling, their voices breaking.* Ferrante's army rounded up those barons not present in the castle and stripped their palaces of their contents. *The king was so eager to get his hands on everyone's stuff that he even had the mules the prisoners had brought led away to his stables, as if they too had been in on the plot.* Coppola's wealth was a particular target. *Everything he had greedily worked for and hoarded over all those years he rashly lost in a single day.* The less portable property was brought in later from the castle in Sarno *and when the king's agents brought the rich spoils to Naples, onlookers thought it seemed like an ancient triumph.* People were particularly struck by Coppola's military hardware, *147 pieces of artillery mounted on military carts*, placed to defend his castle in a confrontation with Ferrante's army.

Their property may not have been the first thing the imprisoned barons themselves had on their mind. *They were shut up in the castle's filthiest and most fearsome prisons*, or in the words of a more recent historian than Camillo Porzio, who was born forty years after the event, *most disappeared into the dungeons of Castelnuovo to become the subject of grisly legends.* Coppola's whole family was seized, *even his women were imprisoned with him*, and no more or less happened to the secretary, *his sons and their wives.*

Ferrante hunted down the conspirators *as if he wanted to cancel the barons' very names.* After a prolonged trial—in case people thought Ferrante was interested merely in getting revenge and seizing their wealth—Coppola, Petrucci and Petrucci's two sons, the counts of Carinola and Policastro, were sentenced to death. The sentences were carried out on different days, to maximize the effect. Carinola, who was insolent at his trial, *was dragged around the busiest parts of the city by a pair of oxen and then drawn and quartered in the Market Place . . . divided into several pieces he bore witness for a long time at the main gates of Naples to his thoughtless treason.* Policastro was simply beheaded. The brothers did not put on a good show at the end. Amid snivelling, Carinola blamed Policastro and Policastro blamed Coppola for what had happened. Their father and Coppola made better deaths, after a long time in the dungeons, on a platform erected in the castle courtyard, *high enough to be seen from the city.*

Niccolò Machiavelli, who from Florence followed events in Naples closely, later quoted a phrase of Ferrante's that the barons should have borne in mind when they were out hunting with the king, that men *often behave like certain small predator birds, who are so eager to pursue their prey . . . that they fail to notice another larger bird about to kill them from above.* Machiavelli abhorred plots like the barons' failed attempt and despised even more the treachery of favourites like Coppola, who *had attained such power that he thought the only thing he lacked was the kingdom itself and wanting that too he lost his life.*

Ferrante in his last years was preoccupied with warning Italy's other rulers, the small predators, about the imminent danger of an invasion by France, the big bird of prey. He died in 1494, before the French marched south. The Aragonese dynasty in Naples collapsed with amazing speed in a fragmented and unstable Europe. Burckhardt wrote that Ferrante had kept the executed barons embalmed in a *museum of mummies* and pronounced *the end of this cross-bred house . . . clear proof of want of blood.* Five different kings of Naples followed Ferrante in less than three years. One of them was the king of France and the last, who stayed, was the king of Spain.

Machiavelli was more interested in Ferrante's betrayal by the two men he had made great and in his ferocious revenge than he was in the long struggle between the central power in Naples and the looming powers of the barons in the rest of the territory. The former had its decisive resolution. The war between Naples and its barons dragged on, despite the dispatch and disappearance of the leaders of the plot against Ferrante. Machiavelli thought the feudal barons *men utterly hostile to any kind of civilized life* and this was a city view of country people. Things had never been quite so simple and they soon became more complicated.

Duchess of Amalfi

One of Ferrante's ten illegitimate children was Enrico of Aragon. Enrico was already in his early forties when Ferrante in 1473 gave him the feudal rights to Gerace in Calabria and so made him one of that class of feudal barons Ferrante warred with. Enrico was out on a mission collecting taxes for his father in Calabria five years later when he died, along with several others, after eating a meal of poisonous mushrooms. He left a pregnant wife and four small children.

Enrico's youngest daughter Giovanna was a year old when her father died, and barely in her teens when she married the duke of Amalfi, the former maritime republic just south of Naples. The duke died soon after, leaving Giovanna pregnant, hardly more than a girl and with one small child already, to manage the affairs of Amalfi and rear the children.

The duchess Giovanna acted as regent for her baby son, and steered Amalfi through the difficult years of southern Italy's invasion by French and Spanish forces. She reduced the load of her late husband's debts, and was helped in managing the duchy's finances by a Neapolitan named Antonio Bologna. Bologna was a member of the still exiguous professional class in Naples. His grandfather had been one of the most active and distinguished intellectuals at the brilliant court of Ferrante's father Alfonso. Bologna had managed the affairs of the last king of the line during his moment on the throne, and it was probably this service to the family that recommended him for the Amalfi appointment, beyond his reputation as being *honestly rich* and an excellent man in money matters. People realized only much later that relations between the widowed young duchess and her financial advisor had turned into love. They married—secretly, knowing enough about her family's baronial values to see trouble ahead. While outwardly all remained entirely professional, *their marriage stayed secret for many years and during that time they slept together nearly every night.*

Giovanna had two brothers and one of them was a powerful cardinal. When she had a second child by Bologna the brothers had her spied on in Amalfi to identify the father. Bologna feared they would have him killed and told his wife *You know better than I do what they're like* before he left for Ancona with their two children in 1510. Ancona was on the Adriatic coast near Loreto, and toward the end of the same year Giovanna set off on a pilgrimage to the shrine at Loreto. She was *pregnant for the third time and couldn't bear to live without her dear husband and was so unhappy while he was away that she was on the point of going mad.* A visit to the venerated shrine was quite normal, but people found it odd that she didn't return to Amalfi. After she had been living with Antonio Bologna for some time in Ancona and their third child's birth was imminent, her relatives in Naples realized she was well established in a new family.

The lovers had known from the start that Bologna's bourgeois status made their relationship unacceptable to the duchess's brothers. Dismissing her *astonished and confused* servants in Ancona, apart from the maid who had witnessed her marriage and a couple of grooms, and going in great detail over the personal and financial arrangements she had made for them all, Giovanna explained that *I'd rather live privately with my husband signor Antonio than go on being duchess.* Her former servants, who had to live with the consequences, made sure her brothers were informed immediately. Naples at the start of the sixteenth century was no place for private happiness, on or off the territory. It was a matter of caste, and Giovanna's eagerness to join Bologna had been intensified by the fear that if her brothers found out about her third pregnancy *they would do something bad to her.*

The brothers used their connexions to have the couple expelled from Ancona. The expert administrator Antonio Bologna *made so many legal appeals that the case dragged on* but he also

knew that in the end he would be expelled. He had a friend in Siena and in order not to be caught off guard he got a permit to stay there with his family . . . [and] sent his children on ahead so that the very day the order was served to leave Ancona within a fortnight, he and his wife and his household left for Siena on horseback.

The brothers then used the cardinal's church connexions to have the family expelled from Siena too. Antonio and Giovanna were heading for Venice when the family realized they were being overtaken by a large posse of horsemen, and *not seeing how they could escape alive . . . driven by fear they rode faster and hid in a small house.* Information was specific about the family's mounts. *Bologna was riding a fast Arab thoroughbred and his eldest son another . . . the two youngest children were together in a bassinet. His wife was riding a good cross-country hack.* Convinced by his wife to make a break

> Bologna and his son and four servants with good mounts got away and changing their mind headed not for Venice but Milan. His intending killers took the woman and her baby son and her daughter and all the others.

The most detailed information about what happened was in one of the two hundred or more *Novelle* written around this time by Matteo Bandello. Like Boccaccio two centuries before, Bandello often wrote his stories about real people and real events. He got to know Antonio Bologna in Milan and his account became more detailed in its later part. For Bandello, Bologna was a cavalier, handsome, brave, lettered, musical—

> a very gallant and virtuous gentleman, and beyond his fine presence and personal bravery, he was a splendid horseman . . . a well-read man who played the lute and sang sweetly—

as well as the accomplished professional businessman and administrator who emerged through the affair. And the discreet, courageous and devoted husband and father. Bandello's report was not impartial. Giovanna and her children and her maid were all taken back to Amalfi and murdered, but Bologna didn't know this. He refused to listen when a man contracted to kill him arrived in Milan and *not wanting to be anyone else's butcher . . . warned him that his wife and children and her maid had been strangled for sure and there was no way out for him.* Bandello thought Bologna believed that when the brothers' anger against him subsided he could be reunited with his wife and children. It was a stratagem to keep him in Milan and in harm's way.

Bologna had spent most of his adult life working for the family of Aragon and might have been expected to know something about their temperaments and how they represented the baronial class they belonged to. Yet again and again he expressed his conviction that the Aragonese brothers would never harm their sister or her children, that in time they would let her enjoy the private life she desired with him. It became the fixation which destroyed him. Bologna was hardly more than the trigger for an intrafamilial tragedy and yet he emerged as its most fraught and complex participant. Giovanna compelled interest and concern when she broke the class barrier for love, but only Bologna sounded like someone who might have belonged in another story altogether.

Giovanna knew her brothers. When she urged her husband and their boy to escape their pursuers on the road to Venice, she too seemed to believe it was only Bologna they wanted to kill. But the story—so much in half a dozen pages—showed that really she knew how it would end.

My lord, go. My lords my brothers won't hurt me or our children, but if they catch you they'll kill you . . . their pursuers were now so close that there was no way his wife could escape.

Bandello heard Bologna sing at a social gathering in Milan about his experience and was struck by his plangency. Learning who he was and knowing what had happened to Giovanna and their children, he went up to warn Bologna *there were people in Milan out to kill him.* Bandello knew Giovanna and her children had been murdered, even while Bologna remained in denial and convinced they would meet again. He knew that Bologna too would soon be killed and decided then, before the dreadful story was over, that he was going to write it up—*he wanted to put it in one of his stories, knowing for sure that poor Bologna would be murdered.* Soon after that he

ran into Bologna riding a fine jennet on his way to mass . . . preceded by two servants, one of them carrying a lance and the other Our Lady's book of hours . . . Bologna looked quite lost and [someone said] *he'd do better to have them carry another lance instead of that prayer book, seeing the danger he's in* . . . they heard a great noise . . . Bologna was attacked by captain Daniele da Bozolo and three heavily armed associates. He was attacked on all sides and died horribly before anyone could help him.

The *lost* look on Bologna's face as he rode distractedly to his death on his *fine jennet* was enough to break your heart.

Bandello in his last sentence remarked that the killers then left in a leisurely manner, unconcerned about being followed.

The apprentice

In the archives of Capodimonte in Naples is a slight undated sketch from about 1600 signed by a C. Belisario. Belisario Corenzio was famous then in Naples. He had arrived in Naples from Greece in 1570 as a boy of twelve and stayed. As a man he quickly insinuated himself into the business of painting in fresco those vast areas of blank wall space offered by the new churches and convents that were going up everywhere as the city doubled and trebled its population. And by the public reception rooms and private suites of the showy new palazzi of the newly urbanized barons. He did façades, ceilings, walls. Arches, vaults, lunettes. He worked fast to fill any blank space. Mostly he put images on the walls of churches and chapels and cloisters.

Corenzio was a fresco painter on an industrial scale. His facile late mannerism lent itself to speed and duplication by his talented apprentices. Some said the quality of his work was *proportional to the fee, sometimes careful, sometimes skimped.* He had a stranglehold on the market for fresco painting in Naples and tended to abandon an unfinished job when a richer commission appeared. He began a vast fresco cycle for the Jesuit church in Naples but *he never finished, since he so often found it convenient to interrupt it and paint elsewhere.*

His Roman analogue was Giuseppe Cesari, the painter who had given the unknown Merisi from Caravaggio his first steady employment on his still life assembly line. Cesari—the *cavalier d'Arpino*—was no less facile, prolific or decorative but he was much richer, far more talented, ten years younger and glowed with the special allure of papal patronage. Corenzio kept an eye on what Cesari was doing in Rome, especially after Cesari unforgiveably won two major commissions in Naples, fresco cycles for the monks at San Martino, in the fifteen nineties. One of these he left unfinished as he hurried back to other work in Rome. Cesari too used to take on more than he and his team could handle. A few years later he was overextended again and had to renounce his commission to decorate the Contarelli chapel in the French church in Rome with paintings of Matthew. He did the chapel's ceiling but not the altarpiece or side paintings. Cardinal Del Monte, who lived next door, snapped up the commission for his little-known protégé Merisi.

The *Matthew* suite was a sensation and in 1600 made Merisi famous overnight. Corenzio would have had a special interest in what was going on here, been curious about Cesari's affairs and piqued by the clamour Merisi's new art had raised in the painting world. Corenzio went to see for himself. The sketch now at Capodimonte was a quick little reprise on paper of the moneylenders sitting around in the first *Matthew* painting. In a couple of details—mainly the position of a couple of prominent legs in different parts of the picture, which were stretched out and not folded under the sitter's stool—Corenzio's sketch differed from the painted canvas in its final form. When x-rays were directed at the painting centuries later, they showed that this was how Merisi had originally done it. Corenzio had seen the unfinished painting in studio, in the Del Monte palace across the alley, before the image had evolved into its final form. Either Merisi or the cardinal had given him a sneak preview of the work in progress. Unlike most painters in Rome, Corenzio was unimpressed, or at any rate unaffected, by what he saw of Merisi's work. He went back to Naples and continued covering blank spaces in religious buildings with frescoed images in the same late manner with the same elegant and productive facility and the same professional success for another forty-five years.

One of the assistants in Corenzio's fresco workshop was a Neapolitan named Giovan Battista Caracciolo. People called him *Battistello*. Born in 1578 and just married in 1598, he did a fresco of some *putti* for Corenzio on the façade of a chapel in 1601, and a little later he did some work inside the same chapel. Corenzio must have talked to his assistant about Merisi's revolutionary painting in Rome and the strong opinions it was stirring up among the painters. Maybe he took Caracciolo with him to see the *Matthew* paintings when he made his sketch. In the next five or six years, while he was still working for Corenzio, Caracciolo made at least one more trip to Rome to look at Merisi's newer and ever more controversial work.

None of these visits to look at Merisi's Roman paintings was recorded. But in 1607, the year Merisi's *Seven Works* went up in Naples, Caracciolo painted a canvas of his own. It was an altarpiece of the *Immaculate Conception*, practically his first known work. It was in many ways utterly unlike anything Merisi might himself have conceived. It showed the ghastly dragon Original Sin as a baby dinosaur breathing smoke, on whose broad head a devoutly yearning Mary's feet were firmly planted. Mary stood in the upper right quarter of this canvas, left hand humbly clasped to a chastely covered breast, eyeballing God the father in the sky. Next to the dinosaur was the skeleton Death. The painting's lilies, its mirror, its rose without thorns and palm frond belonged like the dragon and the skeleton to *the completely developed iconography of the Immaculate Conception*. By the early twentieth century this relic of the counter-reformation had been consigned to the sacristy.

It wasn't all bad. Bearded Adam, sprawling nude in the painting's bottom right—dragon paw and skeleton fingers dangling over him as he grasped the apple and pointed at Caracciolo's neatly lettered name—had a farm worker's sun-darkened hands and calves and antecedents in Merisi's Roman work—in the *Matthew Killed* of 1600. Saints Dominic and Paul in the bottom left were straight from Merisi's *Rosary Madonna*, and God the father descending to take Mary's hand top left, and the young intervening angel, reprised the mother and child in the *Seven Works*. Merisi would have recognized the crowd of jostling nude street children, with or without wings, each doing his bit with a symbol, and he would have found the old men saints and the labourer Adam familiar. He would have seen that Caracciolo had learnt from him how strong raked light could unify this confusion and lift the gaze to Mary, God and angels at the vertex of a pyramid. These were the two things Caracciolo had learnt from Merisi. How to build an image and how to look at people.

Caracciolo had understood the optical structure of *Seven Works*. His painting was also full of signs that he had been looking very intently at the other *Matthew* paintings and Merisi's great rejected painting of the *Mary Dead* sprawled on her back in Rome. And at the *Pilgrims' Madonna* and at the *Rosary Madonna*, with squirming child in arm and street people in blankets at her feet, which was in Naples and for sale. He had assimilated the revolutionary *Seven Works* at once because he knew the Roman paintings that led up to it. The late-maturing apprentice, already nearing middle age and the father of several young children, was still on Corenzio's fresco team, but he soon got several more commissions and started to make his own name as a painter in oils. He worked happily with the imagery of the counter-reformation—like Ribera's his intelligence was all visual, though subtler and more restless—and people liked that. The church liked it especially. Corenzio didn't seem to mind. Caracciolo's growing passion for the existential drama of Merisi's dark planes-of-light oil painting made him less of a potential rival.

While Caracciolo was getting to know Merisi's work in Rome he was getting close to the man himself in Naples. He did a *Madonna and Child in Glory* and based its group of mother, child and street angels on Merisi's original version for *Seven Works*. He saw this unfinished in the studio, because Merisi later painted over the group and finished the painting differently. The grouping Caracciolo copied showed up centuries later under x-rays. Caracciolo did a *Crucifixion* structurally modelled on the *Andrew* painting Merisi did in 1607 for the viceroy Benavente, another painting he could only have seen in Merisi's studio because it then went straight to Spain with the returning viceroy.

By 1610, when Merisi was back in Naples after his brilliant and disastrous foray into Malta and Sicily, Caracciolo's path was coinciding ever more closely with the master's. Merisi the optical experimenter and meticulous painter of life had developed—working on the run and maybe conscious that time was running out—a whole new style of phantasmagoric rapidity, reducing images to essentials, sketching the barest details of a face, a limb, a garment as they emerged from enveloping darkness. Large areas of his canvases he now left entirely dark, and the details themselves were reprised memories of canvases done years before. Rapt, Caracciolo followed him. He threw out what remained from his early training and started painting fast himself, working directly on to the canvas as Merisi had always done. He did a *Salome with John the Baptist's Head*, just as Merisi did that year. He did an austerely sketched painting in 1610—just the two half-figures against the dark—of *Christ Baptized by John* that was exactly like Merisi's own last works.

In May 1610, in what would be the second last month of Michelangelo Merisi's life, a letter went from Naples to Genoa about one of the last paintings Merisi did, his just-finished *Ursula Transfixed*. *Signor Damiano has seen it*, wrote the letter's author Lanfranco Massa, *and he's stunned by it, like everyone else who's seen it*. Whoever Damiano was, Massa was the agent in Naples of the Genoese prince Marcantonio Doria, the first and most eager collector of Merisi's work outside Rome. Doria had commissioned the painting. Merisi had worked for him in Genoa five years earlier, and turned down a huge offer to paint in fresco.

In his letter Massa continued, without a break in his sentence, that *as for Caracciolo, as I have already told your Lordship we haven't yet reached agreement on the Martyrdom of saint Lawrence your Lordship desires.* A couple of lines later he suggested Doria propose a new subject for a painting, because everyone in Naples was competing for his work. A lacuna in the text left it unclear whether the sought-after painter Massa was talking about was Merisi or Caracciolo. By this point it might have been either. Massa's letter showed that serious collectors of Merisi's work quickly became interested in Caracciolo's. The link with Merisi was known and it now gave Caracciolo's career an enormous impetus. Even now, while Merisi was still alive, Caracciolo was suddenly a favourite among enthusiasts of the new art. Then in the summer of that year Merisi left Naples. And then Merisi was dead.

V

Shadow

*The soldier's boy. Planes of light. A den of vice. Children
and shadows. A matter of conscience*

The soldier's boy

The barons who troubled Ferrante, and all the kings of
Naples before him, found it harder to resist the empire. Spain
had clout, a resolve to centralize and in Toledo a viceroy
determined to bring troublemakers to heel. Plenty of noble
families in the South threw in their lot with Spain; some
continued quiet intrigues with the French as a way of keeping
their options open. The servants of power had less room to
choose. Courtiers were an overcrowded group hovering on
the edge of the aristocracy, and subsisting as administrators
and soldiers. Their livelihood depended on the favour of the
powerful, whether family or state.

The Tansillos were one such family. They were from Nola, an ancient and distinguished town strategically placed thirty kilometers east of Naples on the rich agricultural soil inland of Vesuvius. Luigi Tansillo was in his mid twenties when he got a posting in 1536 to the personal guard of the recently appointed viceroy Toledo, and for fifteen years he served the Spanish empire as an officer on campaigns against Islamic forces in North Africa, the Aegean and the Balkans. Toledo's death in 1553 saw him bumped from the viceroy's guard to a job in the Naples customs office, but eight years later he won a solid posting as governor of Gaeta.

Professional soldier by necessity, Luigi Tansillo wrote poems all his life. He was quite prolific, though as a member of the court he never bothered to put out a collection. In his early twenties, around 1533, a few years before landing his place in the viceroy's guard, he had written a long erotic poem that became known as *Il vendemmiatore*, or *The Grape Harvester*, described with a slight leer by its author as *verses for workers in the field of women*. It was much enjoyed and for a while Tansillo was a minor sixteenth century celebrity.

Twenty-five years later, times were changed and the values of the counter-reformation were being enforced. In middle age and already at a low point in his career at court, Tansillo saw the fruit of his younger erotic exuberance condemned in 1559 to the Index of forbidden books. It was very unfair. Tansillo was more uxorious than reprobate. With military dispatch and a courtier's adroitness he moved to recover lost ground by launching into a new long poem called *The Tears of Saint Peter*. He made sure the right people heard about the work in progress and it may have helped swing the governor's job in Gaeta. After that, whether the poet's administrative duties became too demanding or whether his heart wasn't quite in it, the new poem languished. When Tansillo died in 1568 after seven years as governor, *The Tears of Saint Peter* lay unfinished. It was later set to music, and enthusiasts of early religious song are the only people who remember Tansillo today. His real vein, harsh and vivid notes on a soldier's life on the Mediterranean, radiantly realistic glimpses of country life on the bay of Naples, planting and harvesting and rearing children, has receded into oblivion.

Tansillo had a cousin who was also making a living in the Spanish military. The other Tansillo was an officer in the count of Caserta's regiment and he was friends with a fellow officer from Nola named Giovanni Bruno. Bruno had risen fast in the service, and out of courtier's prudence or genuine enthusiasm had named his only son Filippo after the future Spanish king. Bruno became friends with the poet–soldier Tansillo.

Coming home to Nola from Spain's foreign wars was a relief and an anticlimax for these professional soldiers. Shared reminiscence bound them together and Giovanni Bruno's son was an eager audience. The boy was bright, preternaturally articulate and impatient with the mindless grammatical drill of his schooling in Nola. The eleven-year-old Filippo Bruno was probably impressed when Tansillo's erotic poem was put on the Index. He would start his own work *in the field of women* a couple of years later. His father and his father's military friends brought the boy Filippo news of a world beyond Nola, beyond Italy, beyond Christendom, but the thing that most impressed young Bruno in Luigi Tansillo, who was knocking fifty at the time and not yet out of the customs office, was the power of words.

Tansillo's vein would rise at surprising moments in things written by Filippo Bruno as a man. The pleasures of sex were not Bruno's main subject but they surged into mind and on to the page even when he was most abstractly and acrimoniously engaged with the forces of intellectual stupidity. Bruno shared Tansillo's eroticism. In 1592 he was telling people that *he liked women a lot, though he'd not yet had as many as Solomon*, still hoping at the age of forty-four to outdo the Old Testament king's mighty score of sexual conquests and insisting that *the church was very wrong to make a sin out of such a good way of serving Nature, one which he personally highly approved of.* Every word was reported to the Inquisition and taken down.

From the old soldiers' talk the boy Bruno also gathered a sense of how imperial Spain worked as its power spread in the world and how it would end. Years later he wrote

> They've discovered how to disturb other people, violate the spirits of other regions, mix up what bountiful Nature kept separate, make things twice as bad for the sake of business and join one people's vices to the other's. They spread new kinds of lunacy by violence and plant unheard-of madness where it never existed before. They believe the strongest are the wisest and keep developing new techniques of oppression and killing. But things will change with time and their victims will learn how to do the same or worse back in return.

The conversation of his father's male friends went beyond old soldiers' tales and stayed in the boy's memory. Twenty years or so later, his father and Tansillo and other long-dead friends would reappear as talkers in Bruno's philosophical dialogues.

Bruno's parents had few resources—his father's meagre army pay and maybe something from a little land outside Nola his mother's family owned—but in 1562, when Bruno was fourteen and his father was away with the army in Apulia, they found the money to send their bright boy off to study in the capital. It was an effort of love he never forgot. Naples was only thirty kilometers away, but the teeming metropolis drew the adolescent into a different life. He stayed there fifteen years, and five years after leaving, when he published his first real book in exile in Paris, he prefaced it with an enigmatic letter to a married woman whose identity would never be known for sure, *wise, beautiful and generous*, perhaps from Nola, and *the tiller of my spirit's field*. The words recalled Tansillo's genial *doubles entendres* and made *Morgana B.* sound like an older married woman in his home town who gave him his first sexual experience before he left for the big city.

When Bruno arrived there, Naples was sixty years into its life as the Mediterranean metropolis of Spain's global empire and the strategic centre of the sea war against Islam. It was the main exit point for the resources that flowed to Spain from its Italian possessions. The port seethed with military and commercial traffic, and the waterfront quarters were crowded with visitors and temporary residents from all over Italy, all over Europe and Mediterranean Africa and Asia. Neapolitans were still largely excluded from the circulation of goods, money and military hardware in their city. Spain controlled the territory, and financiers from Venice, Genoa, Florence and from the Low Countries and the Balkans controlled the trade.

People in Naples were ever more numerous. The country people on the run from rural poverty and baronial abuse wandered the streets bemused, without shelter or connexions or useful skills, and tried to adjust to city life.

Productive labour was in the hands of a few specialized craftsmen who made goods for a city of conspicuous consumers. Baronial families put on a brave show and jostled for the power and prestige that were now in the gift of Madrid's viceroy. Power-sharing with the locals, as Spain tightened its grip, was more and more a matter of show. Spain entangled the poor in diabolical taxes on life's needs, and imposed Spanish values by force of arms. Kissing was forbidden in the streets and two men were burnt in the Market square for Protestant opinions a couple of years after Bruno arrived *to learn humanities, logic and dialectic.* Naples had more churches, more convents, more monasteries, more patron saints, more religious orders, more roadside shrines, more clergy, more miracles and more ecclesiastical wealth than almost any city in Christendom. The clergy were exempt from taxes, and taxes were what Spain wanted from Naples and Sicily. And Naples was one of Italy's great centres of the arts of living. *Naples and Rome and Venice . . . the whole world's source and image of all kinds of nobility* were also, as Bruno later said through other mouths, *plentiful in whores.*

For two years the boy Bruno stayed with a family friend and took private lessons in logic and metaphysics with two formidable teachers in Naples, who tempered his mind and encouraged him to think. Nearly thirty years later he remarked that *when he was a boy he began to be an enemy of the Catholic faith.* But Bruno at seventeen had no financial or social resources of his own to continue his studies. The formidable Dominicans, who in Naples ran what was perhaps the best university in Italy, represented a way of going on. And they taught you how to speak. In the intellectual theatre of San Domenico, Bruno was overwhelmed by the compelling power of the logic and eloquence wielded by the Dominicans, and wanted to learn from them. *After hearing them debate at San Domenico in Naples . . . he said those were gods of the earth.* It was the power of words again. He too wanted to be a crowd-compeller. San Domenico held irresistible promise.

Eloquence under pressure—talking your way out of a tight corner—was a peculiarly Neapolitan gift, and Bruno was a natural. The Dominicans would teach him control—how to hold a crowd, how to clearly and confidently articulate abstract questions, how to convince your listeners. The Dominicans were famous for their preaching, and understood how much it mattered. It was the first thing they taught. For at least a year, the seminarians' day began with rhetoric. Aristotle and Cicero were plundered for what they wrote about the clear voice, the inventive phrase, the commanding gesture, and how the ancient skills could serve the church. Every week each student had to make a short *declamation* to the others. This was always on the wisdom of the church fathers, but the arts of memory and rhetoric came from the pagan classics. If the church could use ancient skills to further its ends, Bruno could make use of the church's skills to further his own. He entered the seminary. He stayed eleven years, mastering the intricacies of a learning he never believed in, and it made him and unmade him. Disillusion followed immediately. *Then he discovered they were all asses and ignorant and said that the church was ruled by ignorant asses.*

Planes of light

Caracciolo tracked Merisi like a shadow for nearly a year, in technique, subject, clientèle, and probably—though there were no records beyond the record of their art—as a friend, but Merisi left Naples and vanished in the summer of 1610. The living instance was gone and Caracciolo could only wonder where that amazing hallucinatory minimalism of Merisi's last things might be taken.

After Merisi's disappearance Caracciolo's devotion to him as a painter was even stronger, and now that he was on his own he gained some of Merisi's own intractable assurance. A new daughter was born. He frescoed a room in the royal palace with the exploits of Gonzalo de Córdoba, the general who had taken Naples for Spain; and into the scene he inserted a little portrait of his vanished master. Another of Merisi's clients came knocking, and the most prestigious: the insatiable cardinal Borghese, the pope's nephew. In April 1612 a new son was born and the same month Caracciolo personally delivered a *David with Goliath's Head* to Borghese in Rome. Maybe he had a chance during the visit to see Merisi's version of *David* from six years earlier, of David holding the painter's own severed head, still showing the injuries of the fatal street fight. And all the other early and late works of Merisi's that Borghese had snaffled up for his enormous personal collection. Caracciolo did yet another *Salome with John the Baptist's Head* that year. Now he had done about as many as the master.

A couple of years later Caracciolo made another visit to Rome. He was still tracking Merisi, looking into his past. In 1614 he went to see Orazio Gentileschi, Merisi's older associate, his first disciple and codefendant from the heroic days at the turn of the century, when reality irrupted into the stifling world of Roman rhetoric and everything changed. Caracciolo was looking for the early Merisi, the painter of the revolutionary optical style in its first flush. The earlier Merisi, who had converted Gentileschi and dazzled the young Caracciolo on his first visits to Rome, had been a richer and more painstaking artist than the rapid, tensely inventive painter Caracciolo had known in Naples at the end. Gentileschi, the man closest to Merisi in those first brilliant years, knew the secrets of that time. And he had his own. Gentileschi too had trained in decorative late mannerism and done years of work in fresco before being won over by Merisi's new optical art. Gentileschi had been nearly forty then and his new work had its own distinctive take on the Merisi revolution. Gentileschi's way of painting was

> personal, lyrical and exquisite . . . the realism of the light, the surfaces, the flesh . . . the facial features and expressions met with a brilliant and mostly light colouring and strong design, a rigour of composition that was almost classical.

This was something Caracciolo shared in his own personal history and his own practice, and it was why he could learn from Gentileschi now. Seeing Gentileschi paint deepened his understanding of the master's art. *[Caracciolo] told me he knew Gentileschi's style from working with him in Rome about ten years ago*, wrote his agent in Naples to prince Marcantonio Doria in Genoa in 1624. Orazio's daughter Artemisia was no longer working with her father, two years after the rape trial of Agostino Tassi. In 1613 Artemisia had moved to Florence, where she began her wholly independent life as a major painter, and it was in Florence that she and Caracciolo would meet several years later.

Caracciolo returned to Naples and the next year he received a deeply intimidating commission. It was to paint an altarpiece for the church of the Pio Monte della Misericordia where Merisi's incomparable *Seven Works* had been hanging for the last eight years. Caracciolo's painting would be in sight of the master's. The huge notoriety of *Seven Works* and Caracciolo's deep mental bond to Merisi's art must have filled him, at least for a moment, with dread. Then, splendidly, with Merisi–like resilience and in a complex and exquisite recognition of what he owed the dead master, Caracciolo met the challenge.

The clamour around the *Seven Works* had not lessened over the years and not all the attention was enjoyed by the painting's owners. Two years earlier the Spanish count of Villamediana had *repeatedly asked* to be allowed to have a copy made of it. Villamediana was a dangerous loose cannon in the viceroy's court and a person of great influence among the intellectuals of Naples. He returned to Spain in 1617 and five years later was murdered in Madrid, in a killing ordered inside the royal court. He was a satirical man with a savage tongue and pen, but his mortal offence was to be gay. His sexual life was being probed by the Inquisition when he was killed, and the Spanish government feared a scandal. Sex was probably why he had secured a posting to Naples, a famous destination for people fleeing the Spanish Inquisition's sexual persecution, famous enough for Neapolitans to claim, without expecting for a moment to be believed, that gay sex in Naples was a Spanish import.

In 1613 Villamediana's insistence was worrying. The charity's governors met in the dog days of summer and formally resolved firstly that the painting *may not ever be sold at any price but held in perpetuity in said church*; and secondly, that Villamediana be allowed to have the copy made, as long as this were done by one of three approved painters, one of them Caracciolo, but making clear *that said painting may not be removed from said altar.* Seven years later, the pressure from Villamediana removed, the governors resolved more strongly that *no person at any time or for any reason whatsoever be allowed to make copies of the paintings in our church, particularly that over the main altar. That* being the *Seven Works.* It was still under siege.

Caracciolo's stipulated subject was Peter being freed from his prison by an angel. Carlo Sellitto had been the governors' first choice a couple of years before. Sellitto was three years younger than Caracciolo, like him powerfully affected by Merisi's art and at that point he was the more brilliant success. He was enormously in demand. He was so busy with other commissions that the painting was still undone in late 1614 when Sellitto was hit by a fulminant illness that killed him in a couple of weeks. For people who wanted Sellitto, Caracciolo was the obvious second choice. His *Peter Freed* was delivered promptly and its proximity to *Seven Works* did not diminish Caracciolo. His new work had stupendous beauty and power, closer than anything else he did to Merisi's own style and yet assured and vigorously individual. The master would have liked it. It was late Merisi, with a great darkness hovering over its reduced figures, lean minimalist brushwork, a sense of uncertainty in the conflicting gaze and a spare dramatic urgency in the angel leading Peter to safety from his prison. Caracciolo's painting reflected, in the wingless angel's youthful nervousness and Peter's anxious glance down at the sleeping soldiery, Merisi's now lost image of the resurrected Christ, *a thin man who has suffered, done from life*, leaving his tomb *not in the air but passing his guards on foot . . . like a convict escaping from his jailers.*

It was, too, a masterpiece in which something of Orazio Gentileschi was clearly perceptible. The lessons of the last year's visit showed. The surrounding darkness was Merisi's but the radiant colours in the knot of figures at the centre, soldier, prisoner, angel and saint, were Gentileschi's—the play of light on the many folds of the angel's white satin, and the contrast of that with Peter's overlapping light-absorbing dun blanket and with the strong red of the cloth around the sleeping prisoner's waist. And the extreme delicacy of the almost touching faces of old saint and young angel.

Jusepe de Ribera, arriving in town the next year and thinking to have the field to himself as a radical realist, would have been shocked on revisiting *Seven Works* to find *Peter Freed* hanging nearby. He might not have recognized the artist, and wondered who this unexpected blood brother or deadly rival might be. Ribera needn't have worried. A year later his rival Caracciolo left town, on a long working trip to Rome, Florence and Genoa, and he came back a changed man. *Peter Freed* was the culmination and the conclusion of a painterly passion. Caracciolo had produced the greatest painting by any of those early followers who had known the master, and he never again came quite so nakedly close to Merisi's own style. Caracciolo himself was freed now to pursue his own painterly interests.

One of those interests, which he never repudiated even in his most intense allegiance to the new art of Merisi, was the art of fresco in which he had been trained. Fresco and the related arts of draughtsmanship, which were a necessary preparation for painting rapidly over large areas of wet plaster before it hardened. Battistello Caracciolo had a way of embracing contradictions. He straddled two visual cultures. In his deep fascination with Merisi's new art of planes of light in darkness rendered directly in oil paint he never forgot the way of making images he had learnt with Corenzio. The renaissance principles of perspective and the renaissance art of drawing remained a part of his way of thinking. After *Peter Freed*, he gradually reverted, for the last fifteen years or so before he died in 1635, to his own earlier ways. But even when he went back to painting mostly walls in fresco he incorporated Merisi's optical perceptions into his fresco work. He went on lifting parts of Merisi's image structures into his own pictures, and more than once they were early ideas for the *Seven Works* which Merisi had then painted over, but not before Caracciolo had made drawings for later use. He was an assiduous and expert artist with a pencil.

They wanted Caracciolo everywhere. He was in Florence by 1618 and painted for the grand duke Cosimo II. He saw what Artemisia Gentileschi was painting there, and Jacques Callot was etching. Then he went to Genoa and worked directly for Doria, and on a return visit in 1618 he painted the loggia of Doria's country villa in fresco, the job Merisi had refused a fortune to do nineteen years before. By then Doria had twelve paintings by Caracciolo in his collection. The grand duke of Tuscany was so pleased with the portraits Caracciolo painted of himself and his wife that he wrote a letter of recommendation to the viceroy Osuña for Caracciolo to take back to Naples. Resorting to capital letters in his enthusiasm, the grand duke told the viceroy that *having highly appreciated* Caracciolo's skills, *especially in the portraits THAT HE HAS PAINTED OF ME AND HER MOST SERENE ARCHDUCHESS my wife* he had *taken a more than usual liking to him* and asked *Yr Excellency . . . to receive him under your true protection.* And the commissions followed from powerful institutions in Naples. Caracciolo painted big fresco cycles in the viceroy's royal palace and the charterhouse of San Martino next to the Castel Sant'Elmo.

Caracciolo clearly didn't care about the hard-edged social and human realism that made Merisi's work so thrilling. He made over Merisi's optical insights, which he understood as well as anyone, into conventional religious images which nobody ever objected to. In doing this he developed a realism of his own that was subtler and more inward than Merisi's confronting drama, a psychological truthfulness encased in the acceptable scenography of the counter-reformation.

A den of vice

San Domenico Maggiore, with its Aragonese kings of Naples stacked on shelves in wooden coffins—don Ferrante now lying slotted a couple of boxes away from Antonello Petrucci, the favoured chief administrator he beheaded for betrayal—looms at the top of a sloping piazza that descends into *Spaccanapoli*. The huge and now almost empty monastery at its back reaches up to Via Tribunali. These narrow parallel streets, each straight as a die, follow the lower slope of the hill down toward the flat ground at the eastern edge of the city and the old gates of Porta Nolana and Porta Capuana, the sandy ground where people went for country picnics outside the city walls, where streams used to run off into the sea and boats landed fish and produce at the Market. They are the founding traces of Naples, laid down by the Greeks nearly three thousand years ago. Naples grew along their axes—the ancient city's market place and forum, the austere and magnificent great churches of the middle ages.

San Domenico in Naples was the liveliest and least submissive intellectual centre of counter-reformation Italy, at least outside the Venetian republic. It had the best library in Spanish Italy, strong local ties, and was fiercely protective of its own autonomy. The novice Filippo Bruno entered the order in 1565, took the name Giordano and found books in its library by the ironical and anathematized Erasmus of Rotterdam and other works forbidden to public and private collections, books unobtainable anywhere else in Naples. Students read for themselves—*in their cells by lamplight they can read, write, pray, sleep or stay awake all night*—and talked about what they read.

Along with the Bible and the church fathers, Bruno read Ovid, Sappho, Horace, Virgil, Lucretius, Epicurus—pretty well all the extant Greek and Latin poets and philosophers. He already knew the poetry of Petrarch, Ariosto, his contemporary Tasso from Sorrento and his father's friend Tansillo. He also knew a mass of popular verse and popular stories, robustly comic stuff dealing in the domestic and country life of his own childhood, as well as the obscenely witty and subversive work of Aretino. Later he would quote and use them all. Bruno lost none of his familiarity with the pagan, the vernacular, the erotic, the obscene and the comic during his eleven years with the order of San Domenico.

Life in the Dominican convent was neither tranquil and studious nor withdrawn from the city which hemmed it in. It was not a world apart, a demure and pious milieu of silence and prayer, of the low voice and the averted gaze, of clasped hands and measured steps, of knees bent in worship and minds absorbed in meditation, of intense study and earnest dialogue. Or not only. It rented part of its premises to the secular university of Naples, whose riotous and disorderly teenage students carried weapons—the viceroy outlawed them, on pain of torture, on account of the *trouble and scandal* the students were causing—and brawled in the cloister and in the church and in the neighbouring streets. The racket was deafening in the cloisters and the alleys. Novices mixed with loose women, who were hard to avoid in the middle of Naples. A youngster called Santori was a decade or so ahead of Bruno. He would culminate a brilliant ecclesiastical career as the grand inquisitor who sentenced Bruno to be burnt, and at the very end of his life cardinal Santori recalled his own sexual lapses from the true way when he was a boy of fifteen at San Domenico Maggiore. As a novice Santori was wounded by cannon shrapnel in the Spanish bombardment of Naples during the revolt of 1547 against the Inquisition. Someone said of Bruno, probably untruly, that he was admitted to study for the priesthood only on account of his fresh face and the order's ignorance of his early history as *a lookout boy for whores.*

The San Domenico complex had been expanded, rebuilt and added to again and again until it covered a large city block. Its high windowless walls loomed over the narrow alleys and made it easy to defend. Inside, the order's members were doing their own things, not always a great example for the novices. Around the end of 1568 two priests from the convent were convicted of thefts committed *many times, against many people in many cities and other places,* and several more were charged with copying keys and letting novices get out of the convent at will. Others, now *spoiled and rotten sheep,* were variously expelled from the order and sentenced to many years hard labour rowing on the galleys for being *incorrigible rebels . . . fugitives and vagabonds . . . fathers of illegitimate children . . . whoremongers . . . a scandal to the lay community and a disgrace to their religion.* In 1568 too a Dominican attacked another with a sword inside the convent, and others with his fists, after brawling and killing in streets and convents all over Italy.

Things got so wild inside the Dominican convents that in 1571 to control the damage it was made an offence to reveal outside their walls, in writing or by word of mouth, what crimes were committed inside. The punishment was *excommunication and ten years' jail, or worse*. Nobody must mention that the venerable master of the novices, for instance, had been stripped of his habit and sentenced to seven years rowing in the galleys for *repeated wicked and unspeakable acts*. Outside, a monk was dragged off to jail by six policemen, and two others were nearly killed in front of the church in a revenge attack by an enraged Neapolitan husband wielding a pair of pruning shears. One of Bruno's classmates was sentenced to ten years' jail in 1572, having been found at night in the streets of Naples *armed with an arquebus and a double-edged knife* and in the company of a whore. People were *deeply shocked*. Long sentences incurred by monks for violence inside could be hushed up, even a murder, but a monk's knifing of a young Neapolitan outside could not, and the monk would get sixty years, or *life on the galleys* if his victim died. Or another monk's ripping a gold chain from the neck of a praying woman, *witnessed by many people*. He got an exemplary sixty years.

The criminal situation in Bruno's convent was no worse than in the other convents in Naples. Priests and monks were sentenced for acts of theft and violence and for constantly reported acts of rebellion against their order and the church. One priest was repeatedly excommunicated for his *many scandals in the city and innumerable rebellions*. He didn't bother to show up for his trial, let alone the sentencing, and simply continued in his priestly office. Acts of violence including manslaughter and murder were the commonest crimes of all and mostly happened inside. Others were *lapses of the flesh with members of both sexes*. Things were *especially serious* in the nunneries but the aristocrats opposed reform on the grounds that *a delicately brought up Lady would flee such a harsh regime* and that *knights with many daughters* would then be landed with the extra expense of keeping them at home.

Outside Naples the smaller country convents were often given over entirely to banditry. The pope was not infrequently *gravely pained* at having to suppress entire monasteries which had become headquarters for organized crime, the crime being organized by the monks. Monks would shelter bandits on the run and end by joining them. Banditry could be many things. The years of the militant counter-reformation were hard times for country people south of Rome. When Rome and Naples signed an agreement in 1585 to combat the mass banditry spreading through the country around both Rome and Naples, they listed among the outlaws *heretics, rebels, blasphemers, counterfeiters, coiners, kidnappers, disturbers of the peace, robbers, murderers, killers and street breakers*. Religious, political and criminal offenders had overlapping identities, and the authorities viewed crimes of conscience much as they viewed crimes against the state or against the person.

What made the Dominicans—the Dominicans of Naples in particular and those of San Domenico Maggiore above all—stand out was *rebellion*. The word occurred again and again in the disciplinary registers, usually applied to individuals. But with the Dominicans rebellion also involved the whole Dominican *family*. The Neapolitan aristocrats who governed the city, mediating between the Spanish and the locals, were intensely nervous about the Dominican presence.

The Dominicans' intellectual freedoms, their all too intimate ties with the people they lived among and the frequent lawlessness of their lives were all equally worrying to secular and religious agencies of control. Nerves snapped in 1586, ten years after Bruno had left.

After the killing and mutilation of the people's representative and wheat speculator Starace the year before and the hideous repression that followed, it was felt the time had come to clamp down on the Dominicans. The city administration dispatched one of its aristocrats to Rome, to discuss with the pope how to remove the refractory occupants of San Domenico Maggiore and replace them with compliant *counter-reformed* Dominicans. And those of a second Dominican convent as well. The pope agreed instantly and ordered the Dominicans to comply. The authorities tried first with a smaller convent, as more vulnerable, but the replacement Dominicans were knocked back briskly.

The police were called and one of the defending monks stabbed and killed an officer trying to arrest him. He was immediately hanged in the Market Place with Rome's full support. The locals threw themselves behind the Dominicans and rushed off a petition to the pope, who ordered an investigation. Nothing was found to hold against the Dominicans of this convent. The pope bided his time for a few years and ordered a new assault, this time directed at San Domenico Maggiore itself and planned with more care and resources. The pope issued the order at the end of 1594 and with the viceroy's support the convent was surrounded by police while the papal nuncio ordered the hundred and fifty monks inside to leave.

Caught off guard, the Dominicans complied. But days later they returned, *carrying pistols, knives and sticks under their habits*. They threw out the counter-reformed interlopers and stockpiled arms in their cells. They barricaded the doors, manned the high windows, *ready with rocks to hurl on anyone who attacked below*. People massed outside to support their stand, *happy at this exploit*, and influential citizens warned the viceroy that if the siege went on, *all of Naples will be in arms*. Many reasons for anger in Naples found a focus in the siege. Faced with a popular revolt, the viceroy prudently decided not to force matters, and the pope, who meant to excommunicate the monks and have them thrown in jail, quietly changed his mind. The monks stayed.

The Dominican freedom was in some ways illusory. Ideology was more closely policed than crimes of violence, and Bruno's years among the Dominicans were the grimmest and most punitive time of the Catholic call to order. Bruno often blurted out what he was thinking in a very direct way and spoke unguardedly with his fellows. Dominicans were not necessarily bright, despite the order's efforts to filter the intake, and Bruno's explosive energy and critical eagerness, his readiness to think new thoughts and his contempt for received opinion were rarely governed by tact. He got into trouble in his very first months as a novice in 1565, with a scathing remark about some devotional drivel a fellow seminarian was reading, a pamphlet called *The Story of the Seven Happinesses of the Madonna*. He cleared out devotional images of saints from his own cell. The authorities were not pleased and called him to order. *My master when I was a novice wrote a report in order to terrify me . . . but . . . tore it up the same day*. Bruno was an opinionated, articulate and assertive novice who needed keeping in line. Other charges followed and were less easily dealt with.

In 1566 the Dominican Michele Ghislieri became pope. Ghislieri was the ideologue and enforcer of the counter-reformation, and as Pius V he remained active in the Inquisition. Romans had partied in the streets when Paul IV Carafa died some years before, trashing the offices of the Inquisition and destroying its archives. Ghislieri had been Carafa's grand inquisitor. He had presided over the Spanish massacre of thousands of heretic men, women and children in Calabria in 1561, and in 1566 he began his papacy by having fifteen heretics burnt in Rome and setting up a major new headquarters for the Inquisition. During his time as pope—Bruno's first six years in the seminary—over thirty people were executed for heresy. The regime was hardening, and in Naples Bruno was already showing an impetuous tendency to misread the signs.

Toledo had introduced preventive censorship and public burnings of *infected* books to Naples when Bruno was still a child. His motive was political control. Rome now extended the control as Ghislieri had an extensive new Index of prohibited books drawn up. The account books at San Domenico Maggiore recorded a payment in 1570 *for making white paste to remove things by Erasmus and other heretics from the books in our library*. Other ancient manuscripts were scored through, crisscrossed with lines to obliterate commentaries and annotations in texts edited by Erasmus and other humanists. The works of *pagan* writers and philosophers were banned to save students from *the evil doctrine and depraved morals* of their humanist editors. Bruno read Erasmus and *made secret use* of books edited by Erasmus he found outside the convent.

At the same time Bruno quickly made his mark at San Domenico. He mastered the speaker's essential aid, the arcane and ancient art of memory. At the end of 1568, a year after facing his first threat of charges, they took him to Rome *in a coach* to demonstrate his memory skills to pope Ghislieri himself. He recited a memorized psalm in Hebrew, gave some intensive coaching to a leading cardinal and cheekily presented the pope, who was then burning people at the rate of more than one a week, with his own first written work, a pamphlet called *Noah's Ark*, which later disappeared without trace. Bruno was twenty and had never travelled further than the thirty kilometers from Nola to Naples. The art of memory, the information technology of a time when even printed books were few, would be Bruno's bread and butter in his years on the road, the subject of some of his earliest books and the main source of a personal notoriety that would eventually be his downfall.

The brilliant student and Dominican show pony was not always able to contain his contradictions, and in moments of exasperation at ignorance, superstition or sheer *asininity*—soon a central term in Bruno's discussions of religious belief—his opinions would erupt in naked expressions of contempt and dislike, undoing months and years of assiduous outward conformity. In the spring of 1572, a group of prominent Dominicans came down to Naples from the North and were liberally entertained at the convent and taken on outings and boat parties to visit the antiquities. One of the distinguished visitors was holding forth on the ignorance of the church's early dissidents when Bruno—not yet ordained or even a graduate—intervened sharply in a way that made the senior clerics *jump out of their seats saying that I was defending heretics.* It was a trivial incident, but Bruno's energy was always suspect. The vehemence and the impatience would leap out from his dramatic dialogues, and later from the transcribed delations of the spies, enemies and tale-bearers who circled him once he was caught in the Inquisition's net. Several years after the spat with the visitors, when Bruno's rapid advancement was stirring up resentment, someone dug up this incident and the earlier one to raise doubts about Bruno's adherence to the dogma of the Trinity. Did he believe Christ was God or man? The question mattered. It was essential to any kind of Christian belief. People were being burnt over much smaller issues. Yet even to save his life Bruno would never quite be able to persuade people he believed Christ was God. By the time he was handed over to the Inquisition in Venice twenty years later, he no longer really cared about hiding his thought at all.

On the face of it he was doing well at San Domenico. By 1572 he was an ordained priest and in 1575 he graduated in theology with a thesis on Thomas Aquinas. But at the end of 1575 Bruno came under investigation and the next year he was listed in the order's records as one of thirty Dominicans being proceeded against in Naples. His reading of the evil-tongued, lascivious and irreverent Erasmus was probably one concern. The other was the question of the Trinity. He was worried enough about his case to report in person to the order in Rome. While he was in Rome, Bruno heard from friends. *I received letters from Naples informing me that certain books had been found . . . I used to read them secretly and*

I threw them in the latrine when I left Naples because they were forbidden. The books contained notes by Erasmus. Bruno was now in serious trouble. Rome in 1576 was in the middle of a crime wave. The crowds of foreign pilgrims drawn by the jubilee were easy prey for criminals. When an unidentified Dominican monk murdered someone and flung the body into the Tiber, Bruno came under suspicion for that too. Things seemed stacked against him. He abandoned his monk's habit for civilian clothes and left Rome, heading north.

Children and shadows

The only person who wrote about Battistello Caracciolo's paintings for about three hundred years complained, of Caracciolo's Merisi phase, about *the crude forms of low life* and objected in particular to a painting where *Christ and saint John could be taken for labouring people rather than noble, let alone divine* and where the angels' *legs . . . seem more like farm workers' than angels'*. Caracciolo was charged with painting figures of the Christian pantheon as Merisi had, *using the same gross life models . . . though in their faces he tried to give them a nobler look than his new master Michelangelo [Merisi] used to.*

The notion that Caracciolo gave an ideal or divine look to the faces in his paintings was a curious one. If he ever outdid *his new master's* realism, it was in the subtle, various and not particularly beautiful faces he painted. Above all, of the very young and the peripheral. Caracciolo offered whatever clients might want in the way of counter-reformation imagery, but faces, especially the usually skimped features of celestial hangers-on—the angels and the putti wheeling around the protagonists—he realized with incomparable art. He might not have shared the austere rigour of Merisi's understanding of Gospel events and saints' lives, but he caught the human uniqueness of his models. When he didn't have to include heavenly flights or fancy iconography, he painted, in 1622, the *Christ Washing the Feet*, whose serenely tragic foreboding was entirely human, full of drama and monumentally still.

He was famous and sought-after for his portraits, all later lost but one. The vivid pairs of people in his small horizontal easel paintings were seen up close and personal and from disconcertingly intimate places, close to a waist or a bare foot. In Florence he painted *Joseph and Potiphar's Wife*, with two very Neapolitan-looking models, a dark-haired boy and a wife who was not the usual lustful middle-aged woman but a cheeky and provocative teenager. Joseph, who looked about to give in, still wore his plumed hat, and a gorgeously brocaded dark red outer dress, perhaps his coat of many colours. Potiphar's wife lay in a simple neutral nightdress even more finely rendered. Decorative exuberance in clothes and flesh—a late *Judgement of Solomon* was a welter of inlaid helmets, plumes, patterned carpets, elaborately wrought urns, gold jewellery, rich brocades and fancy sword hilts—sometimes distracted.

Other paintings, like *Lot and His Daughters* in tones of brown—they were in a cave—stayed much closer to the austere model of Merisi, not least in the details of the picnic meal. The drama of the three differently directed gazes and the bravura display of five bare feet in the foreground were entirely Caracciolo's own. There was a half-figure *Noli Mi*

Tangere of Mary Magdalen meeting the newly risen Christ, who was bare-chested, holding a hoe and wearing a broad-brimmed gardener's hat. She had understandably mistaken him for the ground-keeper.

Caracciolo was prolific in these close, intense easel works and like Merisi he was most revealingly himself in them. A *Joseph and the Child Jesus* was an unadorned domestic image of a bearded working man and a small son huddled into his protective arms. Caracciolo married at twenty, had at least ten children, two of whom themselves became painters, and the juvenile population of his work extrapolates the domestic presence of children of all ages. The play of looks always animated Caracciolo's pictures, and subliminally conveyed a sense that people had interests which did not necessarily conflict but which didn't coincide either, not in the intimacies of domestic life, nor in the social life of a stressed and crowded city.

Peter Freed had been Caracciolo's most intense Merisi moment. A couple of years later he did a painting which showed where he was now going. It was an *Earthly Trinity* which showed Christ at puberty walking hand in hand with his parents. Mary's oval face was turned lovingly down to her son. Joseph was a vigorous figure of a working man, with sunburnt face and clipped grey hair and beard, a rough tan cloak knotted around his shoulders, looking out for his family with a wary, protective gaze. Between them, the long-haired boy Christ, in a long tunic the same wine colour as his mother's dress, looked up with a partly open mouth at the white dove hovering just overhead. The three had the look of a country family visiting the metropolis—parents perhaps, coming to see their son the new seminarian—and the alert boy's intense curiosity for something his preoccupied parents hadn't noticed was somehow more striking than the fact that what he saw was the Holy Spirit descending. The son of man was delicately backlit by the only real halo in the history of Christian art. The young Christ's face, its intense, fearless apprehension, was incomparable.

Above the three, God the father looked down on them—an older grizzled working man, with leathery hands and weather-wrinkled brow—emerging from a turbine of teenage angels and wine-coloured bed linen that brilliantly and more complexly redeployed the aerobatics of the night alley drama in Merisi's *Seven Works*. The angels were seen with a social acuteness that made them as readily recognizable as God. Only one of the three had remotely angelic looks. The other two were Neapolitan *scugnizzi* with narrow faces and short dark unwashed hair. One of them seemed to have a bad cold. Unlike Merisi's *Seven Works* and its strangely compelling unity of higher meaning and very low reality, the *Earthly Trinity* was cut clean in two between top and bottom. In Caracciolo the strangeness came from tension between the beautiful still-ness—at once everyday human and sublimely monumental—of the lower earthly part and the impending proletarian energy and confusion of the heavenly part just overhead.

At the top left a pair of putti had the job of dropping roses on the holy family. They were like the putti of Caracciolo's first paid work, and such as he always found a place for when he could. These two children were absorbed in their own game, too intent on a tussle for control of the remaining flowers to notice God the father hovering right next to them, let alone the holy family making their cautious way below. Parts of the putti's arms and legs caught the focused light coming from somewhere upper left. Most of them, including their faces, was seen in a penumbra of indirect light, clearly visible against the enveloping blackness, but less intensely lit than the divine figures. The older angels were something else again, faces and bodies fragmented by stronger contrasts of intense light and deep shadow. Merisi had already played with half-shadow like this in Naples, though he used a penumbra that was so dark it almost obliterated the face, like the corpse bearer's in the *Seven Works* and the face of one of the torturers in the Naples *Whipping*. He did it more subtly later in Sicily—the gravediggers in *Lucy's Burial*, Christ's face in *Lazarus Raised*.

Caracciolo never saw Merisi's Sicilian work. He found a play of intermediate light through his own images. It was part of his way of reconciling Merisi's optical radicalism with the gentler shading he had mastered in fresco. This indirect lighting did more than soften the increasingly frightening contrasts in Merisi's work between what was caught in a blaze of light and what was invisible to anyone looking at his pictures, even when he had painted the image into the darkness. Caracciolo's lighting flooded whole pictures with an almost underwater look. Skin took on a livid faintly greenish sheen in direct light and a more bronzy look in shade. It happened quite early, as in the double portrait he did in Florence of the physician saints *Cosmas and Damian* as two young bourgeois intellectuals dressed in black. The word bronze—*bronze light*—would recur in descriptions of Caracciolo's paintings after his rediscovery and Caracciolo would be the *grave bronze patriarch of seventeenth century Naples . . . an archaic personality.*

Swimming in a diffuse bronze light, the livid glare of their pale flesh caught for a moment by the sun, was how the children of the poor looked in Naples. A *Child Jesus* by Caracciolo had a puffy, sallow face like an old man's and eyes reduced to slits under swollen lids. An infant Christ, perhaps the same child a few years younger, had a large head and no neck to speak of. Adolescent angels had scrawny limbs, distended bellies, bad teeth. All of them, like their beautiful or simply pleasing counterparts, were vividly alive, closely observed and unmistakeably themselves.

A matter of conscience

A man called Vandel delivered a message to the mayor of Geneva in June 1551. It informed him that a foreigner had arrived in the city. The new arrival was staying at the Black Head hostelry in Gold Cross Street and was reported as being *an Italian marquis who comes from the emperor's side.* All Italians were suspect in Geneva, and an Italian noble who served the Catholic emperor Charles V was one of the enemy. The visitor had arrived knowing nobody in Calvin's city and bearing no letters of introduction. Everything about him was a ground for mistrust.

Geneva, which a generation earlier had been a smallish fun town of taverns, brothels, theatres, bath houses and a showy Catholicism, was now a walled citadel peopled by the dour members of the most austere and intransigent Christianity in Europe. It was an easy city for an Italian traveller to skirt on his way north into France or Switzerland or Germany, which made it likely the marquis was a man with a mission, whether a spy or an emissary.

His name was Galeazzo Caracciolo. He was thirty-four and he came from Naples, the son of a baron lately enriched and ennobled for his active loyalty to the Spanish emperor and his viceroy Toledo. The baron had become even richer through his marriage to an underage cousin, whom he had abducted and raped, when her immensely rich father died leaving her sole heir. He was an intimate and a regular gambling companion of the viceroy's. Presented at the imperial court, the baron's son Galeazzo became the emperor's *gentleman of the mouth* when he was eighteen. He served the emperor at table, attended him on ceremonial occasions and went with the court on its disastrous military adventure in Provence. At twenty, invested by the emperor with the Order of the Golden Fleece and on home leave in Naples, Galeazzo married Vittoria, the daughter of an even richer and more powerful Neapolitan family, the Carafas. Before long he was the father of four sons and two daughters, and a happy man.

Galeazzo was a serious and reflective man who had *a naturally severe and scrupulous mind* and he had friends much influenced by the new ideas of the German Reformation that were circulating through Europe. His closest friend, Gian Francesco Alois, was an early follower of the Spanish reformer and mystic Juan de Valdés. Valdés, fearing the Inquisition in Spain and in Rome, had come to live in Naples and drawn a circle of intense admirers. The young soldier and imperial courtier Galeazzo Caracciolo, nephew of the Carafa who would become the pope of the Inquisition and the counter-reformation, was convinced at the age of twenty-five of the rightness of the reformers of the Christian church. His inner reflection evolved into a total and irreversible rejection of the Roman Catholic church.

Both Galeazzo's father the baron, abruptly aware of a threat to the dynastic hopes invested in his only son, and Galeazzo's devout wife Vittoria saw early signs of danger. They failed to move him. For several years Galeazzo thought, read, discussed with friends at home in Naples. He observed and listened as he travelled through the ideologically divided countries of France and Germany with the imperial court. He felt the only thing he could do was leave Italy, and in the spring of 1551 Galeazzo left Naples, telling his family he was returning to service with the emperor. As he was. He took a tiny amount of money and rode north with a group of friends who shared his religious intent. When they reached the Italian frontier, all the others but one lost their nerve and turned their horses back. The one who persisted in her conviction was a woman.

Charles V was in the Alps at the time and for several weeks Galeazzo did rejoin the imperial court. But another courtier overheard him speaking with a friend from Naples about their secret beliefs and reported the conversation to the emperor. Charles V ordered the two Neapolitans placed under house arrest but Galeazzo slipped away in time. He headed for Geneva *to live there according to the Gospel*. He arrived on June eighth with a single servant whose name was Antonio. The young noble from the biggest, the most splendid, the most festive and the noisiest city in Europe found himself alone, unknown and without resources in a chill and silent town of pinched grey houses, huddled between the mountains and a windswept lake and inhabited by a few thousand pious souls. Among them were refugees from all over Catholic Europe. Many of Geneva's newer houses built to accommodate these contained stone fragments of broken religious statues. The city's once-adored relics, a piece of Peter's brain and one of Antony's arms, had been thrown into the Rhône and residents were annually interrogated in their homes about their beliefs. Two years after Galeazzo's arrival, Calvin ordered Geneva's first public burning of a dissident.

Anyone would have gone through a few bad moments in the Black Head hostelry, had a sense of cold fingers clutching at the heart, knowing he had thrown everything away—wealth, power, friends, a loving family, a loved wife—irrevocably. If Galeazzo had such a moment nobody knew about it. He was never seen to falter in his decision. He soon won the trust and respect of the Calvinists, became a friend and advisor of Calvin himself and lived in Geneva for the rest of his life.

He still felt the loss. So did the people who loved Galeazzo in Naples. The old baron sent Galeazzo's cousin Ferrante to Geneva to call him home. The two had been raised together as children and were as close as brothers. The family's emissary found the man once attended by an army of butlers, servants, cooks and grooms living in a narrow dark house with two servants. Galeazzo was unmoved. Ferrante and his cousin wept and parted. In the spring of 1553 the old baron, tireless in trying to save his son and his dynasty, sent Galeazzo a safe conduct from the republic of Venice. Galeazzo came down from Geneva to meet his father in Verona and later the baron went on to Brussels and pleaded with the emperor. Remembering the loyalty of both father and son, Charles V promised that Galeazzo's fortune, seized by his Carafa relative, the inquisitor archbishop of Naples, would be restored to his children.

Two years later Galeazzo's uncle Carafa was pope Paul IV and the old baron tried again. He wrung from the pope a promise that his son would be allowed to live in any city of the Venetian republic, unmolested over matters of conscience. Father and son met again on neutral ground in 1555, and Galeazzo gently pointed out that the pope's offer was at best an attempt to seduce him away from the rigours of his conscience and at worst a trap. The church did not feel bound by promises made to heretics. How the pope replied when the old man told him this was not recorded, but two years later, in the autumn of 1557, the Venetian ambassador reported a savage papal outburst against traitors to the faith and in particular Galeazzo, *son of a daughter of our own sister . . . and married to our own niece . . . gone to Geneva to live with those dreadful people and lose his body and his soul*. The pope seemed most angered that Galeazzo was living a wretched bourgeois life in a miserable Swiss town and had abandoned his power, his bella figura, his palaces, the vast tracts of southern Italy he owned and the income these brought him—all his family interests. Six years after Galeazzo had gone to Geneva, the Carafa pope insisted he felt *holy and perfect hatred . . . but nothing personal* against all heretics, family or not. He told the Venetian ambassador that *if our own father were heretic, we'd bring the faggots to burn him with*.

A few months later, around the end of 1557, Galeazzo's wife Vittoria, who had never stopped writing to her husband, wrote again asking to meet Galeazzo on Venetian territory as his father had. A meeting was arranged on the island of Lesina in the Adriatic, just off a part of the Dalmatian or Croatian coast which belonged to the Caracciolos and where they had a castle. For whatever reason, Vittoria failed to appear. Galeazzo met happily but inconclusively with two of his sons, and then returned to Geneva. He was hardly back when a new letter came from Vittoria asking for a new meeting on the island. Despite diplomatic obstacles, in the summer of 1558 Galeazzo went. His Calvinist friends were afraid that this time, lonely and longing for his wife, he might give in. Calvin himself wrote a tense and anxious letter which intercepted Galeazzo in Venice, and reminded him that he had *long grown used to placing your will above your affections, however good those might be.* The next day Calvin wrote to another correspondent that Vittoria *loves him enough to drag him to perdition if she can.*

Again Vittoria failed to appear. She claimed to have been let down by the Venetian aristocrat who had promised to take her and their sons to the island in his galley. But the priests, following her every move like hawks, had forbidden her to meet her husband alone on the island. Galeazzo waited, just across the water from the family castle where his wife was with his father, his children and the cousin Ferrante who had visited him in Geneva. Then he did what Calvin feared. He crossed the water and landed on Neapolitan territory. His old father sent sons and servants to welcome him but again Galeazzo knew it would fail. His wife would not leave Naples and he would not leave Geneva. The old man saw it

other branches of the vast Caracciolo family and life seemed back to normal.

Nevertheless, through the fiercest years of the counter-reformation, Colantonio stayed in touch with his father and helped his father's heretic friends. He was particularly close to Gian Francesco Alois, the friend who had drawn Galeazzo to religious dissent when they were young. Over the years, remaining in Naples, Alois had been forced to abjure his beliefs and later been imprisoned. In 1564 he was finally beheaded and burnt with another dissident at the Market. Colantonio had been unable to help him. A display of fanaticism like this was unprecedented in Naples, which was not Rome, and drew appalled crowds to the great waterfront Market Place. The Inquisition made a surprise raid on Colantonio's palace and found the shining prince burning letters from Alois. Colantonio had lately dealt contemptuously with the church—though he was less an ideologue than a southern baron who considered himself the only law on his own estates—and was tried and imprisoned in Rome. In the dungeons of Castel Sant'Angelo, wrote a contemporary, he stayed true to form and *seemed more of a lord than a prisoner . . . always surrounded by a lot of poor people . . . to whom he always gave something . . . the jailers took orders from him as much as they did from the magistrates.*

After a year and a half of this, the church decided he was *purged* and sent him home. In Naples he went on speaking frankly, *telling everyone openly how he had been wronged, more threatening than complaining and blaming the viceroy for all kinds of things.* The viceroy Alcalá in response tried him, jailed him, banished him from Naples. Colantonio moved to Venice. In the republic he lived magnificently among the local aristocracy and set up as an entrepreneurial corsair. It offered plenty of action and brought in good returns, though Colantonio's business activities made trouble for the most serene republic. Returning with a Turkish cargo in tow from one of his raids in the eastern Mediterranean, he died suddenly in Palermo in 1577. He was not yet forty and his father Galeazzo had nine years to live.

Galeazzo in Geneva remained a close advisor of Calvin's until Calvin died in 1564. Soon after his divorce from Vittoria in 1559, which created a legal precedent, he married a Calvinist widow and worked among Geneva's exile community of Italian Protestants, and helped the ever fewer new arrivals from Italy. It must have been tough. Calvin had political designs on France, and Geneva was no more free than Rome or Naples and in some ways less. It was a city of book burnings. The anarchic, various, humanistic views of the Italian exiles found no space in Geneva. The burning of Miguel Serveto in 1553 profoundly shocked the Italians. *Physician and philosopher . . . this daring Spaniard offered a spiritual conception of religion* and found a more terrible fate in Geneva than he might have at home.

VI
Underground

Candle and brush. Cuttlefish and haircut. Washed up.
Snivelling over a gnat. Gennaro trouble

Candle and brush

Bruno was a philosopher, yet his first real book was a play.
It was published in Paris in 1583 but it reeked of Naples and
showed that Bruno had learnt no less from the low life around
him in the city than in the great library of San Domenico.
Candleman was a philosopher's play and it had, deep down, a
philosophical argument that was easy to miss in the street life
of its action. This came rough and fast and foul-mouthed and
it involved thieving, violence, fraud and sex among the bottom
feeders in Naples—monomaniacs, crooks and imposters, and
put-upon wives, servants, students, girlfriends, neighbours,
prostitutes.

The play's *candleman*—someone you stuck your candle into—was a lethargic middle-aged homosexual. The candle was the young manservant's, who visited his employer at night. But now the married candleman, excited by new fashions in love poetry, wanted to move on to a vaguely conceived involvement with a woman. Not his pretty and neglected young wife but a glamorous neighbourhood sex worker. The candleman needed advice and intermediaries to guide him in this new erotic venture. Only a bourgeois could be so *insipid*. One of his neighbours was obsessed with creating wealth by alchemy. *A man without silver and gold is like a bird without feathers. Anyone who wants to can catch him and eat him. But with feathers he can fly, and the more feathers he has the farther and higher he flies.*

Alchemy was magic aspiring to science. A fixation on wealth creation was hardly surprising among have-nots in Spanish Naples, but it inhibited sex. While the alchemist worked maniacally with alembics and furnaces, his wife was sleeping with local lowlifes, as indeed she'd been doing since she was twelve. She told her lover if it weren't for him she'd have been through a seven-month drought, sexually speaking. Still fond of her obsessed husband, she missed their younger days when they *spent all night and part of the day* playing games she fondly remembered as *leg on the neck, squeeze, stick it in, split the fig, little mouse, limp and lame, back to cunt, come together, four pushes, four bangs, three holes and little opening.*

Another way of making something from nothing in Naples was through words. A third neighbour was a babbling pederastic schoolmaster with a willing student in tow and an obscure sense that knowing Latin mattered even more to getting on in *the world . . . as it is* than understanding alchemical formulae or turning a love sonnet. Using words to control reality, or people's perception of it, meant power in the church, law, politics, the academy. Europe was fixated on words in the late sixteenth century. Bruno's own vernacular, like the impetuous prose coming out of Elizabethan England at the same time, was learned, slangy, arcane, domestic, obscene, exalted, changing register and syntax in the space of a phrase.

Through the printers and publishers of Europe, information and *thinking* of all kinds was escaping the cage of monastic libraries and aristocratic collections in a disorderly liberating rush no church or government could entirely control. Bruno was showing *the world as it was* and aiming his polemical energy at people who tried to control knowledge. *Versifiers, doctors of anything, masters of medicine and philosophy, theologians who think they're the only ones who can read . . . difficult writers.* In *Candleman* he put their dupes on stage, to show a real world and its real people trapped in a cage of dead art, cod science, linguistic gobbledygook and sexual absurdity.

In *Candleman*'s sixteenth century Naples a swarm of dealers, fakes and middlemen, traffickers in nonexistent influence and information hovered like blowflies over the slimmest of material pickings. Fakery and perversion offered a livelihood. Desires and delusions were serviced by vague operators touting expertise in writing, science, magic and the occult arts. The realest skills on display were in the language of fraud, and the cement binding this fragmented society was local organized crime. The gangsters were connected with everyone and they were the real winners at the play's end. They succeeded as criminals by passing as police. For the locals it made no difference whether the thieves and standover men were real agents of order or crooks in disguise. It was a lot like Naples and Italy four hundred and fifty years later. Spanish Naples was a trap its inhabitants could never escape from, for all their furious movement. The play's only outlet for everyone's manic verbal energy was a climactic show of farcical moralism. Everything ended in humiliation and vicious beatings. The old gay was cruelly punished for meanness, fatuity, slothful self-absorption, the alchemist and the pedophile teacher were cheated, beaten and humiliated over and over. *Candleman*'s prison humour, pungent words, garrulous nonsense and potent silence were the real life of the same streets of the same city hundreds of years later. *Candleman*'s comedy of life in Naples wasn't always very funny, though it had its moments—Benedetto Croce insisted it wasn't art at all—and it was unforgettable.

The biggest winner when the farce wound up was the painter Gioan Bernardo. He was the play's sexual chore-ographer and its disabused if not disinterested realist, and he leavened male drive with female sensibility. He was the play's touchstone of sanity and he got the girls. In *Candleman* the main girl was the candleman's neglected young wife. The cunning painter was a figure who turned up often in Neapolitan comedy, if not always as a sane realist. But Gioan Bernardo Lama was a real painter and man about town when Bruno was a student, and a wistful admiration enveloped the play's lucid-minded ladies' man. Lama's image seemed to have stayed in the mind of the slightly built and easily excited young seminarian—Bruno all his life would strike casual observers as cutting a slightly comic figure—as the kind of person he would like to be himself. Lama had style, looks, intelligence, independence and a brilliant record with women. Young Bruno had little more than his intelligence and energy.

The dashing real-life Lama painted portraits of men and women, especially the latter. *He never picks up a paintbrush*, said a contemporary of Lama, without first giving his subject *a really good look from top to toe* and *making sure it's going to work out right for him*. The double entendre became harder to miss when the writer mentioned Lama's *disegno*, which might have been his *drawing* or his *plan*. A not very gifted amateur poet the same age as Bruno wrote of Lama, *Ladies, you'll see Gioan Bernardo / with a single look / do a lady's or gentleman's / fine likeness from life / with all the beauty / of their own eyes and tresses*. Bruno's play emphasized the lively private portraits, though Lama's only works known to survive were the impeccably counter-reformation religious paintings he did for Neapolitan churches. They were pretty good for the time, which was not a good time for painting, especially in Naples. Lama, *whose art though not his life was inspired by the counter-reformation*, was remembered as *a great friend of literary men* and he was at the peak of his fame when young Bruno arrived in Naples, celebrated for being *quite extraordinary at painting a portrait from life*. Alongside his work with private sitters he turned out *Madonna and Child* canvases on an industrial scale as the canny proprietor of a big and busy workshop.

When he was an apprentice painter of twenty, Lama had briefly worked for Polidoro Caldara from Caravaggio, who himself had been an apprentice of Raphael's in Rome. Though not yet thirty, Caldara was doing well when Rome was occupied and sacked by Charles V's mercenaries in 1527, in a spasm of France's and Spain's endless Italian power struggle. Polidoro fled the violence to Naples, where he had worked briefly a few years earlier. He didn't stay long and Giorgio Vasari, writing Caldara's life some years later, had no doubt why. *Polidoro set off for Naples but when he arrived there he found those gentlemen had little interest in excellence in painting and he nearly died of hunger.* Vasari had just visited Naples himself and was full of Tuscan contempt for the Neapolitan art scene in the fifteen forties. The aristocracy wouldn't pay for good work. *They set more value on a horse that could jump than on someone who with his own hands could make painted figures seem alive.*

Vasari wasn't the only observer to be struck by how philistine the barons of Naples were. Just before Polidoro's arrival one of the city's own intellectuals had remarked that the rulers of Naples had far less interest in painting than *in weaponry, jousting, horses and riding goods and hunting, loving and rewarding only the makers of these things.* The barons in the fifteen twenties were hardly urbanized at all, and their tastes showed it. A great original talent like Polidoro Caldara's could blow into town and hardly be noticed. Nothing Polidoro did in Naples survived. Finding no reason to stay, Caldara kept on moving south and by late 1528 he was in Sicily. He set up in Messina, a rich and cosmopolitan trading city with more sophisticated tastes in art than Naples then had, for fifteen busy years. He was making ready to return to Rome when one of his studio assistants robbed and murdered him.

Cuttlefish and haircut

Toledo was one of at least five streets radiating from the messy little nexus of the Carità—maybe even seven or nine, according to how you looked at it. The least visible led off from an obscure corner at a slight angle to Toledo and was its busiest tributary. Pignasecca was Toledo's link to the Metropolitana and anyone coming by train to the centre walked down it. A steady foot traffic struggled up toward the Montesanto station: descending traffic arrived in surges from each underground train and fed into the narrow cutting of Pignasecca.

In the mornings Pignasecca doubled as a produce market. Oranges and dark green leaf vegetables pushed out over the narrow footpath. Grocers' discreeter hams and wheels of cheese, strings of *salame* and blistered boulders of bread stayed behind glass. Living shellfish, squid, octopus and cuttlefish looked up through water in shallow wooden tubs, spread out on the road almost under the wheels of cars and scooters. People on foot had to dodge not only vehicles but the tubs of fish and the squirting hoses with which the sea creatures were refreshed. Sometimes an octopus briefly slithered free among the wheels and heels. Other tubs held heaps of glittering silver anchovies. Larger fish were laid out over ice on trestles. The fishmongers tramped around in aprons and gumboots that were wet and black like the cobblestones, squirting sea water from hoses, and the air around them was briny and ammoniacal. Tubs were painted white or pale blue inside, to better display the wares. The largest actual establishment was the *Grotta Azzurra* and its cavelike opening was a dazzle of electric blue paint and livid neon light.

At alley corners were little kiosks where you could buy a glass of blood orange juice or fresh lemon whipped into a fizz with bicarbonate. Or a paper cone of rubbery gelatinous chopped-up bits of boiled ox tripe, tongue and muzzle. On one corner an old woman in black sat on a stool selling *odori*. Her herbs were bunches of basil or rosemary or oregano wrapped in tin foil and she was part of the family whose men and boys played with water at the fish tubs on the opposite corner. Whether she was there to keep a controlling eye on them, whether she was being made to earn her keep or being allowed to feel useful, or whether they all just liked keeping family company, I never worked out.

Montesanto's centre, in the space that opened up beyond the dire New Pilgrims hospital, was a decrepit station with a splendid open verandah on the first floor overlooking another street junction. The verandah was edged in rusty wrought iron. You could feel a breath of sea air and look down at olives and lemons, *baccalà* and *stoccafisso*. Idle youth perched on parked Vespas or lounged in knots under lamp posts, waiting for the action. The action in those languorous days before Naples joined the market in hashish, heroin and cocaine was a new surge of passengers arriving down a side street from the Metropolitana deep under the hill.

A few doors up the gentle curve of Montesanto were two fiercely competing outlets for secondhand comics. Further up, past outlets for pasta, hardware and beauty products, was don Virgilio's. Virgilio was a barber and he cut my hair for fourteen years. He later moved over the road, just up from the carpenter's where I bought a trestle table, to a fancier new place more salon than saloon and yet gloomier than the sunny old barbershop opposite. It was low-ceilinged and burrowed into the sacred hill, most of it underground like the carpenter's shop but without the smell of fresh wood shavings. From somewhere beyond the artfully lit and endlessly self-reflecting mirrors and the glossy black tiles, somewhere behind the glittering ranks of hair care products and the purple tanning lights, came a throat-catching whiff of mildew. From deeper still, beyond the mouldy airlessness, seeped the deep sulphurous reek of the city's volcanic bowels. Dark patches soon grew under the new mirrored surfaces and corrosion spattered the sparkling new chrome.

The years passed and Virgilio found less and less to work on. He snapped scissors at the air around my ears and severed single hairs, and devoted increasing attention to eyebrows, nostrils and ears. Instruments used in more exploratory work were taken from a surgical case of assorted small scissors with variously curved blades of differing lengths. The last resort was to lather up a brush and strop a cut-throat razor for the nape fuzz. At no additional cost he one day worked an extract of cow's placenta in alcohol into my scalp to stimulate new growth. My head felt on fire but nothing came of it.

A boy in a white jacket brought coffee from the bar and the contents of a tiny white jug were distributed into tinier white cups and gravely consumed while the boy waited and lightly drummed the tray against his knee and watched the movement on the street. The client's shining skull was then blown dry, a two-handled mirror wielded at many angles, the neck refreshed with a squirt of bay rum from a vaporizer with a rubber bulb held in the other hand, and the encounter consummated in a cloud of talcum powder, the flick of a white towel and a distribution of tips.

Virgilio the barber was the only Virgilio I knew in Naples. Yet Virgil was the Latin poet who made Naples his home. It was Virgil who wanted to be buried there and Virgil who for well over a thousand years was almost a local god. People in Naples told stories about Virgil and they had turned to him in bad moments. He was a presiding deity, a guardian spirit as Gennaro became later, who might inform or intervene when disaster threatened. Gennaro was still one of the commonest boy's names in Naples but Virgil lived on only as my barber.

No sense of special power emanated from Virgilio the barber. Special powers, in any case, were posthumous. Don Virgilio faced problems of pressure in the here and now. He said—all obliquity and little silences and rapid murmurs as he snipped at the air—he was resisting efforts to enlist him into politics. The friendly approaches, the unwanted invitations, were already shading into requests and demands that might become threats, which is why he wanted to talk about them and yet was reluctant to. The salon was patronized both by silent and beady-eyed older men who were received with great respect and by petulant and endlessly demanding youths. Either group might come to mean trouble. Virgilio's quiet voice entered many ears and you could see why people thought he might be useful. Virgilio's unspoken worry concerned that intricate and precarious tangle of relationships that made up neighbourhood life in Naples. A tweak at any point quivered through the network. A knife through a single strand could bring everything down. You could not afford to displease powerful neighbours.

The other Virgil too had faced political pressures and requirements that ran against his inclination. He was a country boy from the northern periphery near Mantua, big, raw-boned and girlishly shy, a stammerer who wrote incomparably melodic hexameters. In Rome for his education but disliking Rome's power milieux of law and rhetoric, he went to the Greek city of Naples, where Epicurean philosophy and life on the bay suited him better. After a few preliminary efforts, which may or may not have included a little epic on the death of a gnat, he wrote an artful and slightly precious cluster of pastoral dialogues on the Greek model, threading them with deliciously oblique allusions to the new order in Rome. The allusions were noticed. A poet needed to oblige the powerful and Virgil had done this almost too well.

The political hints were realer than the languid and mannered farm workers given voice in the dialogues. Young Virgil's subtle way of working politics into art appealed to a regime looking for legitimacy after its victory in the savage internecine wars that followed the murder of Julius Caesar. The final victor Octavian was now the emperor Augustus. His chief administrator Maecenas was rich and discriminating and took over as Virgil's new patron, guiding the work in directions pleasing to the new order. The shaping hand of power supplied the bashful genius with its needs. Virgil needed to be away from Rome. He was left alone in Naples to enjoy his private life. The tension of distance, separating Rome's requirements of triumphal destiny from Virgil's private longing in Naples, produced the empire's retrospective founding epic.

The *Aeneid*'s story of ancient times was an ersatz myth of origins and full of thrilling hints that swept its first readers forward almost unawares to the fulfilment they were living under the man for whom the poem was written. It was not quite licked into shape when Virgil took ill on a visit to Greece and died at Brindisi on his way home to Naples.

He told them to burn it, as he lay dying of sunstroke, and of course was ignored. Meanwhile he wrote his own epitaph, life and work in two lines. *Tenet nunc Parthenope, Parthenope holds me now* he put in the first, knowing his body would complete the journey and be in Naples forever. The epic was snatched up by Rome, no one caring about a few ragged lines in its twelve books. Contemporary relevance and imperial promotion ensured a clamour of attention when the *Aeneid* came out. Its pervasive hints about the new regime in Rome were picked up by everyone. The ground was well prepared and the *Aeneid* became Rome's instant classic.

People could hardly miss the point. Telling his story of Rome's origins, Virgil had deployed more than subtle suggestions, oblique references and implied parallels. The heart of the poem was its prophetic vision of Rome's greatness under a leader who would *bring back the Age of Gold* and *expand his empire . . . to a land beyond the stars, beyond the wheel of the year, the course of the sun itself*. It was clear who the leader was: *Caesar Augustus!* On his journey from the smouldering ruins of Troy to the site of future Rome, Aeneas made landfall on the Italian peninsula at Cuma on the bay of Naples. In a cave at Cuma was the Sibyl, the female seer. She took Aeneas down to the underworld of past and future life, to meet the shade of his father, who had sailed with him from Troy and died in Sicily. And in the underworld his father Anchises showed Aeneas a phantasmagoria of the men who would make Rome great, culminating in the one who had commissioned Virgil's poem. *Here is the man, he's here!*

As it needed to, the poetry around this kernel of political statement fixed itself more powerfully in readers' minds than any other. It was pure Virgil that the unforgettable power of the journey to the underworld should have derived from all the wrong things. And that nobody, least of all the pleased emperor himself, should have given any sign of noticing or caring that his message of imperial power was haunted by a sense of irrevocable human loss.

Washed up

Behind the station with the verandah was a funicular leading up the steep hill toward the Castel Sant'Elmo. It was permanently closed. Inside the station was the terminus of the *Cumana*, a little electric line whose other end was twenty kilometers away at Torregaveta. Torregaveta was on the sea. You could see this from a mildewed map under glass next to the ticket grille by the verandah. It was on the sea and out of Naples, close enough to reach in the rickety little train and far enough for the water to perhaps be clean. One day at the very end of that late summer of my arrival I caught the little train. It must have been a weekday. The rattling train was jammed with housewives and young girls and tiny children in joyous discomfort. The mothers generated a heady rush of Mediterranean armpit in the closed carriage as the train burrowed through the dark under Sant'Elmo. They deployed infants, the infants' disposable nappies, bottles and dummies, miniscule sandals, furled beach umbrellas, buckets, spades, mineral water and plastic containers of cold macaroni. The cold macaroni glowed red and gold under the opalescent lids. Faces glowed with radiant anticipation. It was the look you saw on all the outward-headed trains and on the ferries to the islands from April to October, the look of Neapolitans briefly scrambling from the crumbling city toward the sun and sea.

The little beach was crowded and grubby, but you could swim. After a while I wandered inland up the little beach road and along the side of a lagoon. There was a fork in the road and a yellow metal road sign pointed up a narrow rising track to the *antro della Sibilla*. A hot and disoriented day reassembled itself in a jolt of lucidity. I was at Cuma, where Aeneas had landed in Italy, wading ashore where the Neapolitan mothers were planting their umbrellas and gouging their macaroni out of plastic boxes and their smaller children sat peeing in the water. The road sign was pointing to the entrance to the underworld. The honeycomb cave where the Sibyl, wild-eyed, wild-haired, foaming at the mouth and convulsed by the spirits who were making her their medium, had shouted out to Aeneas, himself sweating with fear, what he needed to know.

The track opened out in sight of the Tyrrhenian sea glittering afar. Higher up was a sandstone ledge and a view of the scintillating water right below. It was now blazing noon. The high ridge caught a slight refreshing movement of the air. On the ancient ledge a plaque was set in concrete with the

Aeneid's lines describing how Daedalus landed there after his escape from Crete and the labyrinth. You could see Daedalus now, if you stared out to sea, descending gently like a great sea eagle on his wax-fastened wings. His son Icarus had drowned in that sea, after flying too high and too near the sun, melting the wax which held the smaller feathers of his wings in place. Circling back to look for his son, Daedalus found only a few loose feathers floating on the water. When he arrived safely alone at Cuma he dedicated his own wings to Apollo and built the temple on whose remains I was standing. This was where the Sibyl lived in the cave. Italy's first Greek colonists had settled at Cuma and made the place a city. Replaced by Neapolis, the *new city* of Naples a few miles away, Cuma had already receded into myth by Virgil's time, remembered as a place where the Argonauts had landed in their pursuit of the golden fleece, and where Hercules had passed droving the red cattle he took from Geryon. The Sibyl remained.

A tunnel cut into the ridge of tufo behind the ledge was a recession of tapered pentagonal openings, archways five meters high shaped like a sequence of big upended coffins. They were lit with brilliant shafts of light: at intervals the rock opened to the sun above or the sea and sky to the side. This was the cave and from its depths the Sibyl told Aeneas his fate in Italy—the violence to come, the fields of blood and the Tiber running red. There was no trace of the Sibyl now. The underworld lay below the dead volcanic lake of Avernus, a kilometer from where I stood that bright late summer day. Avernus was a small and perfectly oval volcanic crater and in Virgil's time it still exhaled a poisonous sulphurous gas. The dead black water and the birdless air of Avernus, in the middle of the green opulence of the woods growing right to its edge, imaged that other world of the dead and gone which underlay the sunny landscape of the here and now. Unlike the Sibyl's reverberating chambers in the rock, the water no longer held any sense of menacing otherness. The entrance to the underworld now looked a pretty ordinary pond.

In the underworld Aeneas found people milling in the darkness, the unquiet and unburied dead. Familiar faces appeared in the shifting crowd, faces from his own past, the faces of his own dead. The innumerable dead were waiting to be ferried across the river, like great rustling banks of fallen autumn leaves or the vast wheeling clouds of swallows that swirl over Naples at the end of every summer on their way to Africa. He found Palinurus the helmsman, lately swept overboard and murdered on the beach, Misenus the drowned trumpeter. The shade of Dido, who had killed herself for love when Aeneas abandoned her in Africa, turned away from him now and left him sobbing. Anchises his father, saved from the burning ruins of Troy and now dead, was found for a moment again. Those absences, time lost and the ghosts of the people and places who stood for private happiness, were always what readers remembered about the journey to the underworld. It was the unforgettable centre of the poem and imperial Rome had no part in it. Virgil gave a preview reading of Book VI for Augustus and his intimates. The emperor was presumably gratified by the mention of himself and his role. When his wife heard the lines on their only son and heir, who had died young, she collapsed in a faint from which the doctors had trouble reviving her.

My companions on the journey back were sated, tearful, somnolent, flushed with sun and smeared with salt and sand and oil. Sand in the crotch and sand between the toes. Stomachs full of cold macaroni. Eyelids drooped and heads lurched as the train rattled along the perimeter of the bay and into the underground darkness, heading for the heart of the warren.

By staying Greek and not being a political player in the region at all, Naples became everything Rome was not. The price of its security involved a psychic diminution for the more ancient city, but the arrangement was also immensely liberating for Naples. Neapolitans were free not to be serious. Free to cultivate their Greek garden, and not unaware how deeply Romans remained in awe of Greek culture. Being Greek was a kind of revenge, a soft power of its own subtle kind.

For Augustan Romans, Naples was insidiously close to the capital and the place where many found themselves preferring to be. Virgil's choice was hardly original. Romans built villas on the most beautiful bay in Europe. Lucullus set up house in Naples. Former general in Asia, Roman consul and failed politician, introducer to Italy of the cherry and the apricot, before succumbing to dementia he turned the tiny island of Megaris at the foot of the city's promontory—the island where Parthenope washed up—into a pleasure dome with, among other features, *great ditches cast by force to make the sea passe and runne through his houses to keepe fishe therein and lodgings also that he built in the sea it selfe.* Five hundred years later Romulus

Augustulus, the boy who was fleetingly the last Roman emperor in the West, was sent to live and die on Megaris.

When Virgil made his move to Naples, villas were already strung along the shore from the Phlegrean Fields to the Sorrento peninsula. Other Romans gathered into wealthy settlements like Pompeii and Herculaneum or had hobby farms on the lower slopes of Vesuvius. Cicero had a villa at Pompeii, relatives of Augustus and Caligula had property in the area. A son of Claudius choked to death on a pear at a villa party in Pompeii. Tiberius, emperor after Augustus and no keener on Rome than anyone else, took over Capri as a citadel of private pleasures. Virgil himself built on the water on the other side of Naples at Posillipo, where a wooded hill dropped steeply to deep clear water and looked across the bay to Vesuvius and Capri.

A few years after Vesuvius destroyed the settlements on its slopes in 79, Martial recalled the vanished green shade of the vineyards, the wine that used to overflow the barrels, the dancing satyrs in the hills, and the *homes of Venus* in the town. The area was soon flourishing again, even if Pompeii itself was remembered only vaguely as *the town* which had been buried. Centuries later the medieval *Chronicle of Parthenope* demurely reminded readers that Naples and Campania were *apt for the things of Bacchus and Venus*.

Somewhere in a crowded Greek town in southern Italy, two new arrivals were lost in a maze of alleyways. They couldn't find the lodgings where they'd just left their things. Enquiries

NEIGHBOURS

OPTIMIST

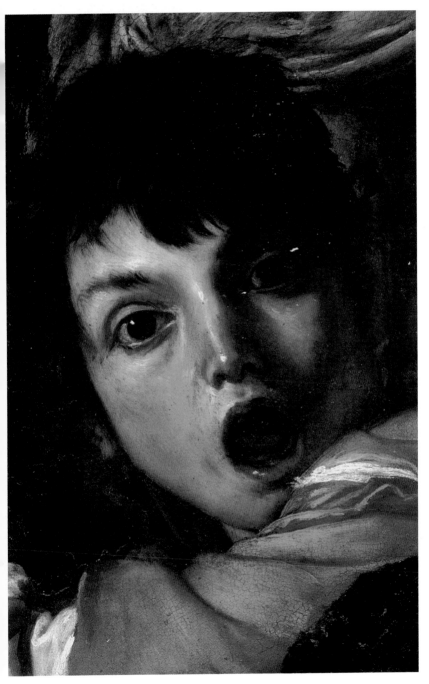

SCUGNIZZO

Ritratto d' Masaniello.

MARKET MAN

VISITORS

DAUGHTERS

PARENTS

DROVERS

of an old woman selling fruit and vegetables on a corner took one of the visitors to a neighbourhood brothel. His friend was propositioned by the distinguished middle-aged man he stopped to ask the way. A brief street corner affray was followed by massage, sex and flagellation. Several devious lawyers and a gross middle-aged transvestite showed interest in the new arrivals, who were struck by everyone's highly theatrical behaviour. People seemed to be acting out their lives on the stage. And their young boyfriend had vanished again.

The strangers in town were thieves and murderers, cultivated young men with an interest in contemporary writing, *students*, as Fellini's film wonderfully had them call themselves in 1968, like the students of sixteenth century Naples. The *graeca urbs* may have been Naples under Nero, or more probably Pozzuoli a few kilometers away, where the Romans had their main port. This was thirty years before Vesuvius exploded and buried the big towns at its base. Two millennia later the scene remained oddly familiar. Only the priestess of Priapus lacked an analogue.

The caves under the hill of Posillipo had been enlarged into a tunnel around the time Virgil lived there, linking Naples and Pozzuoli. The new arrivals in town had disturbed an underground orgy there, celebrating Priapus, that phallic god who was peculiarly at home in Campania—the caves were a busy place for sex until the last world war. Near the quarter where the three interlopers were staying was the villa of the immensely rich former slave who invited them, as visiting literary men, to dinner. Trimalchio was the kind of person who was building up big in the Naples area in the first century. Some of the fancier places at Pompeii imitated the *Golden House* Nero had just built himself over several hundred acres in central Rome freshly cleared by fire. The house with the revolving dining room. Trimalchio, having got his start in life as his owner's toy boy, now owned most of southern Italy. *What I'd like to do now is add Sicily, so I could sail to Africa direct from home.* He also had property at Pompeii, though he only learnt about it over dinner.

Beyond sex and conspicuous consumption, Trimalchio's special interest was in how he would be remembered after death. Following the imperial lead, arrivistes in the Roman empire were almost as energetic about arranging their own immortality as they were in pursuit of sex while time remained. Trimalchio tried out possible versions of his funeral over dinner. He had been to consult the Sibyl in her cave at Cuma. In the last hundred years the Sibyl had sunk from Virgil's sacred prophetess to a popular sideshow attraction, an ancient hag *dangling in a bottle.* Children were taken to see her, and Trimalchio reported that when some small boys asked her what she wanted, she told them, in Greek of course, *I want to die.*

The emperor Nero was at this time making himself over for eternity on an almost daily basis, constantly rewriting the script of his life under the guidance of the Petronius who wrote about Trimalchio. Petronius was *arbiter elegantiae*, and to be Nero's advisor in the finer points of lifestyle and leisure arts was more delicate and dangerous than any political appointment. When the inevitable invitation to commit suicide arrived, Petronius wrote a careful inventory of the emperor's intimate habits and broke a particularly beautiful wine dipper that the emperor coveted. Then he opened his veins in a leisurely manner and went out while chatting with his friends.

While Augustus had used the arts of the not always amenable Virgil and Horace as instruments of his own immortality, Nero felt he was himself an artist, whose special strengths were lyric and tragic. He made his début in Naples, singing on like a true pro through an earthquake to an amphitheatre full of rounded-up locals and military. Moments after the end of the concert, Tacitus recalled, *the theatre . . . now empty, collapsed*. Naples was Nero's favourite city. In the waters of its bay he tried to drown his mother. The murder attempt with the collapsible boat failed but not the later one using knives at home. Naples was *practically a Greek city* and for Nero *only the Greeks had a real ear for music and were worthy of his art*. When Nero sang in Naples exits were locked and his secret police scanned the audience for signs of flagging enthusiasm. Sometimes by popular request Nero sang for days on end. Later he moved on to Greece itself, and it was during his prolonged absence *en tournée* that everything unravelled at home.

Trimalchio's dinner party blurred toward the end with wine. He kissed a slave boy, setting off an ugly moment with his wife. He stumbled off to take a bath, and returned to run through salient moments in his rise to mega-riches. Then he checked off arrangements for death and after, the monument, the embalming, the shroud, the legacies. The visitors escaped from his vast and labyrinthine house—four dining rooms, twenty-something bedrooms, two marble colonnades and guest accommodation for a hundred—and stumbled into the night. The obscure maze of narrow alleys, the litter of broken crockery, the treacherously irregular stone paving, are

Naples after dark even now, and so is the luxury embedded in the squalor.

Snivelling over a gnat

Virgil's own afterlife glowed in people's minds long after they forgot the politics of Augustus. In the short term his work received the kiss of death. It was taught in Roman schools—the *Aeneid* was the central text in an education system based on rote learning and physical violence. Those forced when young by beatings to memorize it found lines and phrases stuck in the head forever. While villa interiors were being decorated with scenes from the *Aeneid*, out in the streets bits of its exquisite phrasing were scratched on walls, along with parodies and nonsense variants and sexual boasts, insults and declarations of love. These mostly went the way of all ephemera, but in Pompeii the graffiti were preserved. The first line of the first book and the first line of the second were the most vividly remembered parts.

Virgil personally got worked over in an epigram by Martial a few years after Vesuvius erupted. Virgil's celebrity profile had always included the detail of his sexual preference and the episode of his patron's well-judged gift of a beautiful slave boy. The boy was immortalized by a cameo appearance as Alexis, the object of desire in one of Virgil's pastoral poems. Martial parlayed this detail into a claim that it was Alexis who transformed the bashful stammering poet who had once *snivelled about a gnat* into the assured imperial triumphalist of the *Aeneid*. For Martial *Arms and the man I sing* was really a shout of sexual conquest and relief. Rome owed the untiring vigour and surge of its national epic to Alexis and what he did in bed.

Virgil had written about the Sibyl and Rome's future before the *Aeneid*. In another of the early pastoral poems the Sibyl had announced from Cuma the birth of a child who would bring back peace and prosperity to Rome, a promise of reconstruction. In another oblique glance out of the country idyll at the lately ended civil war, Virgil was underpinning his art with dynastic politics again. But the real child died and the dynastic scheme Virgil was delicately promoting failed. A few decades later Christ was born and the zealous early Christians read Virgil's poem as a wonderful pagan intimation of the saviour's arrival. So Virgil alone lived on through the long darkness that settled over the pagan classics, as a prophet and a proto-Christian. Augustine insisted in vain that the Sibyl at Cuma was the real Christian forerunner and Virgil merely her recorder. People hung on Virgil's words, his books being easy to find among the ruins, old bestsellers and school textbooks that they were. Opened at random and properly interpreted by a Christian intellectual, they could foretell the future. Virgil himself was eventually remembered as a person of remarkable powers which had nothing to do with words. Virgil himself had personally rid Naples of a plague of flies. He had made a bronze statue of a horse which could cure any sick horse in Naples that was led around it. Virgil had also made a sexual assignation with the emperor's daughter, who had left him swinging in a basket like a fool when he was being hoisted to her bedroom. He got his revenge by putting out all the fires in Naples, fires which could only be reignited by holding an unlit torch to one of the emperor's daughter's lower orifices.

That Virgil's underworld and Dante's inferno were the same, that Dante's *dark wood* was by Lake Avernus and was the place where Aeneas found the golden bough were demonstrated with mathematical precision several hundred years after Dante, and a millennium and a half after Virgil, by the rising young mathematician and physicist Galileo Galilei in a lecture which began from the premise that the circle of the mouth of hell passed directly by Naples.

At sixteen I struggled through *P. Vergili Maronis Aeneidos Liber VI* in T.E. Page's little slate grey Elementary Classic at the back of the school bus. Parts of it I really did read, and they stayed. The book was a wartime twenty-third printing of a school edition first published in 1888. Introducing it, the late Victorian T.E. Page was brutally dismissive of the dutiful imperialist Aeneas, in a way that seems strange in a schoolmasterly spokesman for a high imperial culture that liked to look to Rome for leads. Page found it *hard to take any real interest in his acts and doings* and underlined that Aeneas *is not only unreal and uninteresting, he is displeasing . . . as a human being he is contemptible*. But the robust public school classicist Page, who grew up in the great age of the Victorian novel—the age of the individual, the social and the real—was also a late romantic who had grown up in the time of Tennyson. And for Page the Tennysonian music and melancholy in Virgil made up for everything. That powerful undertow of loss pulled the imperial epic into stranger and more powerful areas of feeling than any afforded by its outward action. Loss felt through time and distance, in disappointed love and especially death. The poem came thrillingly close to stating the futility of the very imperial enterprise it was celebrating. *Sunt lacrimae rerum*. Virgil could only explain this emotional overflow as *the tears of things*. His poem was weepy in ways unimaginable in Homer, Aeneas himself often in floods of tears as he went about his task of founding Rome.

The play of its action against the pull of human loss, the heart-stopping melancholy of its verbal music, took a hold on hearts and minds that the poem never relinquished. The *Aeneid* outlasted Rome's fall and survived the dark and the middle ages as a proto-Christian story. Virgil guided Dante through the underworld of his *Comedy* and the *Aeneid* itself arrived at the renaissance as the unifying work of the European imagination. It was better known and more read than the poems of Homer. Even people who couldn't read Latin knew Virgil was a man who made magic and foresaw the future. Especially in Naples. For Neapolitans Virgil was like Gennaro, the early Christian decapitated by the Romans, another familiar figure and like Virgil mocked as often as venerated, mocked because loved and accepted. Both had special powers but otherwise they were two Neapolitans among many and had better not forget it. Virgil's powers had as little to do with his art as Gennaro's had to do with his faith. They eluded, a lot of the time, institutional attempts to harness their powers.

Gennaro was an obscure latecomer who may never have existed at all but he eventually eclipsed Virgil after vigorous promotion by the church and his naming as Naples's patron saint. His image was enhanced with Old Testament touches. He had emerged unharmed from a fiery furnace and had tamed wild beasts in the amphitheatre. He was insistently shown in a bishop's robes and mitre, especially after the counter-reformation. Virgil's life in people's minds as magus and clown had been mostly limited to the small number of people who could read and write. Opening a book to find a prophecy could hardly match the public theatre of Gennaro's liquefying blood, which began to occur on a reassuringly regular basis at the end of the fourteenth century. But Neapolitans still felt free to insult and revile Gennaro in crudely intimate terms if he looked like failing to deliver. Like Virgil's art, Gennaro's death served immediate and practical ends. Neapolitans needed to foresee the immediate future if they were going to have any chance of not being crushed by it, and Virgil and Gennaro both helped. In the end they approximated to Pulcinella in street comedy, the ridiculous and irrepressible Neapolitan born in ancient farce. Pulcinella had no exalted official façade at all. His only special power was the gift of survival, in the end the only one that mattered. Neapolitans loved all three as survivors and despised all three for being like themselves.

A couple of years before Virgil was born, and a few years after the prosperous town of Pompeii was seriously established as a Roman colony, others arrived in the bay of Naples area who were not wealthy and powerful Romans building villas and buying up country estates. A nomadic shepherd from Thrace, *of those contrymen that go wandring up and downe with their heards of beastes never staying long in a place*, he had enlisted or been pressed into service with the Roman army and after seeing some fighting in Macedonia, sick of the discipline and the way foreigners were treated in the military, he had deserted to go home. He was taken and enslaved, as military law prescribed for deserters, and sold to an entrepreneur of gladiatorial shows, who put him into training camp at Capua, twenty-five kilometers north of Naples.

The treatment he received here as a slave being prepared for mortal combat against other trained killers and wild animals was considerably worse than the army's. With seventy other slave gladiators, Thracians like himself and Celts who wanted to go home to Gaul, he broke out of the amphitheatre at Capua and headed across to the heavily wooded country around Vesuvius. Unarmed except with a few farm tools, they nevertheless made short work of a military patrol sent after them and took their weapons. The senate in Rome sent a legion of three thousand, which surrounded the escapees' camp on Vesuvius, but the gladiators slipped through the army cordon at night and annihilated the legion in a surprise attack in the dark.

That a few dozen tough and combat-trained escapees had destroyed a far bigger force of the regular army was instantly known around Campania. All the desperate poor, escaped slaves, free shepherds and farm workers, converged on the fighters to join them, transforming a breakout into a revolt against the Roman order—*divers heardmen and sheapherds that kept cattell hard by the hill, joyned with the Romans that fled, being strong and hardy men.* A second and bigger military expedition sent by Rome was defeated as decisively, the rebels again breaking through an attempt to encircle them and seizing the army's horses and the legions' standards. One of the Roman commanders was having a quick swim in the bay, between Pompeii and Herculaneum, when the rebels attacked. He barely escaped, was soon overtaken and killed along with most of his force.

Now the rebel slaves and farm workers controlled the whole of Campania. They spent the winter undisturbed by the army, gathering their own forces, building up supplies, making weapons. The Thracian leader, whose name was Spartacus and who still just wanted to go home, found himself riding a formidable wave of revolt against Rome. His forces extended their territorial control south of Campania into Lucania and Calabria. Spartacus tried and failed to limit looting, rape and destruction. He was now leading over seventy thousand men, maybe a hundred thousand, and command lagged behind growth. His Celtic lieutenant Crixus made a further drive east into Apulia, but was defeated and killed.

The senate in Rome slowly realized it had badly under-estimated the seriousness of the uprising in the South. By summer the forces led by Spartacus had defeated two further large armies raised and led by the consuls themselves. Moving north, Spartacus destroyed yet another Roman force of ten thousand. Northern Italy was Cisalpine Gaul, outside Roman territory, and now he and his men were in reach of the Alps and free to go home. But wiping out Roman legions had gone to the head of the workers from the South. They wanted to seize the moment and march on Rome itself. Spartacus knew that in the long run the state would rally, and held his forces off from a siege of Rome, but he was unable to impose his strategic vision and limited aim on the tumultuous mass of his followers. He agreed to go back south of Naples to Lucania and thought of trying to cross to Sicily to join forces with a new slave revolt under way there.

Rome sent the proconsul Crassus against Spartacus. Crassus rallied the Roman armies, still far more numerous than the rebels, and restored discipline with savage punishments. While the rebels were trying to cross to Sicily, Crassus cut them off in Calabria. Forcing the blockade, Spartacus headed east into Apulia, perhaps still hoping to reach Thrace by sailing east. Attacked from behind by Crassus, Spartacus won another battle there, but his men were tiring and the Romans gaining strength and weaponry. The rebels retreated to Brindisi, then back into Lucania toward Campania. After a series of savage clashes, the final battle by the river Sele was a massacre. The massed Roman troops lost only a thousand men: they killed sixty thousand rebels and took six thousand prisoners. *In the end, all his men he had about him, forsooke him and fled, so as Spartacus was left alone among his enemies: who valliantly fighting for his life, was cut in peeces.* His body was unidentifiable when it was over. Before the battle he had killed his horse, *saying: if it be my fortune to winne the field, I know I shall have horse enow to serve my turne: and if I chaunse to be overcomen, then shal I nede no more horses.*

The six thousand prisoners taken by Crassus were crucified naked along the Appian Way from Capua to Rome. Five thousand rebels who attempted a retreat to the North were intercepted and wiped out by Pompey's army, lately arrived from Spain. A few scattered groups went east and survived for ten years in Apulia, but they too were wiped out in the end.

The revolt led by Spartacus was not the only uprising of slaves against Rome, but it was the only revolt seriously to threaten the forces of the state. The unlikely and heterogeneous masses of slaves and peasants who joined him over his three-year war against Roman rule were made into a formidably cohesive and effective force by his military intelligence and daring and what everyone remembered as his personal strength, courage and decency. *This Spartacus was not onely valliant, but strong made withall, and endued with more wisedom and honesty, than is commonly found in men of his state and condicion: and for civility and good understanding, a man more like to the Græcians, than any of his contrie men commonly be.* He knew quite well that in time the Roman forces must win, but fought on anyway. It was some time before the Roman owners of the villas and farms on the bay of Naples slept easily again in their second homes.

Gennaro trouble

Vesuvius went quiet after the catastrophe of 79, and the area around it was soon covered again with forest rooted in the mineral richness thrown up by the volcano. People forgot the high, densely covered hill was not a normal hill. It happened over a generation or so. Life resumed and went on as usual for fifteen hundred years.

What terrified everyone in Naples in the middle of the night of December the fifteenth in 1631 was the violent earthquake. It was the shaking that woke them and sent them rushing into the streets. When they got outside they saw Vesuvius and it seemed to be on fire. Giovan Battista

Manso, marquis of Villa—an intellectual and reformer, a founding governor of the charity that commissioned Merisi's *Seven Works*—was in bed in Naples and not inclined to take much notice of his servants' excitement. He eventually got up and went over to his window. He saw, he wrote to a friend in Rome three days later,

> a huge and growing fire . . . part of it rising so fast into the sky that it soon reached above the clouds and part of it pouring down the hill in sheets like a river . . . the earth was shaking almost continuously and at times so intensely that the walls seemed to have a quartan fever.

Over the next days shocked survivors from the country towns around Vesuvius started arriving in Naples with *burnt clothes and sooty faces*, describing their escape from the river of fire pouring down the slopes and seeming to pursue them, choking on the thick smoke as burning rocks and ash rained down. Over three thousand others had died.

Naples was out of range of the burning rocks and the river of fire, but panic grew as a dense black cloud drifted toward the city, occasionally flashing fire. By Wednesday morning it had blocked out the sun altogether.

> People went through the streets shouting and weeping, or stood in the piazzas not feeling the cold of night or winter or the freezing *tramontana* that was blowing, so they wouldn't be crushed when their houses collapsed.

The wind changed and a *scirocco* brought rain that turned the ashes to mud and made the city streets impassable. The mud *increased the horror and prevented the terrified people from taking shelter or preparing to meet the disaster at hand.* In this moment of terror the cardinal archbishop of Naples had a brilliant idea. *To take San Gennaro's head and blood in procession* outside the city's eastern gate, toward Vesuvius, and wave them in the direction of the impending disaster. The effect of Gennaro's relics was miraculous. Manso reported that

> as the holy relics were taken out of the cathedral the rain stopped completely . . . the people in the piazza clearly saw the glorious San Gennaro himself in his bishop's robes appear at the great window over the cathedral door, bless the people and then disappear. I didn't see him myself because as I said I was with the cardinal inside the doorway.

When the *miraculous blood* re-entered Naples on its way back through the Porta Capuana, the wind changed and people saw the fatal black cloud drift away from the city. Gennaro had saved Naples. His stocks peaked.

There are no fourth century records of an historical Gennaro. His life story was written several hundred years later and it described him as the young Christian bishop of Benevento, the hill city inland from Naples, during Diocletian's campaign of repression against the Christian movement. Visiting a fellow activist in prison in Pozzuoli in 305, Gennaro was himself arrested. He was sentenced, along with several others, to be torn to pieces by bears in the local amphitheatre. The governor being away on business, the sentence became a more perfunctory beheading, carried out near the sulphur pit outside Pozzuoli.

Gennaro was buried outside Naples and a hundred years later his remains, apart from his head and a couple of phials of blood, were moved to the paleo-Christian catacombs under the Capodimonte hill above the city. They were later stolen from the caves by the Lombard rulers of Benevento and eventually moved again to a monastery and ultimately lost from view. They were rediscovered by chance during some monastic renovations in 1480, in a lead-sealed marble urn with Gennaro's name on it. They were in Naples by 1497, in a crypt under the cathedral's altar. Gennaro's head and the phials of his blood, gathered up at the execution scene in Pozzuoli, had been in Naples all along. In 1389, over a thousand years after his beheading, Gennaro's coagulated blood had suddenly liquefied, and before long it was melting regularly twice a year.

Gennaro's blood now gained serious influence among the people in Naples. New practices in astrological prediction and magic divination grew up around its liquefaction. It was a process like the one which had grown up earlier around Virgil and his magic book. *People in Naples could do without bread, or a house, or their health, but never without foretelling the future.* Gennaro suited the times better than Virgil. Neapolitans understood a young man in trouble and they understood decapitation. Their relations with Gennaro became intimate, fraught, sometimes brutal and almost carnal. The church hierarchy hoped Gennaro's dried blood and the fixed cycle of its meltings might bring paganism under control and help the curia get a handle on proliferating magic practices. Neapolitans practised magic a lot, especially for sex, as Bruno knew very well and showed in *Candleman*.

Gennaro had already received a boost thirty years after his body rejoined his head. In 1527 he intervened decisively to end an epidemic brought on by French and Spanish fighting in the South. The Neapolitans promised Gennaro in return to build a splendid new chapel to house his relics. This took some organizing. The ecclesiastical machine considered Gennaro *the church of Naples's gift to the universal counter-reformation . . . for the miracle of the blood, proof of divinity*, but Naples wasn't having the church in control of Gennaro. The *Deputation of the Treasure*—the *treasure* being Gennaro's mortal remains and not the massive gold and silver objects that contained them, or the works of art that would surround them—was a lay body. In 1608 work began on the *monumental* new purpose-built chapel to house Gennaro's remains. It was the size of a substantial church, added on to the side of the cathedral. It took nearly thirty years to build and another ten were needed to finish the basic decoration. Building and painting were at their busiest when Vesuvius erupted, Gennaro saved Naples and Gennaromania reached a frenzy. Who was going to paint the *Chapel of the Treasure*?

Belisario Corenzio the fresco painter was eighty-eight when he died in bed in 1646, the year Gennaro's chapel was opened.

The story—plausible but untrue—was that he had fallen from high scaffolding while touching up a ceiling fresco. He had been busy, famous and influential for decades.

> His reputation grew . . . and so did his friendships . . . he made friends with Ribera, who was very influential as an intimate of the viceroy, and so joined Ribera as boss of the painters in Naples, apart from the few who chose a quiet and honest life outside factions. Corenzio flattered Ribera, who loved his pushy insolent ways and got him into favour with the viceroy, who made him a court painter . . .

Ribera was more than thirty years younger, and in his early years in Naples was perhaps intimidated by Corenzio's acquired Neapolitan street smarts. Ribera had knocked around himself once, and left a wild reputation behind him in Rome, but in Naples he was already trapped in the *beau monde* of the viceroy's court—there would be many viceroys, over the years, and all of them his patrons—doing high-toned commissions for the church and the Spanish aristocracy. Ribera was a painter fixated on the hard lines that living left in a face or a body. Corenzio would have brought him back to the kind of world that left its marks on a person. In life only however. If Ribera was a high-living dirty realist working at court in oils on canvas, Corenzio was a gutter-fighting exponent of late mannerist charm in fresco. He was ruthless in keeping his grip on the market.

> His commissions were so many and so frequent, it's amazing . . . how many large scale projects he carried out.

He got the big jobs because other painters were scared of him—everyone found him hostile, frightening and overbearing—and they used to claim credit for letting him have the work they knew they couldn't get for themselves.

In fifty years Corenzio covered vastly more wall space in Naples than anyone else. He was determined that

no other professional be allowed to have a higher reputation than his, that no outsider be given preference for work done in Naples, especially in the most conspicuous sites. He pretended to be promoting Neapolitan artists . . . to win allies to discredit and drive off painters from outside Naples. The methods included using violence and death threats when necessary. He used everyone in this way, to get the most prestigious and best-paid work for himself and leave the unimportant jobs for others . . . who were all too scared of him and Ribera to dare to complain.

Gennaro's chapel was a challenge made for Corenzio. The money was excellent, the prestige incalculable and Corenzio wanted a piece of it. In 1618, a couple of years after Ribera's arrival in town, the Deputation of the Treasure was commissioning the paintings and sculptures and the deputies wanted the best for Gennaro. They wanted the chapel painted in fresco and though Corenzio was the fresco man in Naples, they were inclined to think the best man for the job was Giuseppe Cesari, the cavalier d'Arpino. An *outsider*. Why Cesari never did the

Gennaro frescoes was not clear. Everyone agreed he was the deputies' first choice. At fifty in 1618 he was newly married, a child was on the way and he may not have wanted to leave Rome. Cesari's earlier encounter with Corenzio when they were both working at San Martino might also have been so unpleasant that it put him off ever returning to work again on Corenzio's turf.

So the deputies turned to a really major figure, Guido Reni from Bologna. Reni was the greatest painter then working in Italy, nervous, withdrawn, a high stakes gambler and said to be a virgin. He arrived in Naples in 1622 and

had just done a few preliminary drawings and begun a bit of fresco when he left everything as it was and fled. He went home because he felt threatened by the people there. He thought they were hostile to outsiders and would conspire as a matter of policy against any professional who wasn't one of themselves. There were many grounds for believing this, mainly the severe beating given to a servant of Guido's, who was told that *anyone should expect that treatment if they went to someone else's city and took the locals' livelihood away.*

The writer who claimed this had known Reni well. It was confirmed a year later by a painter contemporary of Reni's in Rome. The second version added that the attackers were after Reni when they *mistook a servant of Reni's for the painter himself, beat him up at night and left him wounded.* Reni, the first report went on, was so shattered when his servant staggered in from the darkness to the house where they were staying that he slipped away from Naples the same night with his assistant and the servant, leaving only a note on the bedside table.

Corenzio was arrested for having ordered the attack on Reni's servant, but *released for lack of evidence*. After a couple of years the deputies, taking the hint, commissioned an elderly local late mannerist to do the job. Fabrizio Santafede wasn't up to it and was dismissed in short order. Reni's assistant Francesco Gessi returned to work with him but was also sacked, after being followed in the streets by sinister figures who seemed to be armed, and receiving anonymous letters warning him of plots against his life and advising him in his own best interest to give up the work. Corenzio kept up the pressure and, weakening after three more years, in 1628 the deputies let him fresco a corner of the chapel on spec. Juggling other commitments, and working with his old apprentice Caracciolo, he took a year to do it. The deputies, by now in a total funk, couldn't decide. They gave Corenzio another trial run in another corner. This time they said no and Corenzio's work was painted out.

VII

Market

Morning Market. Another blow-in. Lenders and collectors.
Masaniello arranges himself. What drovers saw. Convent at
nightfall

Morning Market

Somewhere in Spain hangs a large panoramic painting of
the *Market Place in Naples*. It was done just after the middle
of the seventeenth century and showed a morning in spring.
Trading was well under way. The air was clear, the sky a
striking blue with a crisp dry tramontana sending shreds of
beige cloud and some wisps of white haze scudding out of
the picture past the mauve outline of Vesuvius, rendered with
the clarity that in Naples came only when a tramontana blew.
Dry sunny air and high barometric pressure meant energetic
activity on the ground and revealed in unusual detail the

choral business of the Market and its people. Detailed low life and large-scale topography melded into something that felt like real life. An odd mix of aims and genres came alive in the splendour of the weather.

Thieves were being arrested, or running off amid a clamour of Market women. Bare-legged and barefoot children were brawling in the dirt or picking a fortune teller's pocket or crawling among buyers' legs to steal fruit from the sellers' shallow baskets. Monks slung heavy sacks over their shoulders, a priest proffered a holy image for adoration. A donkey mounted a mare. The mare seemed not to mind but the loaves of fresh bread in her saddle baskets went flying and a bystander sprawled on the ground. Order was restored with sticks, men looked on with interest, women scattered, one snatching a glance over her shoulder at the stallion's attributes as she hurried off. A one-legged beggar importuned a pair of nearby drinkers and mounted police led off a couple of hunched and shrinking arrestees on foot.

The incidents were immersed in the fascinating ordinariness of a working morning. An old woman laid out her meagre offering of root vegetables on the ground with an artist's care, their tails radiating from a hub of tops, grouped by type and flanked by mounds of rounder and smaller vegetables on the side. Her tiny still life became part of the picture. Knives were sharpened, cheese weighed out on scales, wine casks tapped while fussy buyers picked over produce. Little dogs skittered through the interstices, a dozen of them, leaping up at each other and at the children, hanging round the food shops, nosing the ground or keeping an eye on human movements.

A couple of them seemed to be having sex as a smaller third dog looked on. Animals were everywhere, donkeys bearing people and produce or waiting to be loaded up again, sheep and goats nuzzling the dirt for a blade of grass, oxen drinking from shallow tubs, donkeys drinking likewise on the other side, oxen pulling carts, horses ridden or pulling coaches, red-combed hens sitting in a basket on someone's head. Some of the human drama—a brawl and a couple of people laid out cold on the ground—was rendered so faintly and from so far away that you could hardly see it.

The radiant sky and the purple hulk of the mountain invested the people and their dealings below with vastness and meaning. The low range of hills reaching inland from the volcano was where the Market sellers came from, and the hills' rich soil produced the goods laid out. They were ordinary people and daily life as a benign and heavenly eye might see them. Or an eye with some human failings. The little foreground figures, picked out with a lot of red and blue, showed in the tiniest detail and behind them details gradually blurred, just as the colours faded toward the back of the Market Place and the handsome church with its jutting spire. Or a benign and distant monarch's eye, gazing on an image of life in a part of his empire he would never visit. Or the eye of a viceroy, looking back from retirement in Spain at the peaceful busy productiveness he had once overseen, and his own deeply rewarding years of service in one of the most beautiful and entertaining places on earth.

The nearest sides of the rawly unfaced buildings framing the scene were still in shadow. Some parts caught the morning sun, all glowed with old sunlight trapped in the porous tufo.

Washing on the rooftops, pots of herbs on ledges, women's faces at windows, simple wood or canvas awnings over the shopfronts at ground level. In the square, the white canvas and the light battens protecting the wares looked like boats and sails on the sea of people. *The painting of the Market fair in Naples is so delightful and curious that the eye never has enough of looking at it.*

The Market Place in Naples had grown from a patch of flat ground on the outskirts of town where a stream ran into the bay. Sea and beach were just out of sight behind the row of tenements on the painting's right. The church of the Carmine and the big Carmelite convent adjoining it were practically on the beach. The Market was supplied from the flat sandy beach where fishing boats unloaded their catch and market gardeners from around the bay brought their produce directly to point of sale by boat across the water. Many of the buildings lining the Market space in the painting had six storeys and one had seven. Naples was now a megalopolis of over half a million people and the Market was its belly.

> The Market is perhaps the vastest space you can see anywhere in Italy . . . in this place every week on Monday and Friday buyers and sellers come together and a mass of food can be seen: grain, flour, stock feed, green vegetables, animals of all kinds for slaughter, according to the season, and every other kind of goods to meet human needs, so that its fame and size match any other fair held in our kingdom.

Two hundred years later it was still *packed at all hours by people buying and selling food and other supplies . . . a variety of people, different cries ringing in your ears, a universal commotion, especially on Fridays and Mondays.* Today it is a crowded desolation.

Domenico Gargiulo, who painted *The Market*, was called *Micco Spadaro*, being the son of a sought-after swordsmith in Naples who was keen for Micco to follow him into the business. Amenable Micco obliged, *for years sadly cleaning swords, then beating and tempering them himself, to please his father.* Forced to leave home for persisting with his art, he apprenticed himself to the painter Aniello Falcone. Salvator Rosa was another apprentice and close friend, who shared Gargiulo's avant-garde interest in landscape painting. Like Falcone himself, neither had any interest in the grind of religious commissions.

Falcone was only a few years older than his students. He had learnt painting with Ribera and his first work was a grim study of a punitive *Schoolmarm* holding a raised whip in one hand and a book in the other and towering over two plain and wretched small boys in fearsome disproportion. *Lucy Giving to the Poor* was a sunny open scene on the edge of the city and its dispossessed had the monumental dignity of the architecture framing them. Falcone was famous for battle paintings and in the trade they called him the *oracle of battles*. The immensely rich collector Gaspare Roomer particularly liked these and got Falcone to fresco his magnificent new out-of-town villa on the sea with panoramic battle scenes. He sold Falcone's war paintings all over Europe. They were always a *battle scene without a hero*, collective images of men fighting which *showed not the fighting but the making ready* and war as *part of daily life . . . almost ordinary realism, real movements of horses and riders, vivid portraits and accurately observed clothes . . . figures fully and inwardly shaped, objects handled almost as in still life . . . some of the settings recognizably places around Naples . . .* Falcone still seemed happier, and more himself, with a group of middle-class people improvising a *Concert.*

Gargiulo was comfortable in the social landscape of figures at work or play. His friend Rosa, except in the smouldering drama of a *Self-portrait* against a lowering sky, reduced human figures to near invisibility among forests, rocks, clouds, beaches. People for Rosa were details in the greater mineral, vegetable, meteorological scene, pretexts for a title. Gargiulo painted people tiny in their masses. Both started out painting real people where they lived and worked in the country and on the coast, and then diverged, one toward the landscape and the other toward its people. *His main interest was real life, and so he often went out into the country in company with Rosa and sometimes with his master himself . . . soon the name of Micco Spadaro was famous.* Gargiulo never left Naples. Rosa, a restless protoromantic ahead of his time, got away quick and hardly ever came back.

Gargiulo was fascinated by the work of his contemporary Jacques Callot, the French photojournalist of an age before photography. Callot made rapid, vivid sketches of the many figures in street life, festivals, performance improvisations of *commedia dell'arte* or the horrors of the thirty years' war, then engraved and printed them for sale. In a working life of fifteen years or so Callot produced over fourteen hundred prints and a couple of thousand preliminary drawings. The prints set their many figures in the deep space of carefully rendered urban or landscape settings. Some were unbelievably complex. *The Fair at Impruneta*, done in Florence in 1620, included over thirteen hundred distinct single figures of people and animals in an image smaller than forty-five centimeters by seventy.

Callot the engraver, who never painted, died in his early forties in 1635. Gargiulo, a painter who never engraved, gathered as many of Callot's prints as he could get his hands on and studied the energetic economy of the few lines Callot took to show a miniscule figure's age, sex, class, activity, feeling and bring these together in a striking stance or a gesture, a calligraphic stroke that made everything one. Gargiulo thought about the ambiguity in Callot's art, the way the eye danced over people seen as clearly defined individuals, however tiny, and saw the larger movements of social togetherness. The vastly panoramic little prints led your eye from single figures, pairs, knots, huddles, clusters—intimate, hostile, or momentary and inconsequential—to the larger crowds that were always coalescing and disintegrating, moving and re-forming and never the same, like the clouds gliding soundlessly overhead across the sky.

Gargiulo the Neapolitan came to understand the dynamics of crowds even better than the French master he never met. It took a while to show this in his art. Early in his career he formed a partnership with a northern Italian painter of his own age who worked in Naples and specialized in studies of monumental architecture and ancient ruins. These were fashionable among private collectors, who were often amateurs of antiquities. Viviano Codazzi would paint a monumentally inert scenography of mellowed antique pillars, steps, porticoes, rotundas, and Gargiulo would bring it to life by flicking in his little human figures sprawled on the steps or gesticulating in the street. As their partnership progressed, the human presences got tinier and tinier within their architectonic cage, more and more subversively alive. Less was more. Each painter liked what the other did and customers liked what they did together, Neapolitan images of darting low life framed by austere grandeur. Then in 1647, after nearly fifteen years in the city, Codazzi abruptly left Naples and never returned.

Beside painting fresco on the endless walls of the charterhouse of San Martino, along with other inevitable religious commissions, Micco Spadaro—people kept calling him the nickname from *his greener years*—did a lot of small paintings which went straight into private collections. They were quick, sketchlike *capricci* showing scenes of street life in the city and working days in the country and they kept him close to the photojournalist spirit of Callot. The point of these *faits divers* was implied in the paintings' small size: to offer vividly recognizable images of moments in contemporary life, something the owner and the owner's friends would see without that interference of history, religion or morality that grander art entailed. Gargiulo's capricci had bite but no affect, elicited a small shock of recognition. The capriccio was a format in which a painter could be himself, and in attending to details of ordinary working life, Gargiulo *was* being himself.

He abandoned significance like a man throwing off pretentious and uncomfortable formal clothes. People being human together in public spaces were his subjects, not excluding street people, working people, the poor, children, panhandlers, petty criminals, even killers. Even his biblical and mythological scenes looked like real life events. He was a painter of energy and movement whose paintings were full of small momentary flares of violence. His Christian martyrdoms looked like outbursts at a country picnic, and when he had to do a massacre of the innocents what *move[d] viewers* were *the mothers weeping over the little slaughtered bodies and other children in their death throes and others torn from the breast of their loving but horrified mothers*. When he had to do formal horror, Gargiulo did the appalled witnesses best of all. They were himself.

A lot of the small paintings were later lost. Among the survivors were *Women Washing Laundry* in a country stream, which included a scuffle with some youths, molesting the young women as they knelt over the water or trying to steal the laundry. A scene of *Fishermen Attacked* bringing their catch ashore in a rocky cove at evening was a moment of violence by bandits trying to seize the fish. There was a scene of *Criminals Punished* led through the streets, one mocked with a paper crown and riding an ass to jail or hanging. There was a *Riding Lesson* for the younger nobility. Looking good on horseback as you went down Toledo mattered in Naples more than almost anything if you were a male aristocrat. In Gargiulo's painting the young blood on his high-stepping white charger got no more attention than the trainer, the knot of onlookers and idlers, one tipping back dangerously in his chair, and hardly more than the tiny thread of other young riders on white chargers being led around the piazza in the distance.

All this fed into *The Market Place*. Transposed into a large panorama, Gargiulo's intimacy with the ways of the people he was painting transformed the banal commission for a painting of record. It charged each tiny figure with its own energy and choreographed the swirling eddies of people into a celebration of their togetherness. *The Market Place* was an image of the choral theatre of Neapolitan life, and like the best Neapolitan art it filled an essentially static scene with a winning dynamism.

Another blow-in

Their new surge of dissatisfaction with old-school locals gave the San Gennaro deputies courage to think big again. This time they thought Domenico Zampieri, familiarly called *Domenichino*. Like Reni he was a Bolognese working between Rome and Bologna and at the peak of the profession. If the deputies couldn't bring Reni back, they were now going for the closest thing. Though everyone in Rome advised him not to go to Naples, in the spring of 1630 Zampieri accepted the Gennaro commission by letter, and the next year he moved to Naples. Before leaving Rome, he received an anonymous death threat by letter from Naples, but he had a major contract to respect and went anyway. Like Reni, only more so, Zampieri was deeply shy and solitary, not a people person at all. Corenzio and his associates were no less hostile than before to incursions by prestigious outsiders. *The workaday painters' rancour* was as strong as ever. Everything was in place for a replay of the Reni episode of nine years earlier.

His paintings were insipid but Zampieri the man was in his quiet way a lot tougher than Reni. As he left his room in the archbishop's palace on the second morning after arriving in Naples *with his whole family . . . he found a strongly threatening message advising him to go straight back to Rome and give up the work he had started.* This was a shock, and knowing what had happened to Reni he went straight to the viceroy Monterrey. The viceroy reassured him enough to keep working, though after this he no longer dared go outside in Naples, and *the only journey he ever made was to go from his rooms to his work, which was so close it was the same as not going out at all.* A few months later Vesuvius erupted and Gennaro interceded, which was frightening but restored a sense of proportion and urgency to Zampieri's work on moments in Gennaro's life. Now the new viceroy Medina demanded he do a series of paintings for the king in Madrid. This meant failing to meet the contractual deadline for his work on Gennaro. The viceroy, having forced Zampieri to break the contract, then refused to help get him an extension. The deputies threatened to cancel payment for paintings not done on time.

In a rage Zampieri threatened to walk off the job altogether and the deputies let him go. He rented a horse at Aversa and rode day and night until he reached the Aldobrandi estate at Frascati—it was high summer—and ended up staying there over a year. In Naples the viceroy had the painter's wife and daughter held under house arrest as hostages against his return. He did go back and work resumed for the now deeply hostile deputies, who never quite forgave him for leaving. The painters' cabal *hated him for coming back.* They ran a campaign of slanderous whispers and anonymous letters and libellous pamphlets. Ribera and Giovanni Lanfranco—an old rival from Bologna and Rome who had arrived in 1634 and immediately aligned himself with the Ribera–Corenzio axis—were both determined to get commissions for Gennaro's chapel, and they rode the anonymous agitation with attacks on Zampieri's work. Ribera proclaimed that Zampieri *was no painter because he didn't paint from nature, only a good ordinary draughtsman*. Ribera added that Zampieri *didn't even know how to use a paintbrush* and that he spoiled the figures in his painting by *overworking* them.

Ribera at least was speaking as a painter. Everything he cared about in painting was opposed to Zampieri's careful idealizations. Ribera had just painted the *Bearded Lady* Magdalena when Zampieri arrived and was not going to see his own fierce naturalism undermined by an interior decorator from Rome. He well knew that in Rome taste had already turned against the real, and that Zampieri's imported elegance was a foretaste of what was to come in painting. Ribera had a vision of the real world to defend against Zampieri. Corenzio had only professional interest.

Zampieri's painting was sabotaged. He would arrive in the morning to find his previous day's work painted over during the night, or that ash had been added to the plaster so his painting fell off the wall when it dried. He kept at it, though the stress was unbearable and made worse by an ugly dispute with his wife's family. Already *uncouth and mistrustful by nature*, he now *turned against himself, went off his food, couldn't sleep, alienated his wife . . . weakened and lost his energy*. He had nearly finished when he died suddenly in 1641. His wife claimed his drinking water had been poisoned. The doctor advised her to keep quiet about it, *since nothing could be done for him now*. Poison was what Reni had been afraid of. Ribera and Lanfranco got their commissions: an undone altarpiece and the cupola that Zampieri had only begun to fresco. Ribera's painting *Gennaro Leaves the Furnace Unharmed* took him five years to finish and by the time it was done Ribera had succumbed so completely to what one twentieth century art historian called *the compositional rigour and richness of expression of the Roman-Bolognese tradition* that another twentieth century art historian dubbed it *Domenichino's Revenge*.

Eight fat cherubs did a well practised and elaborately synchronized aerobatic tumble with linked hands against a cloud-flecked sky of brilliant blue. Ribera's Gennaro emerged from the furnace as a highly institutional churchman, prematurely middle-aged with a puffy—even slightly rabbity—face, fat clerical hands and a bluish shadow of beard showing through his well shaven and pasty indoor cheeks. He was splendidly coped and mitred in gold and making all the right moves with fingers and eyeballs, apparently unaware of the ropes still around him and the jet of white flame at his back. Ribera had painted more of a sashay from the sacristy than an escape from the furnace.

Only in the lower left, among the overwhelmed soldiery and the fleeing plebs, there was a Neapolitan scugnizzo, not terrified at all but yelling his lungs out in the wild drama of the moment, taking time in his lateral flight to look over his shoulder and out of the canvas with a look that wasn't a hundred miles from the *Clubfoot Boy's*—*Look at me, Ma!*—and affording a moment of instant recognition and connexion to anyone who might have just walked in off the street. By the time his painting of *Gennaro* was hung, Ribera was living under protection in the viceroy's palace, but this was not where he'd been for most of his life.

Corenzio at eighty-three was too old to benefit personally from Zampieri's death at sixty, though his people did.

239

When he died five years later nobody was surprised to learn he was immensely wealthy. Bernardo De Dominici wrote about these events a hundred years after they happened. De Dominici would be much disapproved of by twentieth century academics for extravagant errors and inventions in his lives of the painters, branded *the counterfeiter* as early as 1892 and sixty years later a purveyor of *shameless lies* and *shameless mystification*. De Dominici was a man of strong sympathies and exuberant imagination who had a way of shaping a painter's life to fit his own acute perception of the art. And sometimes vice versa. In his account of Corenzio's failure to render light in his painting, De Dominici wrote

> his saints in paradise are surrounded by such dense clouds that the saints seem to be in the shadows of limbo rather than in paradise, where all is splendour. Unhappily he kept this darkness up almost every time he had to paint saints in glory.

He brought his telling of Corenzio's life to a climax, after rising to it through the wars of Gennaro's chapel and then maintaining suspense through a descriptive interlude, in Corenzio's last and most wicked act of all. This was the murder of one of his own apprentices, a gifted young painter whose work was praised more highly than his own. De Dominici's aria on the obscene spectacle of seething, devious senile jealousy concludes with the ancient painter's death fall from high scaffolding, working to the very end.

Since Corenzio died in peaceful retirement, people later believed the poisoning too was *certainly invented by the biographer.*

But the young painter really existed and his name, variously given in the old sources, was Luigi Rodriguez. He was the second son of a Spanish officer stationed in Palermo, and born about 1580. When he arrived in Naples in 1594 he was put in the care of a slightly older Sicilian painter already working there. A few years later he was working alongside Corenzio and the most admired painters in Naples on one of the most important commissions in the city. Around 1600 he married and between 1601 and 1607 had three children. In these years he also did, on his own, a major fresco decoration. After this, he worked in Corenzio's fresco team, sometimes alongside Corenzio's other assistant Caracciolo, who was a year or so older and just starting out. Rodriguez died in 1609, when he was thirty at most, remembered as a notoriously hardworking, intelligent and fast-rising young painter in fresco, who had won major commissions when he was hardly more than twenty and had worked for Corenzio for several years. The fragments fit the murder claim. De Dominici had only the timing wrong. It happened thirty-five years earlier.

I first came across Rodriguez's name not in De Dominici but in a multivolume guide to the buildings and art works of Naples written not long after Rodriguez died. *Notizie del Bello dell'Antico e del Curioso della Città di Napoli*, five volumes in its nineteenth century edition, was written in the late seventeenth century by a sober, unfanciful, unassuming, well-informed and extremely accurate cleric called Carlo Celano. Celano was not writing a study of sensibilities like De Dominici's but simply assembling a compendium of facts for the serious tourist, and his facts have stood up very well. Perhaps a slight tremor registered at the mention of *our Luigi Siciliano*, who was Rodriguez.

Luigi was an assistant of Belisario Corenzio's. The friars called on him to paint the church as mentioned. The master [Corenzio] inquired of these same friars why they had commissioned the assistant and not the master to do the work and was told it was because they thought the assistant was better at painting. Belisario waited until Luigi had finished the paintings in the lower part, and seeing that people commonly praised them as better than his own, he had him killed miserably in the flower of a youth that showed promise of doing marvels in art.

Celano was born in 1625 and lived in Naples all his life. He was a contemporary of Corenzio's for his first twenty years and an informed historian of Neapolitan art and history. Celano was in a position to know. He was De Dominici's source, telling essentially the same story and, in the one detail that matters, more convincingly. De Dominici had the perfidious old painter personally slipping poison to the young challenger. Celano said nothing about when it happened and wrote simply that *he had him killed*. Which was exactly what any boss in Naples would do.

Lenders and collectors

Gaspare Roomer was talked about in his lifetime and for quite a while afterward with great awe and described in that special tone people reserve for the unimaginably rich. A contemporary in Naples described him as

financiers who ran the economy. Southern barons, living off the revenues of their huge estates, thought commerce beneath them, and so, disastrously, did the Spanish, whose thinking ran more on military, imperial, religious, dynastic, bureaucratic and racial lines. The ethos in Naples was non-commercial and outsiders exploited the opening. Increasingly, as the Spanish economy floundered, the vicerealm's administration depended on foreign financiers to underwrite its operations and bail it out of crises. Before long Roomer was lending not only to the viceroy but to the Spanish crown in Madrid.

Roomer's private collection of paintings was huge. By 1630 it was being housed in *a series of twelve rooms*. When he died in 1674 he owned more than eleven hundred canvases. Being Flemish, Roomer liked realism and he didn't mind it rough. Being a businessman, he dealt in paintings like everything else. Buying and selling between Antwerp and Naples during his long collecting life, he was an influential channel for the movement of art between northern and southern Europe for most of the century. Neapolitan painters found buyers in the North through Roomer's activities, and the Flemish work he brought south to Naples showed them what was happening on that other frontier of the real. Like the Spanish empire, only a lot more successfully, Roomer was engaged on two fronts: the Low Countries and the Mediterranean.

Roomer had bought don Marzio Colonna's great palace in Naples after Colonna's death. Don Marzio was the duke of Zagarolo, the Colonna who sheltered Merisi on his estate there in the summer of 1606 after the street killing in Rome, and who took Merisi with him to Naples at the end of that summer. His palace was probably where Merisi lived in

Naples when he painted the *Seven Works*. For Merisi it was a minute or so from Piazza Carità on the edge of the Quarters, where nearly all the painters in Naples lived in a compact and densely intermarried community. Roomer had missed out on Merisi but he homed in on Merisi's Neapolitan followers. He collected Ribera's work with enthusiasm, even or especially the hardest paintings to like. It was Roomer who commissioned the repulsive *Silenus* and he also had *Apollo Skinning Marsyas*. He also bought Caracciolo, not quite so passionately. Roomer liked big scenes too, and went for Aniello Falcone's panoramic and antiheroic battle canvases. And when Caracciolo died in 1635, Roomer was ready—the moment it appeared—to seize on the work of a near-unknown who was the newer generation's very greatest painter. And when *he* died young, Roomer became very interested in the panoramic work of Domenico Gargiulo. He knew his painters.

Roomer had an associate, another Fleming called Giovanni Vandeneinden, who had arrived in Naples penniless—*a very poor shipping clerk married to a collar starcher*—and accumulated his immense wealth, financial power and aristocratic relatives entirely through his operations in the city. With money came art. Advised by Roomer, Vandeneinden built up his own huge collection of first-rate paintings, buying the work of painters in Naples and investing in outside art through his business network in Rome, Venice, Genoa and the North.

The strictly financial influence of Roomer and Vandeneinden and the other outsiders in the vicerealm was eclipsed spectacularly in the late sixteen thirties by the rise of a local—*the most audacious businessman in the history of southern Italy*. The vicerealm was by then in such deep financial trouble from the cost of Spain's war in the Low Countries that the Roomer milieu held back from lending more. Bartolomeo d'Aquino certainly eclipsed Roomer as the richest man in Naples. For a while. He had started as a small businessman, one of three brothers who had a shop in Naples, and then made a lot of money fast through astute and lucky speculation in government bonds. When the usual financiers made themselves unavailable to the Spanish administration, d'Aquino was pressured—he claimed later—into helping out the government in 1636. This encouraged Roomer and the others to come back into play. Over the next eight years d'Aquino personally raised sixteen million ducats for the government in Naples, most of which went straight to Spain or to Milan, which was the operational base for Spain's war in the Low Countries. The others raised another twenty million. The public debt trebled.

The effect on people in Naples and its hinterland of the arcane financial dealings involved in raising these funds for Spain's war effort was not hard to see. In return for their credit the financiers were allowed, as the state's contracted tax collectors, to extort new taxes on everything in sight. New export taxes on silk and oil—Naples's main exports—new consumer taxes on oil, flour and salt, new sales taxes on everything bought and sold, imported and exported. A stamp duty on all contracts was rejected when the aristocracy objected. The tax contractors kept seventy per cent or more of the taxes they collected and d'Aquino's agents deducted his cut before the money went to state or local government agencies. D'Aquino had made himself so necessary to the financial viability of Spain's war effort that his requirements had priority over the government's own.

After five years of this regime, the government's tax office noted that *mothers are selling their daughters because they can't feed themselves*. Men in great numbers were trying to join the clergy, which was tax-exempt. The thugs employed to extort payment did such damage on their raids that the king wrote to the viceroy from Madrid in some distress about their violence. The viceroy Medina, who had run the new financial regime for six and a half years, or had been run by d'Aquino, ended his term two years later in 1644. His successor, the admiral of Castille, resigned after less than two years as viceroy because he couldn't raise in Naples the money Madrid was demanding. By 1646 the city and the vicerealm were squeezed dry. The thirty years' war was still going, the Low Countries were still in full revolt.

D'Aquino later claimed that the system was missing beats as early as 1640 and that he had been forced to sell on his tax credits at a loss. He had to keep launching new speculations to keep up the flow of money north to the war front. Delays in payment were causing alarm and then panic in Madrid. D'Aquino was running a kind of Ponzi scheme whose only investor was Spain. The rest of the financial crowd started keeping their distance from him, but too many people were involved too deeply in his activities to let him go altogether. People did talk about how little of the actual money extorted from the people was reaching the war front, and how much of it went to d'Aquino and his associates. The new viceroy set up a commission of inquiry and at the end of it d'Aquino was arrested, mainly so none of the tangle of interested parties exposed would try to eliminate him. He was a convenient scapegoat, along with the previous Medina administration, though his rise had been enabled entirely by Madrid. The case had already dragged on for years when other events intervened.

After his fall, d'Aquino was reviled by everyone. The aristocracy had always loathed him as a low-rent upstart. D'Aquino was now seen as

> stunted and ugly like his origins . . . a big spender . . . clothes and lifestyle more like an aristocrat's than a businessman's . . . full of squalid little faults . . . lived badly . . . loathsome vices . . . linked with men he made fortunes for in return for unmentionable sexual favours . . .

And so on. But even at the height of his wealth and power d'Aquino revolted the nobility. It was partly his getting above his station and partly the fact that d'Aquino was the viceroy's man at a particularly intense moment in the power struggle between viceroy and baronage. One of the most turbulent and fiercely pro-French barons in 1640—and a brute to his vassals—was Gian Girolamo Acquaviva, the count of Conversano. The viceroy Medina and d'Aquino both thought, for quite different reasons, that a brilliant move would be for d'Aquino to marry one of the count's young sisters. Her name was Anna Acquaviva and she was currently shut in a convent at Benevento. A marriage agreement with enormous dowry was fixed with another Acquaviva brother, who got a twenty per cent cut for negotiating the deal. The count heard of it and a posse of angry nobles gathered to block the marriage. The duke of Atri, who was yet another Acquaviva brother, called on d'Aquino to desist in his low proceeding. *This marriage is costing me fifty thousand ducats,* d'Aquino said, *and I'd pay as much again not to have any discussion about it.*

But several dozen aristocrats and their armed retinues rode in procession through Naples to the palace where the bride-to-be, released from the convent and brought down to Naples for the wedding, awaited her betrothed. A big crowd followed, eager to see what would happen. The viceroy sent a couple of senior judges with military escort to block their way. They were swept aside. The knights invaded the palace and the bride was escorted back to her convent in Benevento by her brother the duke of Atri, and the prince of Torella, who was a Caracciolo, and the duke of Maddaloni, who was a Carafa. The viceroy furiously convoked the ruling council the same night to issue a *fierce reprimand.* The council refused. The nobles showed *a class solidarity worthy of the most demanding causes.*

Masaniello arranges himself

Tommaso Aniello d'Amalfi, known around the traps as Masaniello, was born in the house on the corner of Broken Alley at the Market at the beginning of the summer of 1620. He was the eldest son of a shoe repairer called Cicco d'Amalfi and the woman he had married four months earlier. A brother was born two years later, another two years after that and a sister in 1626. The second of the three boys died quite young and soon their father Cicco too disappeared from the sparse records of the lives of the Market people.

Masaniello's mother Antonia had been a prostitute around the Market. *No longer being any good for that* after starting a family, she then hawked the embroidered headscarves that *married women wore in the Market district.* The house in Broken Alley opened on to the Market square right by one of the excise posts where contractors exacted the duties imposed by Spain on produce bought and sold. This one exacted duty on *grain . . . livestock . . . fresh meat and salt meat, fresh cheese . . . and every other kind of cheese.* It was a circumstance people would remember later.

Tommaso Aniello grew up, as the son of a shoe repairer and a retired prostitute turned bonnet salesperson, outside the cycle of production and consumption. He quickly learnt to live by expedients. He was, the mass of anecdotal evidence converged in agreeing, unusually charming, spontaneous, opportunistic and yet principled, intuitively intelligent and deeply sensitive to the feelings of the people around him, amoral, joyous, unreflecting, histrionic. He was remembered as generous but vengeful, frank and complicated at the same time, sincerely modest and insanely vain, deeply penetrating in his awareness of his own world and somewhat clueless about the larger movements around it. He was a young male Neapolitan of his time and class with no formal education, an unusually attractive presence and an openness of nature that some people exploited but most responded to. His troubles were the usual ones of being poor and out of work. These did not diminish his loyalty to God or the king of Spain or their representatives in Naples. He was against *bad government.*

At first he was one of the swarm of Market kids, filthy, barefoot and often trouserless. Children who supplemented their meagre home diets with ripe fruit given or snitched among the Market sellers, who supplemented the family income with deft liftings from the pockets and purses of country visitors, tavern drinkers and busy dealers. Who watched the animals coupling and the prostitutes and their pimps and their clients and the motherly women who for a small fee brought people together. The card players, the drinkers, the cheats and conmen and the expert older thieves. They saw the comedians and the acrobats on their stages and the fishermen bringing their catch ashore down on the beach.

The children noticed the brutality of the excisemen, and the stratagems Market people used to circumvent them. They saw the ritual humiliations of minor criminals, and since the Market Place was also the site of public executions, they saw ritual death and its class distinctions, beheading for the aristocracy and hanging for commoners and worse for those who offended God or king. For them there was torture, mutilation, quartering and burning alive, and the Market children saw this too. They saw elaborate religious processions to the church of the Carmine and the clatter of military pomp around the viceroy's weekly visit for mass. They went around in mobs, ignored by busy adults but closely monitored by their peers, and developed a powerful collective morality that mutated but did not vanish as they grew. Masaniello's early life left no records. He was part of this formless mass.

Masaniello ran errands, learnt how to make himself useful and how to meet people's not always licit needs. He learnt to make himself liked and to get himself trusted. He also found out how a young man with no social resources behind him could find his own trust abused by thugs or jacks in office who did have some power, and he resented it bitterly. He hated the excise contractors and their private armies of enforcers even as a boy, and he showed it. After his father died an uncle took him in for a while, but had to send him back home because his hostility to the excisemen made trouble for the uncle.

He hung around the fishermen and paid them little or nothing for small fish superfluous to their catch, and he hawked these cheap around the market in paper cones. He didn't always get paid. Once he delivered a parcel of fish to the house of a wine merchant who took the fish and didn't pay. When Masaniello went back later to collect his money the wine dealer told him to clear off or he'd *fetch a hiding*. It wasn't the only time he was cheated of both fish and money. Another time he was beaten up by the duke of Maddaloni's servants when delivering fish to the Carafas. It was a beating he didn't forget. But he did manage to establish a connexion with the convent next to the Carmine church, where they always paid for his deliveries of fish.

He did other odd jobs too. He networked and made himself useful around the Market. The marchioness of Brienza's estate manager, who was a priest and at the Market picking up a consignment of cheeses sent in from the country for the marchioness and her son the prince of Atena, asked Masaniello if he couldn't manage to slip the cheeses past the excisemen. Masaniello could and did, in several sackfuls. He got a couple of cheeses out of it for himself as well as some cash. The cleric was glad to have avoided a punitive excise payment and Masaniello to have made a little money for the day. Hearing of Masaniello's difficulties—he had a wife and child by then, and life was more and more of a struggle—appreciating his smartness and skill, the factor agreed to be Masaniello's godfather. In the always fluid and ambiguous Neapolitan way, an informal but intensely personal connexion was being made across their differences of social class, and its purpose was to circumvent the extortionist state. Don Mercurio Cimmino was not Masaniello's only godfather, but he was the least equivocal. Masaniello needed all the help he could get and the business of the cheeses seemed to represent a step up in the level of his activity, from being a small-time street seller and avoiding the excise collectors and their enforcers on his own account, to working for others, delivering contraband goods on commission.

This increased the unwelcome attention from customs officials and police but it also brought useful connexions. At one point a lawyer saved him from prison for contraband. Everybody practised contraband under that intolerable excise regime. The only question was what you could get away with. When he did end up in jail another time, over gambling debts—he was a mad gambler, like most in the Market milieu—he made a significant friendship. Marco Vitale was an educated bourgeois, the natural son of a prominent lawyer by a bakery worker's wife, and he was some years younger than Masaniello, though already a graduate. Vitale has been described briefly and demurely as *handsome and dissolute*. A Spanish observer from the viceroy's court at the time called him more tartly *a youth of sixteen and a notorious homosexual*. The same contemporary document, presumably expressing views later held privately among the courtiers and hangers-on inside the royal palace, said Masaniello himself was a *mad homosexual clown*. For the Spanish establishment in

1647, *sodomita* was a concise way of saying a lot of bad things about a person and especially about a person's attitude to the proper order of things.

Even in jail, a lawyer had money and connexions: Masaniello had more or less nothing, and prisoners were not fed by their jailers. A Neapolitan contemporary wrote that *Marco . . . took [Masaniello] under his protection as a servant in prison.* The relation was close and it continued outside and it lasted for years. Masaniello for his part would have been a good person to have onside in jail. That he was a few years older than Marco, strong, handsome, articulate, resourceful, funny, uninhibited and street smart—

a witty joking man, medium height, dark eyes, rather lean, with long hair and a wisp of blond moustache, barefoot, with an open-necked shirt and short canvas trousers and a sailor's cap, good-looking and as lively and spirited as anyone could be

—complicated but didn't change the underlying social reality. Marco's reality was more complicated than Masaniello's. Probably, during their time in jail together, Marco expressed a few thoughts about the social order and the way things were at the moment. Maybe his ideas articulated things Masaniello was already thinking in an unformed way. In any case, Marco was connected through his father to a man who had very clear and strongly held ideas about the way things were in Naples, and before long—whether or not through Marco's direct agency—Masaniello and that man were in touch.

What drovers saw

In Fellini's *Roma* of the early seventies, there was a nightmare traffic jam and accident somewhere on the edge of Rome, sheep and cars and trucks in the rain, sheep caught in *autostrada* traffic, a gridlock of animal and metal. The dream of a traffic jam that opened *8½* some years before had merely been the stifling trap of one contemporary life. The later and worse nightmare of the sheep in *Roma* was the collision of the preindustrial with the late capitalist, the slow car wreck of Italy in the fifties and sixties.

The sheep were the woolly white innocents of the past caught in a moment of confused contemporary cruelty. They were terrifically cinematographic and activated the Italian viewing public's faint memories of Catholic iconography. But the sheep were real memories too, for the poor country people from Sicily, Apulia, Lucania, Calabria, Campania, who had gathered in the *borgate* on the edge of Rome after the end of the war, and for the more determined ones who had gone further north to the factories of Milan and Turin. Sheep on the move in large numbers had been a part of life in southern Italy for thousands of years. Sheep had been around even longer in North Africa, the Middle East and South Asia. Their farming had been intrinsic to the earliest civilizations along the Euphrates, the Nile and the Indus and representations of sheep in art were at least five thousand years old.

Sheep arrived in the western Mediterranean countries thousands of years ago too, and in the peculiar crumpled geographies of Greece, Spain, Italy, the Balkans and southern France, where the land rose steeply and irregularly from the sea's edge, where coastal summers were long and hot and inland winters long and cold, the sheep farmers used to take their flocks up to the mountain pastures as the snow melted in spring, and down to the coastal plains when the cold weather returned. Patterns of transfer developed in different places, along established trails to the same pastures year after year, for centuries and then millennia.

There were sheep trails for the seasonal migration of the flocks all over Roman Italy, and particularly in the South. Watched perhaps by Virgil, sheep climbed to the free highlands behind Naples and coastal Calabria for the summer, along green trails that belonged to the Roman state. Along with the empire, legal ownership of the trails eventually vanished and sheep farming became a branch of brigandage. When the Normans gained control of those regions of the South that had been under Arab rule—Sicily, Calabria and Apulia—in the early twelfth century, they offered pastoralists incentives to reintroduce large-scale sheep farming on the great Apulian tableland above the Adriatic coast to the east of Naples. The mighty emperor Frederick II made a home at Foggia in the thirteenth century, the terminus of the great Apulian sheep walk and where the sheep fair was held. He set up the pastoral customs system in Foggia which lasted until the late nineteenth century. It was a great source of income for the kingdom of Naples. Alfonso of Aragon tightened up its operations in the fifteenth century, put a tax on sheep and the use of trails and pastures and forced all buying and selling to be done through Foggia, *with payment exacted all along the line, naturally*. He introduced the Merino sheep from Spain. When the imperial Spanish arrived, bringing their own rich experience of sheep and their migrations and their incomparable expertise in how governments could make money out of them, they made sure its operations didn't miss a beat. After all, *before the riches of the New World were realized, Castilian wool production was the cornerstone of the expansionist economic policy of Castile and Aragon.*

At the end of October the sheep who had spent the summer eating grass in the mountain pastures of the Abruzzi began to come down, over the course of a month or two, to winter on the Apulian plain. For six or eight weeks, resting at intervals in designated layover pastures, they descended along a skein of ancient sheep walks, *green lanes* a hundred meters wide that went on for seven hundred kilometers and ended at Foggia. At the end of the winter their wool, their cheese, skins and lambs were sold at the Foggia sheep fair and the animals made their way back up to the high ground for the summer. By the middle of the fifteenth century there were nearly two million sheep on the Apulian tableland, and the number was much the same three hundred years later.

It was still happening in the early twentieth century, though with far fewer sheep, as malaria was eradicated, the latifundia were broken up and Merino sheep taken to Australia, and the farming patterns of the Italian South were reconfigured. When they came down from the mountains in the nineteen thirties it was still as it had always been.

White dogs went to the front, sides and rear; the flock was led by a shepherd with a crook and a ram with a bell. Beasts of burden followed with tents, poles and nets to make folds, and milking and cheese-making utensils . . . at the summer pastures the sheep grazed slowly upward as the snow melted . . . the shepherds wore large sheepskin jackets summer and winter . . . had a hard and melancholy life, being with their families for only one month in the year.

Around Naples, shepherds brought flocks down for the winter from the Apennines. They came down in September ahead of the autumn rains and went back in June. During the winter the shepherds slept in straw huts by the milking enclosure. Their families lived in villages along the sheep walks, *and except for three nights at home every two weeks during summer, they visited their families only during spring and autumn.* The same observer described a fortnight's trek back to the high ground. The flocks were *driven by fierce dogs and . . . Abruzzi shepherds . . . horses or mules for the baggage.* In Calabria the landowners' families moved up to the mountains with their sheep and went hunting there in the summer.

Everyone who described the lives of shepherds of the transhumance spoke about their social isolation, the separateness of their life even from other country people's—the crop growers' above all, who stayed put and were the shepherds' permanent antagonists, hating them for the incursions of the passing sheep, and trying in turn to encroach with their plantings of vines and wheat on the pathways the sheep needed for their seasonal migrations. The travelling shepherds were separated even from the herdsmen of those sheep and goats and cattle that didn't move with the seasons, and even from their own families.

It was a world apart and without change. *Transhumance is . . . outside society . . . the shepherds . . . are always a race apart . . .*

'untouchable' outcast[s] . . . the lives of the migrating shepherds . . . a totally separate world and civilization. On the sheep walks of Apulia in the nineteen thirties, *shepherd organization . . . was similar to that of the Romans.*

This was the peculiar resonance of the Gospel stories' insistence that it was the shepherds, in the dark loneliness of their winter working nights, who had the first news of the Christ child's arrival on earth, and they who first found the mother and child in the stable. The sheep culture of the Mediterranean pervaded the Christian Gospels—the sheep and the goats, the value of the single lost sheep, and so on and on to the Bible's overarching double image of Christ himself as at once the sacrificial lamb of God and the shepherd of his people. The uniquely hard and outcast reality of the working lives of the transhumant shepherds of southern Italy made the Christian story resonate for anyone who knew, even from a distance, what the pastoral life was like.

Clean white woolly rent-a-lambs, and sometimes for special commissions even huge and majestic rams with powerful curved horns, were permanent fixtures of the painter's studio. They were always useful. Their value was symbolic, but a good painter knew that high recognition value—a real sheep—increased the symbol's impact. Everyone knew the animals were standing in for Christ. Then in the sixteen thirties, something extraordinary happened, something so obvious that nobody at the time even mentioned it. People ignored it for nearly four hundred years, though it was remarkable in itself and embodied in some of the seventeenth century's finest paintings. Christ quietly left. The sheep moved to centre canvas. Not as symbols but as themselves. One sheep's a symbol, three's a flock. The sheep and their shepherds. Not merely as privileged witnesses of a religious mystery but as working people and their animals. Religious painting went secular, and nobody noticed.

Convent at nightfall

It was a winter afternoon and darkness fell suddenly. It hardly mattered. The little corner of the old city had hardly changed in centuries, a pocket of continuity just inside what in the time of Aragon had been the eastern perimeter wall of Naples. I entered under the arch joining the massive cylindrical towers of Porta Nolana. Overhead was a fifteenth century relief of don Ferrante on horseback and around my feet, outside the old city wall, the detritus of the day's produce market. This modest affair was all that remained of the great Market shown in the painting.

After about three intersections I turned left into a narrow street lined with scratched and flaking façades of a darkening dirty yellow and a lot of firmly closed little doors and windows. The street was a famous thoroughfare in young Boccaccio's time, and before that it was an open stormwater drain and before that a little stream at the end of its run down the hill to the beach in front of the Market where the open boats landed fish and produce from all around the bay. The Lavinaio ran past the front of the church of the Carmine and the monastery next door.

Before the church the Lavinaio opened out on the right into a glimpse of the broken-up remains of the vast old Market space, and at this point a narrow alley ran off to the left—*Broken Alley at the Market*. When Gargiulo painted the Market this alley was also called *Pear Tree Alley* and the house and the alley were tiny but clearly visible on the left in the picture's receding perspective from the far end of the Market square. The house on the corner of Broken Alley or Pear Tree Alley was destroyed by a bomb in the summer of 1943, like many other homes near the waterfront in the weeks before the invasion of southern Italy. It was rebuilt, however, on the same scale, the tiny corner site not leaving scope for much else, and the trim three storeys of today look much as they do in the painting, though done up now in white stucco with puce trim and not in pale raw tufo. A large marble plaque was now fixed to the façade's first floor. It hadn't been there last time I passed.

Three and a half centuries after Micco Spadaro painted it, much of the rest of the Market Place is still in part surrounded by that raw unfinished tufo which goes pale gold in the sun and used to delight the landscape painters from the North. Some of the pale tenements are still ruined fragments from the raids of 1943, their amputations roughly cauterized, clumps of weeds forcing their way through the unused parts, third floor bedroom doors opening into space. Fifteen years after the bombing a huge speculators' block broke up the great Market space. The tiny fluttering shreds of washing at the windows high above hardly soften the façade in dark grey Stalinist cement, which was how the developers of the nineteen fifties preferred to finish their work in poorer neighbourhoods. Even before its devastation in 1943, Piazza Mercato was no longer the place where Neapolitans went for their fruit, vegetables, fish, cheese, bread, grain, poultry and their little meat. Today the area does a desultory business in building and decorating materials, paint and cleaners, children's toys and fireworks. The enigmatic desolation of the waterfront itself is now cut off by iron railings and the busy road which runs along the railings.

At the end of the nineteenth century, in the works done after the cholera epidemic of 1883, the wide straight road called the Rettifilo was cut through the lower part of Naples from the railway station to the Castelnuovo. It runs roughly parallel to the other road along the waterfront, and what remains of the Market Place and its periphery are now sandwiched and isolated between the two streams of traffic. Even a century ago, the Castelnuovo hadn't been a major destination in the city for many years, and the road—leading only to a tangle of irrelevant minor streets around the further impediments to flow represented by the royal palace, the opera theatre, the crags abutting the sea and the sea itself—did little to ease the traffic even in an age of horses and mules. Today the Rettifilo and the Via Marina are both gridlocked several times a day and whenever it rains. But the Rettifilo did achieve its purpose of demolishing thousands of the fetid tenements in which the cholera had bred. The swathe cut through the slums was wide. The four-lane road was lined with several kilometers of substantial new palazzi of vast bourgeois apartments, professional suites, commercial offices and the plate glass windows of upmarket shops at street level. Behind these brave new façades shreds of old squalor remained.

The road was more a desperate response to a social disaster than a visionary act of renewal for Naples, bold and enlightened for the time nevertheless. It was a work of strategic beautification on the Paris model, like the other big confused efforts of those years to make Naples over into a modern city, and a whiff of the French fin de siècle still hovers in the Rettifilo's heat and fumes. The new road wiped out that proliferation of old neighbourhoods just in from the waterfront, each a specialized artisan and merchant district around the Market Place, peopled by workers and dealers in wood, stone, textiles, leather and precious metals and the offices of buyers and financiers from the rest of Italy and Europe. Until the panicky spasm of renewal a century ago this flat strip of Naples by the sea hadn't changed greatly since the motherless boy Giovanni Boccaccio found the world there six hundred years before.

The church of the Carmine had a makeover in the eighteenth century and presents a baroque face to the buildings which now come between it and the Market Place. It was almost dark when I got there, but I found what I was looking for inside, the other marble plaque angrily denouncing the theft of a body in 1799. The young man from the Market who had led the people of Naples a century and a half before had left a dangerous memory. In the moment of the *Parthenopean Republic*, an essay in political enlightenment inspired by the events of France and America at the end of the eighteenth century and immaculate of violence, the Bourbon rulers of Naples one night had his remains removed to some unknown place before, with help from Nelson and the Royal Navy, they suppressed the new republic and massacred its ministers.

The church, that recent evening, being still a people's church, was quite busy. Shadowy figures came and went, lit candles, knelt in prayer. In the pews an animated huddle of grey-haired priest in matching jumper and three women was deep in consultation. One woman was elderly, one young and the third middle-aged, and their whispered discussion was compelling in its intensity, surely domestic or criminal. The three women seemed three generations of the same person. They were grandmother, mother and daughter, identical except in age, at vigorous grips with one of those problems that recurred through the generations and the centuries.

Outside black night had fallen and there were no lights. A shadow passed with a slight movement of air. A sandalled African monk was hurrying back with long silent strides toward the convent, wrapped in his dark habit. Face and habit were nearly invisible in the night. I passed outside the cloister where the murder happened and crossed a patch of unlit waste land between the convent wall and the marine road. Noisome smells came from blackness at the base of the wall, the ground was uncertain and unexpected walls rose out of the dark. It was a long way round—the convent is vast—but in the end I was back among lights and cars and people coming out of the closing shops, and in a few minutes was passing again outside the towers of the Porta Nolana through which I'd entered.

Naples is a theatre of inner-directed intensities, and the Market square had long been the scene of some of the city's more terrible moments. It was where *Corradino*, the fifteen-year-old Conradin, last of the Hohenstaufen, was beheaded in 1268, a few years before the first church of the Carmine was built. It was where Protestants were burnt and where the men and women who led the Parthenopean Republic were hanged. Here in the space of a few square meters the captain of the people was born and married, lived, worked, led his people, was followed, adored, honoured, betrayed, humiliated, murdered, beheaded, defiled, abandoned, washed, made whole again, honoured again in death and buried in his church, abducted and made to vanish forever.

VIII

Palace

Children's stories. The orchestrator. Bruno's run.
Masaniello gets ready

Children's stories

The duchess seemed to be floating. She glided silently toward
the main entrance, upper body hanging low, so low that her
beige twinset was hardly visible above the long and ancient
oak table, a table lined with massive and severely upright oak
chairs with studded leather seats and claw-handled arms, that
stood lengthwise along the entrance hall. The eyes of a couple
of dozen male ancestors, most in military or clerical garb,
looked down with imperturbable severity as the duchess flew
out like a genie through the left-hand archway that led into
the far end of the dynastic hall. She negotiated a perilously
sharp turn around the corner of the table without missing a

beat, skimmed down its length with her rope of pearls still out to the side and effortlessly kept enough distance between the row of feudal chairs on one side and the portrait-covered wall on the other to allow free movement to the wide and rhythmic skater's swing of her parallel arms that drove her forward.

I never saw this. I announced my arrival through the decrepit intercom device that was hanging on a bunch of old wires out of the wall of the great stone arch on the street. The duchess from above sprang a little trapdoor in the vast and studded wooden gates to let me in. I climbed the marble stairs that wound around the courtyard to the *piano nobile*, glimpsing a fuzzy outline of the duchess herself through frosted glass across the courtyard as she hurried out of the kitchen. My arrival at the door usually coincided with hers, which was perceptible as a soft, almost inaudible thud on the other side of half a meter's thickness of wood and steel. The duchess built up such momentum so fast that not even her expert flick of the heels could bring her to a complete standstill short of the door itself.

In the minutes before the door opened I could identify the click of smooth new steel locks releasing their grip, then the clatter of ancient iron bolts being slammed back, the clank of rusty metal bars being withdrawn from holes in the floor and brackets in the walls. I was always the morning's first caller, and apologized for disturbing her. The duchess's own greeting, when the door did swing open, was always the same. *It's the maid's day off.* Then she spun around and was off again, back in her low swinging crouch, cashmere cardy flapping as she shot round the table's end and disappeared through the distant archway. Her compact body was shod in giant fuchsia nylon fur mules and they skimmed over the black and white flagstones, polishing as she went. When I caught up with her we were in her study. The duchess had flicked on a lamp and was rummaging through the big brown leatherette shopping bag in which she carried her legal documents.

We had a complicated relationship, the duchess and I, but in principle it was legal and for a long while I never got beyond the legal office. I don't think she had a full-time legal practice, but judges at the law courts used to pass on the odd little piece of work and every little thing helped. Her filing system was rudimentary, and if she couldn't find the relevant documents in the leatherette shopping bag she used to wander off to see where they might be. I was eager to see what lay under the extremely old leather bindings of the many volumes on the study's shelves. The titles on the spines had long been illegible. When she left I whisked a random volume from its shelf, and the binding vanished at the hinges in a puff of tobacco-coloured dust. I was trying to reassemble the book and slip it back when the whole row slumped and disintegrated and I started sneezing and the duchess returned. My hands were black from brushing against the shelf but she was scrutinizing a sheet of *carta bollata* and seemed to notice nothing else.

It wasn't until the reception that I reached the penetralia of the duchess's warren, which went on forever but seemed to have no main entrance or exit, let alone a façade. The massive door into the grand hall that I knocked at turned out to be some kind of tradesmen's entrance. Neapolitan residences, especially those of aristocratic survivals, were often hidden under a crust of mimetic obscurity that was more the work of time than cunning contrivance. It was only at the reception that I reached the private chapel, with its candles and vases of lilies and its Luca Giordano over the altar. Giordano was known as *Speedy Luke* in the later seventeenth century for his unbelievably vast output. He painted a *Self-portrait* in one of the earliest pairs of dark glasses to be seen in art, and he was pretty good if you liked baroque.

In the library proper outside the chapel there were rows of ancient folios but the young people of *Napoli bene* were doing their heavy petting that evening in the dimly lit corners of the incunabula. It was only from the reception that I found the duchess was a duchess at all, or rather from the name that stretched across the dog-eared pasteboard card with which she invited me around. She always made it clear that she preferred not to stand on ceremony and I used to address her informally as *Contessa*. She liked that. *A few friends . . .* she wrote, announcing the reception.

A few friends was alarming and it was a surprise to think of her entertaining on that scale. It was a party for her niece, and the duchess's main involvement seemed to have been to make the premises available. We mature guests were few. Her husband the duke, whom I never met, remained in his castle near Salerno. Most of the castle, the duchess told me, had fallen down in the earthquake, but the duke still seemed to prefer it to Naples. The reception was a no-nonsense affair. The waiters whirling through the crowd on the terrace in white gloves and white jackets were many, and the silver platters glinting above the guests' shoulders were huge, but there was little on the platters. Looking around for a refill at an early stage in the evening I found the waiters had vanished altogether. Like magic.

The terrace itself was hallucinatory, on several levels like the duchess's apartments, and with an Australian gum tree that had grown a couple of storeys high in its terracotta vase. Even in daylight it was easy to get lost. One morning I had stepped out there with the duchess, the conclusion of some protracted negotiations having been marked by a thimbleful of sherry, and found myself looking down on Piazza Dante. This was long before Gae Aulenti had transformed its great semicircle into a postmodern desert designed for sponsored events.

The statue was still at the centre then, people were still sprawling over the many steps at its base, cars inching around it or jammed on the footpaths. The informal parking attendants from the ex-cons' association were prowling for departing drivers, women in shawls were hawking contraband cigarettes, van drivers and motorcyclists delivering trays of fresh mozzarella and fish to restaurants whose cooks were dragging on a pre-lunch cigarette by the potted hedges. Youths were delivering textbooks, boys in white jackets carrying trays of coffee. Girls were trying out makeup, kids on Vespas were whizzing on one wheel, dealers were dispensing drugs, mature ladies were making friends, people were taking coffees, schoolchildren were skirmishing and pairs of unidentifiable people were yelling at each other from a distance or gesticulating in intimate conversation. The palm trees were wilted, the ornamental borders trampled, the exhaust fumes blue. Policemen in white helmets were carefully noticing nothing. I was thinking how slightly unreal and even charming the social panorama was when observed from above, like a spread in a child's picture book, when the duchess sighed heavily and turned away.

The court of miracles, she said and raised her eyebrows in distaste. It was a bit unfair. The duchess's remark about these mostly amiable people in the piazza below us and their manifold doings, made from the vantage point of her own little court, reminded me of *The Story of Stories* and how rapidly, in the seventeenth century, people could move up or down the structures of a rigidly vertical society. They could do it so fast it seemed like magic.

Giambattista Basile was in the same situation that Bruno's father's friend the poet Luigi Tansillo had found himself in seventy years before. A certain social position and expectations to maintain and no money or connexions to do it with. Basile was born at Posillipo in 1575 and well before the end of the century had left Naples to seek a modest fortune where he could. He arrived in Venice and enlisted in the armed forces of the Serenissima. Venice's valuable outpost of Crete was in danger of invasion by the Turks and Basile was sent to help man the garrison there. It was around the time Othello was sent by Venice to defend Cyprus from the same threat. Unlike the seething sexual perversity that Shakespeare's newly married Othello found in Venetian Cyprus, Basile found in Venetian Crete an expatriate community of wealthy and cultivated business people and their families. The young officer from Naples settled in fast. He took part in their entertainments and discussions, fought in a Venetian naval campaign in 1607 and the next year resigned his commission and went back to Naples.

Arriving home, he found his younger sister had become a superstar. Andriana Basile, while still in her teens, had become *La Bella Adriana*, the most famous singer in Italy, the *Siren of Posillipo*. She was immensely beautiful as well as a gifted musician who also played the harp and the Spanish guitar. For the next twenty years she remained Italy's most admired female singer in an age of great artists, and the most sought-after at its courts. The Gonzagas of Mantua, who had already secured Monteverdi, were determined to have her. In a single day in 1610 the duke wrote her seven letters in his determination to conclude a contract.

Vincenzo Gonzaga the duke of Mantua was as discerning as he was acquisitive. He had perhaps the best collection of paintings in Italy and three years before, urged by Rubens, he had paid a huge sum for Merisi's great rejected Roman painting of *Mary Dead*. Adriana was not keen to leave Naples but she succumbed at last and set off for Mantua with husband and family. She gave concerts on the way in Rome and Florence which enraptured her audiences. The duke's twenty-three-year-old son, the cardinal Ferdinando Gonzaga, who at that moment was negotiating Merisi's fatal attempt to return to Rome, wrote ahead to his father that Adriana had *left undying fame and has stunned the city as truly the world's prima donna*. The cardinal kept in touch with her for years, even after he became duke himself, and sent her his own compositions for her to sing. When Adriana first sang at Mantua that summer, Monteverdi pronounced her quite the best singer in Italy. A couple of years later the duke made her a baroness.

Giambattista Basile was swept up into the Neapolitan milieu of his sister the diva and the Gonzagas invited him too to their court. He didn't stay long. He was himself becoming known in Naples as a poet—he began by imitating Tansillo—turning out copious but now forgotten verse, and plying the courtier's trade in administrative work for the viceroy and local barons. By 1619 he was governor of Avellino and in 1626 the viceroy, who was mad about Adriana now that she had come back to Naples, made him governor of Aversa. These were serious postings. Basile's Italian verse petered out around 1618: it was not a great age for poetry in Italy. What now surged through Basile like new blood was the splendour of his own Neapolitan language. He jettisoned the dreary and inert literary Italian of that early baroque moment and began shaping the richness and vivacity of the words people spoke in Naples into something that would last as written art. He did a book of longish poems about life in Naples that were fresh and alive as none of his Italian poems had been.

As a poet writing in Neapolitan Basile was one of several friends working the same vein. What he did next was Neapolitan in prose and it was unique. Basile produced the greatest book of imaginative literature in Italy's seventeenth century. It grew out of his own life in the satellite courts of the large towns and small cities around Naples. The small provincial courts were intimate, and far closer to the country people and townspeople who surrounded them than the magnificent and embattled Spanish viceroy's court in Naples. Basile listened to the people he lived among, collected their stories and transformed these stories into comic and erotic entertainments for readings aloud during the after-dinner diversions at the courts. Source stories shaded into products of Basile's own imagination, and the pungent Neapolitan speech of illiterate tale-tellers blended into the baroque extravagance of Basile's own written language. He did something nobody had thought of before and assembled, in a five-day cycle modelled on Boccaccio's ten, *the oldest, richest and most artistic of all the books of folk tales* in Europe. It became a source and inspiration for the brothers Grimm two hundred years later.

People who heard Basile's stories read around 1630—servants listening in as they cleared the tables or waited in the doorways as well as the nobles and their courtiers—delighted in their ever-changing register, from exquisite refinement to carnal grossness and back again, in the same fable, the same person, the same sentence. A snigger, a sigh, a laugh were all natural responses at any given moment. A lot of Europe's fables were first written down by Basile, though in forms that might have shocked later readers. The original of Cinderella, Basile's Zezolla, the *kitchen fire cat*, was a killer. Basile's Cinders was the only daughter of a widowed prince who had remarried—these were the kind of minor nobility Basile was working for. The new wife was a jealous virago who mistreated her stepdaughter. Cinders complained to her governess during needlework lessons. *I wish you could be my mother. You always treat me well.* The governess devised a murder plot in which Cinders first played on her stepmother's rancour by claiming she wanted to save her designer clothes by wearing old things at home around the castle.

The prince's new wife, rising to the idea of her stepdaughter dressed in economical old rags, raced to the massive chest where the old clothes were stored. Cinders held the lid up while her stepmother rummaged for something really unattractive. At which point Cinders dropped the heavy lid as planned and broke her stepmother's neck. After the period of mourning following her stepmother's fatal accident, Cinders worked on her father to marry her governess and in the end he came round. The former governess and new stepmother then revealed the existence of six daughters from a previous relationship and Cinders was worse off than before. Thereafter the story was much as it remained in Perrault's later and genteeler French version and in all the others that followed, down to Walt Disney's.

But the tone remained Basile's and Neapolitan, that of an unstable social world in which everyone was fighting daily for survival and advancement, where even the rich and powerful faced sudden reversals and where adroitly precipitated deaths were part of the game. It was still, provincialized and miniaturized, the world of don Ferrante's fatal wedding reception. Its arbitrariness generated as much joy as cruelty. Basile's stories overflowed with the life of the material world and the social world he and his listeners knew, rich and poor promiscuously mixed, with lively details of domestic life, animal life, court life, country life—the food, the clothes, the furniture, the language, the plants, the insects, the fish—above all the domestic. Basile had a novelist's love of redundant particularity that looked forward to Dickens and Balzac.

Cinders's slipper, for instance, was no mere slipper, let alone a wholly unreal one of glass. It was a *chianelle*, an immensely high and unstable cork-soled platform shoe of the kind whose last major irruption into the heartland of western civilization occurred in the early nineteen seventies, a precursor of today's faux-leopard stiletto-heeled platform bootie. No wonder she lost one when she had to run. In Naples these platform soles were originally add-ons, to let ladies descend from their carriages without fouling their actual exquisite court slippers or their finely finished dress hems in the reality of the Neapolitan street. They later became the rage in their own right at court, valued as height enhancers, since Mediterranean women, and particularly those of the kingdom of Naples, were not greatly tall. By Basile's time they had been around for well over a century and like all prestige fashions were filtering downward through the social layers. They became almost uniform, first for the high-class courtesans and then—reverting to their original practical use—for ordinary streetwalkers. One of the first Neapolitan words I learnt was *zuoccola*, for a whore. A *zoccolo* is a wooden clog.

When the aspirant women were all trying on the prince's mystery platform shoe and it was Cinders' turn, the shoe not only fitted but *flew to [her] foot as iron runs to a magnet*. This was a graceful reference by Basile to one of the scientific phenomena that the ever curious amateur of science Giovambattista Della Porta, who had died just a few years before and had also been a fellow comic writer, had discussed in his book *Natural Magic*.

Moments of startling cruelty in the *Story of Stories* were often glanced at and then resolved by someone's joke or a sudden transformation. Old women in the tales encountered revulsion edged with fear, like the one flung at dawn from a palace window for tricking her way into a king's bed, screeching, in a last desperate effort to save herself, *But an old chook makes good stock*. She was saved by a fig tree that broke

her fall, and the hilarity of some passing fairies, who had
never seen anything funnier than the old woman hanging
from its branches. As thanks for the laugh, they changed her
into a dazzlingly seductive fifteen-year-old and new royal
favourite. Her nagging and envious old sister, wanting to
know how she did it, was told impatiently *I had myself skinned.*
The old hag, hoping to duplicate her sister's triumph through
cosmetic surgery, got a barber to skin her alive in an operation
recounted at excruciating length, and died.

A king's son out hunting, at the start of another story,
passed an old woman's hovel and casually smashed the little pot
of beans on her windowsill. They were her only food. At the
end, when he married the girl of his dreams—the previously
arranged royal bride, a heavy-drinking Flemish lady of the
business classes in Naples, having preferred to return to the
more generous wine goblets of home—the ghost of the old
woman, now dead from hunger, appeared at the wedding
feast and cursed him. *I'm the shade of the old woman whose pot
you broke and who starved to death.* Sometimes Basile, making
his courtly audience laugh through his masterly shifts of pace
and tone, made them think about things they might not, in
less pleasurable moments, have wanted to contemplate at all.
About aristocrats or merchants in the country, away from the
secure refinements of home, hunting or travelling, falling
prisoner of a local *monster.* The monster's terrifying appearance
and uncouth manner often turned out to conceal a kindly
nature and delicate sensibility. The monsters were the dirty
rural poor, known to Basile's audience as their own brutalized
vassals or the wild displaced persons wandering the streets of

Naples, the wrinkled and wild-haired old people who were being painted as philosophers and saints.

It was the same with animals. His early version of the story that became *Puss in Boots* was a cat's bitter fable of human ingratitude. Basile was a writer who had more in common with Mark Twain than with Charles Perrault. He died suddenly in an epidemic in 1632, and his sister Adriana, who might around this time have been painted by Artemisia Gentileschi, as she certainly was by Battistello Caracciolo, saw the five days of *The Story of Stories* through the press, volume by volume, day by day, over the next five years.

The orchestrator

Marco Vitale's lawyer father Matteo was a friend of another lawyer from the same town outside Naples, an intellectual and doctor of law called Giulio Genoino. In 1647 Genoino was about eighty, white-haired but active, and he had a history behind him. Genoino was a driven man. Twenty, thirty years earlier he had been famous in Naples as a political militant representing those commercial and professional middle classes on the rise all through Europe. In Naples the bourgeois were far fewer and less affluent and had a harder time than elsewhere asserting their presence in the political structures of the state. The Spanish, who did not encourage local initiative, were one reason for this. Another was the aristocrats who had a crushing predominance in the institutions Spain allowed in Naples. The ruling council of Naples had six elected members, five nobles and a sixth representing *the people*, meaning the embryonic bourgeoisie. This was even more skewed than it looked. The five nobles were elected by their fellow nobles, and the people's elected representative was chosen personally by the viceroy from a list of candidates. The only hope of representing the people thus lay in pleasing the viceroy. The people's representative was the viceroy's own representative on the city's governing body.

Genoino was determined to enlarge the bourgeoisie's political space. He was propagandist, agitator, candidate, office-holder, intriguer for the interests of the new class and the Neapolitan aristocracy's implacable enemy. Portraits showed him dressed in sober black, with a neatly clipped beard and a sensible hat. Genoino had a lot in common with his contemporaries in England and the Low Countries, especially with those industrious parliamentarians and regicides who were transforming monarchy into commonwealth. Among the brutes, parasites and raptors of Neapolitan power, foreign and local, he was a lonely presence, lucid, obsessed and indestructible.

There had been a time that looked like Genoino's moment, twenty-odd years before, just before Masaniello was born. In 1619 the Spanish viceroy in Naples was the duke of Osuña, who was having a particularly rough time with the assertive local nobility. The barons had absolute power on their latifundia and behaved as if they had it in Naples itself. For Spain's viceroys, as for Ferrante in the fifteenth century, the landholders were an entrenched interest well aware of the larger struggle for power in Europe, and which still intrigued with France when it suited their interests. They knew Naples needed them to control the South and they knew their estates provided the soldiers to fight Spain's foreign wars.

Osuña was not a politic viceroy. He was given to the big gesture, the bold move, the unexpected initiative, but he didn't think much about consequences. He ingratiated himself with the masses of Neapolitans living on the edge of survival, who now crowded the city in numbers that made them dangerous. They had been badly hurt by the tax on fruit imposed thirteen years before.

> One day the viceroy was going round the city in his usual way, throwing a few silver coins now and then to the mob that followed him. Touring the Market Place and passing the shed where they collected the tax . . . he got down from his coach, drew his sword and cut the cord of the scales used to weigh the fruit. This generous and spontaneous act . . . aroused indescribable enthusiasm in the poor people crowded around, the ones who felt the burden most. They all broke out in amazing shouts of joy and applause . . . and let off fireworks three nights running . . .

It was no skin off Osuña's nose. While the Market crowd were celebrating he hiked other taxes to make up the difference. He improved his rocky personal finances by claiming ownership of galleys and slaves belonging to the Spanish government and selling them back to Spain. A couple of years before, he had given an *al fresco* dinner party, with twenty-five celebrity courtesans among the viceregal guests, and a few weeks later a party for women only at which each girl received a free designer dress. There was always something in his hospitality for the destitute. At the al fresco dinner there was a table covered with food for them. How the guests laughed to see the starving crowd fight over it, while the viceroy personally taught them a few manners with a heavy stick across the shoulders. Carnival was something else again. The viceroy dressed up as a Turk in a turban with a bird of paradise and headed for the Market with several hundred courtiers in oriental costume. Carts were dragged into the piazza loaded with goodies for the poor and not one but six huge Trees of Cockaigne were set up with more food at the top of the greasy poles. The viceroy sat under an oriental baldachin to take the salute at a march-past of three hundred half-naked street people armed with tarred and feathered sticks, and gave the signal for the food fight to begin.

Osuña's idea in 1619 was to create a new power axis to contain the barons by making common cause with Genoino's urban middle classes. It was another quick fix and Osuña lacked imagination to foresee the difficulties, and patience to work them through. His maladroitness and conceit meant his moves always played out badly. They aggravated the nobility's antagonism and made Madrid mistrust him. Genoino the bourgeois lawyer was modest, coherent and disciplined, unlike the indulged and unstable young Spanish grandee. But as a politician Genoino was a man after Osuña's own heart. Each tried to use the other and together they were a disaster.

Osuña had noticed Genoino's presence on the local political scene and decided to promote him as an ally. In 1619 he made Genoino the people's representative in the city government, an appointment swiftly unmade by the aristocrats of the vicerealm's highest body, the *collateral council*, on the grounds that it had not been preceded by due consultation. This was true, and the aristocrats' reaction predictable. Osuña responded by renominating the agitator a year later and challenging the judicial authority of the collateral council. Genoino was now demanding equal representation for the people and even, with suicidal daring, that the nobility pay taxes. The viceroy made Genoino a judge and then reappointed him people's representative. The collateral council annulled these appointments on grounds of conflict of interest. Simultaneously it challenged the viceroy's own authority to make these nominations. Osuña retreated on the judicial nomination but Genoino took office all the same as people's representative. On 29 May 1620 he rode to his investiture at the head of a cavalcade through Naples, *followed by a mass of friends and armed supporters.*

The nobles short-circuited the viceroy's lines of communication with the government in Madrid. They sent their own envoy to argue against Osuña directly to the king, and they got Osuña recalled. The viceroy was enraged when he received the order and hurled a silver platter in his wife's face. Left without political cover and hearing of his coming arrest for high treason, Genoino fled Naples by sea. He sickened with malaria during the summer voyage along the coast, was arrested, taken to Madrid and tried for sedition. He escaped execution, was held a year in Madrid and then, circuitously and interminably, taken back to Naples. They held him in the dungeons of the Castelnuovo and in the autumn of 1622 sentenced him to spend the term of his natural life in the Spanish fortress of Peñón on the coast of Morocco. Thirteen years later he was granted clemency and released.

Four years after that, now in his seventies, he was allowed home to Naples. Ferociously opposed by the nobles and the collateral council when he tried to resume his activities, he was imprisoned briefly in the Castelnuovo after insisting publicly on the people's right to equal representation. The old man took religious orders on arriving home, knowing he needed all the institutional cover he could get.

Genoino returned in 1639, at the start of the viceroy's financial adventure with the speculator d'Aquino. Taxes were being slapped on everything everywhere and the value of small savers' fixed incomes from government bonds was withering as the financial crisis spread. Major businesses in Naples went bankrupt, dealers in oil, silk, wine, textiles, even one of the big merchant financiers—though not Roomer or Vandeneinden—dragging others down with him. The crisis deepened even as Spain's need for war money, troops and ships remained insatiable. *The widespread conviction that Spanish resistance during the final phase of the thirty years' war depended almost entirely on the financial resources of Naples was well founded.* Spain's old enemy France was now looking at Naples with freshened interest, and the new viceroy, without resources, had to look to its defence. At the beginning of 1646 he resigned, unable to supply what Madrid demanded out of Naples.

He was replaced by the duke of Arcos, who arrived in February of 1646. Arcos had been briefed about the financial crisis, about the renewed violence of the barons in the country, about the catastrophic drop in living standards in the city, but the duke was not up to the job. Even a competent administrator would have found himself in a dead end. Toward the end of his first year in office, urged on by a ruling council whose members would be getting their cut from taxes collected, Arcos issued an edict reviving the failure of twenty-five years before, a sales tax on fruit, the staple food of people who were already going hungry.

Genoino had spent the several years since his release from the Castelnuovo spreading the word among the business community and professional people and the lower levels of the city administration. When the viceroy revived the fruit excise at the start of 1647 Genoino also went to work with the people it most affected. He was eighty now. He had been eighteen when Neapolitans rose against the new tax on bread in 1585, so he hardly needed reminding what part hungry people might play. As in 1585, but even more now, the centre of the anger was the Market and the contiguous waterfront districts where the small artisans worked. Genoino was in touch with a couple of the Market district's boss men, Perrone and Palumbo, who perhaps mentioned the name of the young Masaniello from the Market who had already led a few clashes with the excisemen who collected the money. Maybe Genoino knew already that Masaniello was determined to do something serious about the intolerable tax. Maybe he also heard about Masaniello from Marco Vitale and his father. In the spring of 1647 Genoino and Masaniello were already in touch.

Bruno's run

When, in the spring of 1579, a troubled Italian intellectual arrived in Geneva after a series of zigzag flights from Rome through northern Italy, the elderly Galeazzo Caracciolo, as leader of Geneva's community of exiled Italian Protestants, got him some suitable clothes and sounded his allegiances. The man had arrived in Geneva wearing a white Dominican monk's habit, not a good look among the Calvinists.

> He persuaded me to get rid of my habit. I had these clothes made into a pair of stockings and some other things, and then this marquis and other Italians gave me a sword and a hat and a cape and other clothes I needed.

Galeazzo found the Italian a job as a proofreader with the Italian presses in Geneva. The new arrival was another Neapolitan. If the two exiles felt a surge of recognition and nostalgia when they met, they would have soon found they had little else in common. The austere and noble marquis was now in his sixties and nearing the end of a life of renunciation. Giordano Bruno had been three years old when Galeazzo Caracciolo arrived in Geneva. The marquis must have been startled now to meet a battler from Naples, slightly built, fiery, loquacious, opinionated and argumentative. He had battled for his education and fought even harder for his intellectual independence, and from Galeazzo's point of view Bruno was doctrinally most unstable. He quickly got himself into bad trouble in Geneva.

Bruno described his meeting with Galeazzo and his change of wardrobe thirteen years after the event. He knew the value of a precise and vivid detail, and admired the way a painter could evoke a complex unseen whole in the rendering of that tiny part which caught the viewer's eye. He was a brilliant exponent of memory systems based on a sequence of related visual details, and for fourteen years had made his living by teaching these in the courts and universities of Europe. In 1592, under arrest in Venice, with hypnotic art he told his inquisitors about the transformation of his monk's habit into winter underwear and himself into a Geneva bourgeois. His intent was to draw the inquisitors' minds from larger and murkier matters. Like whether he had formally joined the Calvinist heretics. Bruno had in fact joined the Calvinist church, if only to attend their university. But he now told the inquisitors he had gone to Geneva from France—which was on the brink of civil war between Catholics and Protestants— simply *in order to live in freedom and safety.* He told Galeazzo *I had no idea what sort of religion this city's was,* and this was clearly untrue. So he dwelt on the Dominican habit in which he had arrived, *a habit of cheap white cloth with over it the scapular I'd kept when I left Rome.* The heavy overcloak was another link with his Catholic past and reinforced the image of a man who had never really abandoned the true faith or its accoutrements. Bruno by 1592 had lived through moments of acclaim and great danger in most of the major countries of Europe. In Venice he was in worse danger than he had ever been. He was playing for his life and he knew it.

In Geneva the trouble began with his very first attendance at a philosophy lecture. The chair once held by Calvin was now occupied by a shallow careerist. Bruno, whose formal academic qualifications were superb, was already resentful at having to play the student again and appalled at what he heard. Blind to the local forces he was taking on and eager to make a major intellectual impact in Geneva, he erupted in a pamphlet identifying twenty philosophical errors in a single lecture the professor had delivered on Aristotle. Bruno rushed his pamphlet through the press, blithely assuring a local printer he was putting out a purely philosophical argument. The shallow careerist, a French aristocrat called Antoine de la Faye, was shaky on Aristotle but an agile politician and a powerful figure in Geneva's ruling institutions. He swiftly moved the case from questions of philosophy to firmer legal ground. In short order Bruno was *arrested for having caused to be printed certain replies and invectives against M de la Faye counting twenty errors by the latter in one of his lectures.* Charged with libel four days later, Bruno pleaded guilty and agreed to beg publicly for the complainant's forgiveness and the mercy of God and Geneva's justice system. The printer was released and his fine reduced on the grounds he had been misled by *the monk.* So much for the hat, the cape and the sword. Bruno stayed in jail.

He risked staying there for some time. He had offended the authorities of Geneva, since the complainant was one of these. De la Faye had his career to think about and an exemplary harsh sentence for Bruno was most desirable. New charges were introduced that Bruno had attacked the Genevan church on doctrinal grounds. Bruno argued that these were defamatory rumours spread by the complainant. Evidently rattled, he *claimed he was being persecuted . . . and made several other accusations,* but as a blow-in monk from Italy, Bruno, in Geneva, was not in a position to argue anything. Bruno was a nobody. Three days later Geneva's ruling consistory excommunicated him *for having made defamatory statements regarding ministers and a regent of the college.* Bruno was forced to repent on his knees and sent back to jail to mature his regrets. The university was warned *not to tolerate in any way such a person, who might disturb the school.* Bruno himself needed no hint. Released after two more weeks of considered penitence he straightaway left Geneva and headed back into France.

When he said that what he had sought in Geneva was *freedom and safety*, Bruno was telling the truth. He had left Naples and then Rome in 1576 only because the Inquisition was planning to try him, which meant imprisonment. All his movements after that were a search for a safe haven and a means of livelihood. He was utterly alone. He had no friends or colleagues, no contacts to look up, no patrons, no letters of introduction, only his tenuous and compromised link with members of the Dominican order. He had no money and no resources beyond his own intelligence and energy. Each new country meant learning a new language in which to look for work. At least, among intellectuals, there was Latin.

In Toulouse, where he went from Geneva, he spent two tranquil and not particularly productive years teaching philosophy in the university, until civil war between French Catholics and Protestants made it dangerous to stay in the South. Bruno decamped to Paris and taught there too, before moving to London. In Paris the French king heard about his art of memory.

I became so well known that Henri III had me called in one day and wanted to know if the memory system I knew and taught was natural or a magic art. I satisfied him—I demonstrated to him personally that it wasn't a magic art but a science . . .

Learning, knowledge alone, was never the only thing Bruno was after. The boy who had been enthralled by the power of Dominican eloquence still wanted to convince others by the force of his written and spoken words. Yet in some ways the speaker's art—the art of winning over a large intellectual audience—eluded him forever. Bruno's lectures and debates in Oxford and Paris were unmitigated and humiliating disasters. In Oxford even as he began to speak the Anglican academics were tittering at his appearance, manner and his Italian way of pronouncing Latin. One supercilious Oxford don, later archbishop of Canterbury, called him *that Italian Didapper . . . with a name longer than his body . . . the little man*, a didapper being a small darting diving bird found near rivers. The Oxford man wrote twenty years later with undimmed hostility that in 1583 Bruno's

hart was on fire, to make himselfe by some worthy exploite, to become famous in that celebrious place . . . he had more boldly than wisely, got vp into the highest place of our best & most renowned schoole, stripping vp his sleeues like some Iugler . . . he vndertooke among very many other matters to set on foote the opinion of Copernicus, that the earth did goe round, and the heavens did stand still, wheras in truth it was his own head which rather did run round, & his braines did not stand stil.

They accused him of plagiarism and suspended his lectures. It was England that made him think for the first time with brief but intense regret of home, the small and ancient town of Nola on the lower slopes of Vesuvius and the teeming slums of Naples. For an instant he sounded faintly lost. Oxford was bad enough. *[I] was born and raised under a kinder sky*, he wrote after lecturing at a university where he found *a constellation of the most stubborn pedantic ignorance and presumption mixed with a peasant uncouthness that would try the patience of Job. And if you don't believe me, go to Oxford.*

But it was the impersonal brutality of London which really got to him. With a fairly extensive and intensive experience of Italian, French and Swiss city crowds gained after leaving Naples, Bruno found people in the streets of London

the most disrespectful, uncivil, rude, crude, uncouth and ill bred on the face of the earth . . . knowing you're a foreigner, they sneer at you, laugh at you, jeer at you, blow raspberries and call you in their own language dog, traitor, foreigner—and this last name is to them a real insult and it means they can do you every wrong in the world.

He had been living in the French embassy and his diplomatic protection in London ended with the ambassador's recall. Back in Paris—now a difficult and dangerous place for Bruno—an Italian who worked for Henri III and knew Bruno well described him in a letter as *a most pleasant little companion and he knows how to enjoy life*. Everyone remembered Bruno as *little*. His major intervention on Aristotle—it was Bruno's farewell appearance in France and he was even more concerned to leave a major impression in Paris than he had been in Oxford—turned into a brawl. Bruno was interrupted, challenged and, when the fighting started, allowed to slip away through a side entrance only after promising to return the next day to answer his critics. The next day he was on the road to Germany.

Bruno taught for two years at Wittenberg in a free community of minds, where his student Hamlet found *more things in Heauen and Earth . . . Then are dream't of in our Philoſophy*. A shift in the political climate forced him on to the road again. Leaving, in the spring of 1588, he spoke in Latin to his gathered students and colleagues. Bruno thanked them at the end for giving him the only secure and friendly home he had known since fleeing Naples. For a moment the fierce and brilliant mask of self-assurance slipped. Fleetingly, he let himself be seen not as a great thinker sure of his mission, but a man like any other, homeless, friendless, a lonely man with troubles. There was no shadow of self-interest over his words. He was already on the way out.

> Though I was a foreigner, an exile, a refugee, the play-thing of fortune, small in stature and poor in worldly goods, quite out of favour and pursued by the hatred of the crowd . . . you did not despise me . . . you welcomed me . . . for two years you protected me . . . you sustained me and did not listen to my enemies.

His German academic audience would have recognized his reworking of Matthew's *Gospel* here, and the implied identification of himself with Jesus, who had said *I was a stranger and ye took me in . . .* He knew they knew he was being anything but self-deprecating, and that they would be moved all the same. And they might have sensed that they were moved because they knew he knew these too were the words of a man going out to face a bad end.

After a futile visit to the emperor in Prague and a few brief engagements in Frankfurt and Zurich and Brunswick, at the end of a decade of fierce productivity in his philosophical writing, in late 1591 Bruno went back to Italy. He went because he sensed that things were about to change. A new king in France and a new pope in Rome seemed to promise movement in Europe. He had been living precariously and often dangerously in alien places for fifteen years. Once again he misread the signs.

The short-term reason was another memory gig to earn badly needed money. Zuane Mocenigo was a Venetian who invited Bruno to stay in his palazzo in the spring of 1592 and instruct him in memory techniques. Bruno found his host so bigoted and obtuse that for a while he moved to rented rooms to get away from Mocenigo, and found reasons to make a trip to Padua. Things came to a head when Bruno showed signs of leaving. Mocenigo felt cheated of the promised memory skills, and with half a dozen of his servants one evening he locked the house guest in an attic. The next day Mocenigo rushed off a letter of denunciation to the Inquisition in Venice. It impressed the inquisitor enough to arrest Bruno the same evening. *My profession is letters and every science*, Bruno said when they arrested him. Not religion.

He said that Christ was a fraud and that since he was carrying out fraudulent acts to seduce and fool people he might very well foresee he'd end up on the gallows . . .

that Christ seemed to perform miracles because he was a magician . . . he said it was impossible for the Virgin to have given birth . . . he said our opinions are donkeys' doctrines . . . that he's amazed how God puts up with all our Catholic heresies.

Two days later Mocenigo wrote a second letter recounting what Bruno had shouted through the door of the room he was locked inside, when Mocenigo called out—it was like a scene from *Candleman*—that he was going to report him to the Inquisition as punishment for not teaching the memory techniques as promised.

He said he wasn't afraid of the Inquisition because he didn't harm anyone the way he lived and that he didn't recall saying anything bad to me and that even if he had he'd said it to me alone . . . that the worst they could do was prevent him rejoining his order . . . *So you've been a member of a religious order*, I said . . . *and how do you reconcile that with not believing in the Holy Trinity and all the bad things you said about our Lord Jesus Christ?* . . . he only replied that he had already packed his things and wanted to leave . . . he said if I let him out he'd teach me everything he knew and leave me all his things, except for one little book . . . and I found it among his papers . . . .

Mocenigo was now in trouble himself for not reporting Bruno earlier, and trying to strengthen his position. He wrote a third letter, adding details to provoke the inquisitor and rubbing in Bruno's impiety.

I told him to shut up, since I was a Catholic and he was worse than a Lutheran and I couldn't stand him . . . he laughed and said, *Wait for judgement day and you'll get the reward you deserve* . . . he also told me he liked women a lot, though he hadn't yet had as many as Solomon did and he said it was very wrong of the church to make a sin out of something that served nature so well and that he thought was a very good thing indeed.

Mocenigo also made muddled but piercing mention of ideas that were central to Bruno's thinking.

I heard Bruno say in my house . . . that *the world is eternal and there are infinite worlds* . . . that nature makes created souls pass from one animal to another . . . he's planning to start a new sect he calls *new philosophy* . . . He says . . . *all the best theologians in the world won't know how to answer him.*

Even channelled by Mocenigo, Bruno sounded at the end of his tether.

I heard him say . . . *the world can't go on like this because there was nothing but ignorance and no religion that was any good . . . soon the world was going to be reformed because corruption like this couldn't last* . . . He said . . . *that in this time of greater ignorance than the world has ever known, some people are boasting of knowing more than ever before.*

His salty harangues against Christianity of a few weeks later, to a captive audience of filthy prisoners in the dungeons of Venice, promptly reported by spies and minutely transcribed by the Inquisition, were like all the things he'd ever wanted to fling in the face of his distinguished audiences in all the places he'd ever spoken—Naples, Rome, Genoa, Turin, Venice, Padua, Geneva, Toulouse, Paris, Oxford, London, Wittenberg, Prague, Frankfurt, Zurich—in fifteen years on the road. After nine weeks in jail Bruno felt he'd had enough. He renounced his errors and asked God and the court to pardon him. The court was not convinced and seven months later, after intense pressure from Rome, Bruno was extradited from Venice and transferred to the Inquisition's jail in Rome.

As the endgame played out, Bruno did not lose his intermittent showman's flair. He knew the institutional rules and orchestrated his own trial as a brilliantly alternating sequence of admission, denial, retraction, collaboration and stonewalling. After eight years of this, mutual exhaustion overtook both sides and his death became the church's only way out. The last thing they wanted was another public burning. Sixteen hundred was a jubilee year to celebrate the church's recovered order, vigour and serenity. At the end of 1599 the inquisitors had to report that Bruno said he had *no duty or desire to say he is sorry, doesn't know what he should be sorry for, has no reason to be sorry and doesn't know what he ought to be sorry about.* In late January they were still urging him to *return to the womb of the apostolic Roman Catholic holy mother church.*

Bruno was on his knees when they condemned him, but immediately stood up and *in a threatening manner* told them *You're more afraid to pronounce this sentence than I am to hear it.* Which was probably true and in any case unanswerable. The man who longed to convince with words compelled when *he'd learnt by heart.* Not only because he entertained people, perhaps. As a fishmonger, minor contrabbandiere and general person for hire Masaniello was building contacts with persons of influence around the Market and beyond—*friends, associates, protectors*—and tavern keepers might have found it wise to treat a friend of the friends hospitably. The same connexions and his own growing influence gave him authority to intervene in local disputes, and he was getting known as an arbiter in neighbourhood quarrels and street deals, since *he had nothing else to do all day than settle people's disputes.*

The Carmine at the Market being a major place of worship in Naples, the viceroy was in the habit of going to mass there every Wednesday in his coach, surrounded by courtiers, soldiers and lackeys. Arriving on the day after Christmas of 1646—the fruit tax lately voted but the decree not yet published—Arcos found himself surrounded by an angry yelling crowd. Since his coach was blocked by the press of people, the viceroy nervously emerged from behind the curtains and made a vaguely reassuring speech. No viceroy enjoyed being jostled by an inflamed and smelly mob, and when mass was over Arcos slipped away by boat from the Market landing to avoid a repetition. Back at the palace the tax contractors told him Neapolitans understood only *the big stick* and urged him to stand firm, and he did. Only from now on, Wednesday mass was with the Jesuits, who were a handy coach dash up Toledo. A week later the tax decree was issued with details of the new duties payable on fresh and dried fruits. Armies of collectors, enforcers and *spies* surged into the Market to catch people slipping through the fiscal net. You could go to jail over the tax on a pound of figs. Ugly confrontations became more and more frequent as winter turned to spring. Masaniello made his feelings known.

This was the voice of the angry young man Genoino was so anxious to make contact with. In May a Spanish warship was blown up at the docks, and a week later word arrived of an uprising in Palermo against a similar tax in the Spanish vicerealm of Sicily. The administration there had panicked and suspended all excise payments. Posters immediately appeared on walls in Naples urging action against the Spanish, invoking Palermo and quoting Jesus, *Go and do thou likewise*. The warship was the work of the barons, who were intriguing with the French again and the only opponents of Spain who had the logistical resources and access to large amounts of explosive. But the massive attack increased the tension in the city. The posters sounded like Genoino's work.

A week into June, the excise post at the Market was burnt down in the night. The arson was organized by the current people's representative, Andrea Naclerio, who was trying to ingratiate himself with Market people, terrified of being slaughtered over fruit as the people's representative Starace had been over bread sixty years before. Its executors were the two Market area bosses Genoino was in touch with, Palumbo and Perrone. The former was released from jail for the purpose. Perrone was a gang leader who was not in jail because he had become an abbot in the convent precisely to be out of the law's reach. They were contrabbandieri and *camorristi* and had the contacts and influence in the Market quarter that Genoino wanted. Plus the friar who was Masaniello's contact at the convent—the one who was sleeping with his wife Bernardina—and a couple of others including Masaniello himself. It seemed to be Masaniello who started the fire. He later claimed it was. Soon after that Bernardina tried to smuggle into the city a little bag of flour for home use. The excise agents found it hidden in her clothes and she was jailed. The head of the excise office for flour, a man named Letizia, was a vindictive man and she stayed in jail for a week while Masaniello sold everything he owned, his work tools and a pair of woollen trousers, to pay the fine Letizia imposed.

Early in the summer a group of nine young men in their mid twenties from the Market met at a drinking place just outside the walls of Naples called the *Buffalo's Waterhole*. The food and wine were good and you could enjoy them beside a freshwater spring, surrounded by quiet green and away from the dirt and the noise and the crowds. And away from curious eyes. After a light meal they began to talk about a new move against the excise. The centre of the group was Masaniello, who had a major part to play in the imminent festivities for the Madonna of the Carmine, a great celebration held every year in the Market square on July the sixteenth.

The centrepiece of the show was always a big mock battle between Christians and Turks staged by two armies of Market boys, assaulting and defending a purpose-built wooden castle in the middle of the piazza. The friar from the convent was in charge of events and Masaniello was the captain of the boys' army, responsible for training, choreographing, outfitting them for the day. It was a little extra earner passed on by the friar to keep him sweet. The boys were called *Alarbi* and the Arabs fought with blackened faces and Moorish dress and yelled out Turkish war cries. The plan now was to seize the moment and turn the kids' mock battle into a demonstration against the new tax. The boys' army would lead the crowd in a march on the viceroy's palace, chanting *Long live the king of Spain! Down with bad government!* The kids were brought to the Buffalo's Waterhole and given their instructions, each being paid a small coin and given a long cane as weapon for the day. Training went ahead and Masaniello got very taken up in his mission.

One day . . . he went very angry towards his house, and passing by a Church where the famous Bandito *Perrone* had fled for refuge with a companion of his, being ask'd by these, what ayl'd him? he anwered in great choller, I will be bound to be hang'd, but I will right this City; they laugh'd at his words saying a proper Squire to right the City of Naples. *Masaniello* replyed, Do not laugh, I swear by God, if I had two or three of my humor, you should see what I could do.

Maybe it was the growing heat of summer and the excitement of training hundreds of wildly keen fourteen-year-olds in quasi-military exercises—they were already marching round the city, *ragged and barefoot . . . with a rag for their banner and a broken drum* and shouting slogans—maybe it was the lack of reaction when they marched to the palace and shouted *Down with the tax*, but things suddenly accelerated.

A little after he fell into a great choller, because his fish was taken from him by some of the Court, because he had not payed the gabell, he thought then to make use of the occasion of the murmerings the peeple had then

301

for the Gabell upon Fruit, and being departed from
Perrone he went up and down the fruit-shops that were
in that quarter, advising them that the next day they
shold come all united to the market, with a resolution to
tell the Country-Fruiterers that they wold buy no more
gabell'd fruit.

The *gabella* being the excise. This was the word that went out
before the market day of Sunday July the seventh. Masaniello
had two brothers-in-law who were not inconsiderable figures
in this world. Mase Carrese was a market gardener in Pozzuoli
who delivered his produce by boat to the Market retailers, and
Ciommo Donnarumma sold meat, coal, salt and fruit from
a big store at the Market. Through them the Market people
knew that no excise was going to be paid that day.

Market day began early when the market gardeners arrived
by boat from Pozzuoli and other places around the bay and
unloaded their produce and distributed it to the Market
retailers. Masaniello and his army of alarbi waited around a
corner, watching. The excisemen came forward to collect the
tax. Wholesalers and retailers both refused to pay. A group of
Market people went off to get the people's representative from
his home and Carrese led another delegation to the viceroy's
palace. Arcos graciously referred them to the relevant official,
who made them wait, then insulted and threatened them. The
delegation arrived back at the Market hot and furious. The
people's representative was already there and telling people
they had to pay. Carrese shouted angrily, *God gives us plenty
and bad government brings famine.* He was threatened with arrest.
He shouted *I'm an honourable man and I own my things.* The

chief of police present slapped him to make him shut up and show respect. Furious, Carrese slashed the cord of a big crate of his figs and emptied the crate on the ground and other sellers did likewise.

Masaniello's alarbi swarmed into the piazza with black rags flying on the tips of their canes, yelling their chant, *No tax! Long live the king of Spain! Down with bad government!* The boys grabbed the figs and stuffed them into their mouths, then started throwing others at officials. Police and excisemen chased them around the Market square. The crowd was growing. Older boys arrived and threw stones. One stone hit the people's representative hard in the chest and threw him back. He fell back heavily but was saved from the crowd by Perrone and his camorristi, dragged to a boat and rowed away to the safety of the palace. Masaniello climbed on to a fruit stand and urged the crowd to action. It was the first time he had spoken to a crowd and nobody later recalled what exactly he said. He did tell them he was the man who had burnt down the tax office in June, and the crowd now went over to the rebuilt excise office, broke in, ripped up its records and set it on fire. Soon all the excise posts around the Market were burning. The old agitator Genoino was on the scene but out of sight, giving advice, avoiding exposure and watching to see how it turned out. Little was spontaneous that morning, apart from the free figs.

A column of eight hundred Market people led by Masaniello set off in pursuit of the people's representative Naclerio, who was now hiding in the palace apartments of the viceroy's wife. The people's representative was seen—*You're the one we're looking for, you traitor dog*—escaped through the duchess's window, rushed through the garden and hid in the Castelnuovo. It was now eleven in the morning. Another group of four hundred arrived at the palace, led by a Sicilian veteran of the Palermo uprising in May. Having burnt more tax offices at the city gates, they now disarmed the soldiers on duty at the palace, streamed up the staircase and shoved aside the viceroy's Swiss guards. Discipline was maintained, the double cry of loyalty to Spain and rejection of the tax kept up. But the viceroy was not at home.

Arcos had panicked and been about to yield on everything. Friends, courtiers, advisors urged him to stand firm. First he had to escape from the palace. As the viceroy slipped out by a concealed staircase and headed in a coach for the safety of the convent opposite, an unknown person lunged at him and yanked him to the ground by his hair. One witness improbably claimed it was Masaniello himself. Another said it was Pione, a fifteen-year-old captain of the alarbi. The viceroy flung a handful of gold coins toward his attacker and fled on foot, but the crowd closed in again. He was saved by Genoino's great-grandson, who shouted *Let me handle him*, misdirected the murderously minded crowd, slung the viceroy over his shoulder and got him inside the convent. From a balcony the viceroy scattered little handwritten notes abolishing the fruit tax and they fluttered over the heads of the growing mass of angry people. But it was too late to stop what had started.

in with work often indistinguishable from the master's. But toward the end of the decade the lines of his drawing were tremulous and in 1650, explaining why he had been slow to finish a painting, he wrote that he had suffered from a *weakness in the brain*. He'd had a stroke, or more than one.

A medical event was never merely medical. Ribera's prolonged collapse coincided with the wild years of the financial crisis in Naples and the dealings of Bartolomeo d'Aquino with the Medina administration. It was a time of shrinking incomes, bankruptcies, hunger and hatred of Spain. The Spanish painter who had charged steep fees for decades was suddenly hard up. The obvious reason was his dwindling output, but perhaps not the only one. Ribera's years of prostration continued beyond the end of Medina's long term as viceroy and the short term of his successor Castille. When Naples exploded in 1647, Ribera's long intimacy with Spain, and its viceroys in Naples, exposed him to the people's anger. When Neapolitans took to the streets and Spanish power was vacillating, Ribera and his family holed up in the royal palace. The move to a besieged fortress was stressful in itself and brought its own problems when after fifteen months of violence the uprising was finally over. Ribera painted the dashing young saviour of Spanish power in Naples and temporary viceroy don Juan, mounted on a prancing grey steed against the bay of Naples, as *Don Juan José de Austria on Horseback*, an emblematic portrait of the restoration. The youth then used their proximity to seduce Ribera's teenage niece, and everyone in Naples immediately knew.

This humiliation, Ribera's long failure to establish himself as a Spanish grandee, the physical collapse, the money worries, the litigious unsatisfied clients, the political anxieties—all this was recorded in letters, contracts, diplomatic reports. What slipped from view, because it wasn't documented, was Ribera's connexion to a group of brilliant young painters emerging from his own studio just before his collapse. The young painters themselves soon reverted to obscurity. None lived long enough to establish a real name, let alone become famous. Their work showed their common experience as Ribera's apprentices and they were remembered, more and more vaguely, as his followers. The youngest and most brilliant of them died at thirty in 1648, his name soon confused and forgotten. He was one of the great Italian painters of the seventeenth century.

In 1640 Ribera was commissioned by Medina to paint an *Adoration of the Shepherds*. The work he painted was admired enormously and many years later Medina gave it to the new king of Spain. The protonotary of Sicily ordered one for himself in 1641 and when he still hadn't received it five years later started legal action against Ribera. Ribera did another in 1643, which was in the cathedral in Valencia and destroyed in the nineteen thirties during the Spanish civil war, and a last *Adoration* in 1650. Infants and adoration were a rather new area of painting for Ribera, after years devoted to age and pain. The 1640 *Adoration* was lit by the new Venetian luminosity that had flooded into his work in the thirties. The last version he even made into a daytime scene, mother, child and shepherds against a brilliant afternoon sky. As in the Prado *Philip* of 1639, the *Clubfoot Boy* of 1642, the *Don Juan* of 1648.

The original 1640 *Adoration* was not a daytime scene, though Ribera got something of the same effect. The mother and her child at the centre were caught in a white light. Mary was in pale blue with a glimpse of red undergarment, holding her naked child on a white cloth, their pallor made livid by the light, surrounded by shadowy shepherds. Mother and child were like a swatch of blue sky and floating clouds. The light detached them from their densely pulsing surroundings. Mary looked insipid, her child whitely inert, her blue drapes and the manger, apart from a few individual straws, perfunctory. Were they unfinished, or someone else's work?

A youngish black-bearded shepherd knelt on her left, leaning forward, his head in shadow, his bony knotty shoulder, arm and chest caught in less intense light. He was holding an oddly clean sheep with a marvellously rendered impress in its fleece from his grip. The sheep was not staring as intended at the holy couple, but looking out at the painter like a dog in a snapshot. Behind and above him were two standing shepherds, receding into darkness. On the right was a powerful shepherd with thick white hair and beard, on his knees. Under his ripped and sleeveless leather jerkin he wore a full sheepskin. A thin-faced and eager caped woman craned forward behind him, her vividly articulated hands clutching a basket of chickens. A brown-bearded and brown-blanketed shepherd stood above her, receding into shadow. Hovering low and close and caught by peripheral light, though unnoticed by the figures below, three naked putti in vigorous movement, their wings barely adumbrated, seemed like real children in the sky, realler or more lively than the pale newborn below.

The canvas was *signed by Ribera*. The Merisi who had painted the Messina *Adoration* and the Palermo *Adoration* thirty-odd years before would have been impressed by the vivid new life. But was it Ribera's? Maybe in 1640 the sick Ribera was already signing work by his brilliant young assistants.

In the quiet days of the seventies at Capodimonte I used to stop more often than elsewhere in front of a dark painting of middling size that showed a night huddle of four grubby-looking men, a couple of sheep and a sturdy little red-eyed pony asleep on the hoof. Two of the men were sound asleep, the younger with his mouth slightly open. Another was waking startled and the youngest, already fully awake, staring intently at two infants hovering inches from his face. One sheep likewise had turned its head at the irruption of light and movement in the night air, pausing in mid-chew as a sheep will, while the other ignored the disturbance and went on cropping. One infant was swathed in a floating brown blanket that showed only its head and a hand, the other was completely naked and showing a little grey wing. The canvas on which they were shown being much wider than high and the figures done close in, the children were hovering so low that they would have been no more than shoulder height to anyone standing fully upright. They were all a single compact knot of animal, human and supernatural, out in the dark in the middle of nowhere.

The children were waking the shepherds to announce the birth of Christ. I had a great love of this unknown painter's *Announcement to the Shepherds*, for its real people, real animals, real accoutrements, real lives, and for the way it showed them without rhetoric in a powerfully composed unity of cloth, flesh, fleece, darkness and light, wonderful plasticity in the play of surface over form, animal and human, the flying baby's legs treated with no less depth and feeling than the bare legs and feet of the half-dressed shepherd in the foreground or the wonderfully elegant hindquarters of the watching sheep. Details were exquisite but served the whole—the dirty sole of a bare foot, the wrinkles on the back of a working hand, the grubby irregularities of the fleece on a sheep's back, the crust and crumb of a broken half-eaten loaf, the knot tied on a bundle of belongings. The dense paint, browns and greys from pale skin to black night, shading sometimes into red or blue, folded shadow and dirt, living and inert into a continuous whole, so that the painting was as much unified in its surfaces as in its forms. The deeply naturalistic intent was lightened by the vigour and brio of its realization.

This painting was like Ribera's *Adoration* in the way it was built up, in tone and handling and its detail. There was a similar lean bare-shouldered black-bearded shepherd in the left foreground, though Ribera's sheep was on the other side. The sleeping brown-clad bearded shepherd at the centre was like the dreamy bearded brown-clad figure in Ribera. The young shepherd sleeping with his mouth open was close in position, form and lighting to the shadowy shepherd with the bagpipes in Ribera. And the two infants overhead were like the three in Ribera.

There being no mother and child at the centre of this *Announcement*, all the brightness of colour and lighting, the conventional delicacy of their treatment, were gone too. Here the rough shepherds had surged in from their place as watchers at the edge in Ribera to become the very centre of this painting. Even the hovering babies, drained of Ribera's celestial light, looked like country kids who happened to be a few feet off the ground. This was the painter's choice, not one dictated by the change of subject. In Luke's *Gospel*, the *shepherds . . . keeping watch over their flock by night* heard the announcement from *the angel of the Lord . . . and the glory of the Lord shone round about them.* The shepherds saw *with the angel a multitude of the heavenly host.* In this painting there was no angel, no glorious light, no heavenly host, just black winter night lit by a glimmer and the glimpse of a couple of small children in the air, with sun-darkened lower legs and feet, embodying the message about a child. This was an overnight stop somewhere along the *tratturi* of a sheep's life and a shepherd's, between summer and winter, the mountains and the sea. Which was why the generic *ass* of Ribera's nativity scene was here a sturdy mountain pony to carry tent poles and blankets, food and drink and materials for the overnight stops. Who had painted this great and secular *Announcement*? The painter was identified only as a Neapolitan *Master of the Announcements to the Shepherds.*

For several years in Naples I lived a few doors from the church of the Pietà dei Turchini and hardly glanced at it. It was always closed and its narrow austere façade was easy to miss, but inside were three masterpieces from the early seventeenth century. It was the church of an orphanage and music school from the end of the sixteenth century and named for the turquoise tunics worn by the singing orphans. The church held Caracciolo's 1615 *Earthly Trinity*, Filippo Vitale's *Guardian Angel*, a painting much influenced by Caracciolo, and an *Adoration of the Shepherds.*

This last had no sheep or hovering babies, just the mother and child and in profile on the right a kneeling shepherd with thick white hair and beard. Behind him stood an old woman leaning toward the baby, her head covered by a voluminous white country woman's headpiece. It was not quite straight out of Ribera, but the scarfed woman and the white-haired shepherd were close to the pair on the right of Ribera's 1640 painting. If the sheep painter of Capodimonte had taken the left side of Ribera's canvas—sheep, bare-shouldered black-bearded shepherd, hovering babies, shadowy shepherds in the dark—this painter had taken the right side, the white-haired shepherd and the white-scarfed woman. The old woman here was not holding a basket of chickens, but as if to make up for the absence the painter had placed in the centre foreground, at the very bottom of the canvas, a little basket with two beautifully rendered forms of *ricotta salata*. The earliest description of the painting picked up enthusiastically on the shepherd's felicitous gift of *a ricotta in a most lifelike little basket*. Above the heads was only the deepest darkness.

This painting did have an author with a name. Everyone agreed that it was the work of Juan Do. Indeed it was the only work of Juan Do on which everyone agreed. He was a Spaniard like his master Ribera, but the first thing known about him was his marriage in Naples in 1626 to Filippo Vitale's stepdaughter, when his two distinguished witnesses were Ribera and Caracciolo. Did their presence make him a respected peer of the great Neapolitan painters, or a promising protégé? About twenty was the usual age for a man to marry. Was Giovanni Dò, as he soon became, older and in Naples for years, or younger and lately arrived? The man's face behind the old woman's shoulder was thought to be a self-portrait and it showed a man of about thirty. Dò was talked about and collected by serious people like Vandeneinden, but this was the only painting that survived as surely and identifiably his. Another *Shepherds* painting by him had another old woman in a white headscarf, some very Hispanic faces and finely rendered bread in a basket. It was light in colour and delicately finished, as if done by Dò before the potent darkness of Naples had worked on him. In the foreground were two lifeless-looking lambs with their feet tied. Dò was not a man who painted sheep.

The people's captain

Fifteen hundred barefoot fighters manned the people's army that Sunday July the seventh and its crack troops were arriving now. Three hundred alarbi aged ten to fifteen in torn shirts and trousers to their knees and armed with canes wielded like swords. Rags flying, they appeared and vanished with hallucinatory and scary speed, beating out a fast rhythm on the drum, shrieking and howling and chanting the slogans. *Long live God. Long live the king. Down with bad government.*

The rhythm bounced off the walls, the narrow alleys and tiny piazzas of the city as they raced from Market to palace. The black rags streamed from the tips of their canes and behind them came older boys who were armed *with broomsticks, chair legs,* stakes and pikes and ready to do real damage. As they streaked through the city in the vanguard of the people's revolt, the boys paused at the small market in Piazza Carità where the painters lived. *Having burnt the tax collecting pavilions around the city they ate all the fruit in Piazza Carità and hurled the rest to the ground*, reported the papal nuncio to Rome. Then they thundered and screamed down Toledo with their canes and black rags like a wall of water on their way to the palace. The viceroy Arcos was now safe with his wife and children and his people's representative in the Castelnuovo a few hundred yards from the palace, surrounded by its deep moat and secured by a raised drawbridge.

The Market forces went round the city jails, disarming guards and setting free prisoners. In Letizia's jail, where Bernardina had been held over the flour, they found a man serving four years for evading tax on some broken pieces of biscuit. That afternoon back at the Market the bosses Perrone and Palumbo got themselves elected *captains of the people* and Perrone's first order was to collect all the weaponry held by the city's arms dealers. Masaniello's alarbi, armed now also with broomsticks and chair legs, were being joined by young workers and adults in their actions against the tax collectors.

The Market bosses were using Masaniello as a front for their own moves. Old Genoino stayed out of sight. He decided the next move, to punish the exploiters and profiteers. He drew up a list of houses to be burnt, and Masaniello made sure the first was Letizia's. At nightfall Masaniello had the bells rung in the Carmine's high tower, covered in glittering coloured tiles, to call the people from the Market and the other quarters along the waterfront. When they came he called them to action the next morning against all the taxes that were oppressing them. He gave his younger brother Giovanni the list of houses to burn of corrupt aristocrats, magistrates, politicians and speculators. Giovanni rode off in his fisherman's red hat and barefoot on a mule, bareback and unbridled, to organize the kids into demolition squads and supply them with matches and torches soaked in pitch.

Control was tight. There was to be no looting. Everything had to burn. And that night they *made Naples burn like a Troy.* One of the houses that went up in flames was the palace of the financier d'Aquino. And there was no looting. Processions of monks of various orders appeared as the avengers were setting out, imploring the insurgents to calm their spirits. They were told to *Get back to your church and pray and don't disturb us now the moment's come to get rid of unjust taxes. We didn't see you making any processions when they were being imposed.*

Then Masaniello turned to the heart of the problem. Food suppliers were given lists of fair prices and bakers told to increase the size of a loaf. Not to follow the food decree was punishable by death. Masaniello, contrary to the expectations of Genoino and the other operators who had made him the charismatic front for their manoeuvres, was showing independence of judgement, authority of command, understanding of priorities and a mastery of logistics and tactics. Contrary to their plan, he was taking over as the undisputed leader of the rising. A military observer from the North was struck by the instinctive military smarts of

a low fish-seller who not only commanded a population as large as Naples's and its surroundings, but did so prudently, though he was young, and intelligently . . . soldiers were amazed how a man who had never used a weapon or seen a campaign or a fortress, knew how to organize trenches, shelters, sentries and patrols.

Genoino had thought he was giving Masaniello orders, but Masaniello was merely taking advice from Genoino. The archbishop of Naples, cardinal Filomarino, a difficult and clever man, no friend of either the Spanish regime or the Neapolitan aristocracy—the Carafas had insulted and manhandled him in the street—dealt closely with Masaniello as an intermediary over the following days. Filomarino had already saved the viceroy's neck that morning by intervening outside the convent. A few days later he told the pope

> this Masaniello has achieved such a level of authority, command, respect and obedience that he has made the whole city tremble at his orders, which are carried out by his followers with great rigor and exactitude. He has shown prudence, judgement and restraint. In short he has become a king in this city, and the most glorious and triumphant the world has had.

Masaniello set up in the Market Place and for three days envoy after envoy came from the viceroy, agreeing to one thing after another. Yes to bigger loaves of bread. No to the tax on fruit. No to all the taxes imposed on Naples in the century since Charles V. Diomede Carafa, duke of Maddaloni, and his brother arrived on horseback as emissaries from Arcos. Masaniello grabbed the duke's bridle and pulled him down from the saddle, excoriating Carafa as a traitor to his country. The crowd was in ecstasy.

Many troops had been sent to the war front and Spanish posts in Naples were seriously undermanned. The officers were disoriented and scared. Routed in one clash, foreign soldiers abandoned the city and the people took their arms. Masaniello could have overthrown Spanish power in Naples at this point, but he was perversely loyal to the king in Madrid. All the Market people wanted was food to eat and room to live. All Genoino wanted was power for the bourgeoisie. A king was a king. Like the barons, the churchmen failed to mediate with the people. The church had never cared and the Market received its emissaries with contempt. Arcos tried to bribe Masaniello with a secret offer and Masaniello told the people he had refused the viceroy's money *with a thousand thanks*.

He was moving away from his earlier guide. Genoino, softened by the tax concessions, promises of historic reform and a major role for himself, thought he could dispense with Masaniello now, and the ferocious proletariat of Market and waterfront. The aristocracy regrouped and smuggled three hundred men from their estates into the city at night. The men were posted strategically around the city and told to listen for the church bells of the Carmine pealing from the Market Place. Then they were to take control. In Rome, French agents were poised to move at the moment of greatest Spanish weakness. On Wednesday the tenth Masaniello was at a mass meeting in the Carmine. People assembled to hear a reading of the promised tax reform and the announced amnesty for insurgents and there were shouts of anger at Genoino's deal with the viceroy. At this point Masaniello was shot at by five killers armed with arquebuses. The bells pealed but the killers had missed their target and Masaniello was unhurt. In the confusion they slipped out of the church but didn't get far. Thirty-odd organizers and assassins were seized and killed, among them the boss Perrone, who had been taking orders from the Carafas of Maddaloni. The duke and his brother Peppe were the attack's main movers. They had planned a terrorist bombing—barrels of gunpowder were found hidden in a drain—and poisoning of the Market water supply. The duke eluded a manhunt by thousands but Peppe Carafa was seized, his head hacked off and hoisted on a pike and his body dragged through the city. The duke's head had a price on it and his brother's was hung in an iron cage.

Now Masaniello had a hundred and twenty thousand armed men at his orders. He requisitioned more arms and men from the households of the aristocracy, who obeyed or fled the city. On Thursday, after a mass meeting in the Carmine, when the statement of the city's historic rights was read out and approved, he set out to the viceroy's palace on horseback followed by Genoino and the cardinal in a coach. The cardinal had convinced him with difficulty to change his old red fisherman's cap and shirt and torn-off trousers for the cloth-of-silver suit given by the viceroy and for the first time in his life he wore shoes. He was reluctant to go at all. From horseback as he rode through Naples he urged people to burn the palace and the city if the meeting was a trap. In front of the castle he showed the crowd the documents Arcos was to sign and said

I ask nothing for myself, and seek only the public good. For no other reason would I have given up my waterfront rags, because I was born on the waterfront, I've lived on the waterfront and I want to die on the waterfront.

Again he told them not to trust the aristocrats, to burn the city if he failed to emerge from the palace. When Arcos greeted him, he fainted from the stress. After the signing the two faced the crowd together. *It's all done, my people*, he shouted and the people applauded madly. Extravagantly, he kissed the viceroy's feet and the viceroy made him captain-general and gave him a gold chain. Then he rode home and changed back to his old clothes. He asked the Market people if they'd let him accept the gold chain and they did. On Friday, dispensing justice from his ground floor windowsill at the Market, he ordered the summary execution of speculators, the disposition of troops, supplies and security forces without listening to Genoino, who was pushed aside and jeered at by the crowd. Many still suspected Genoino and the cardinal of involvement in the failed assassination plot of two days before.

On Saturday the articles of the city's rights were solemnly sworn to in the cathedral. While Bernardina visited the viceroy's wife, who gave her three designer dresses, Masaniello showed his first signs of disorientation when he rode to meet the viceroy. He made a wild speech on the way, drank from a water-seller's jar and pissed in the street outside the cathedral, buttoning up his flies as the viceregal coach arrived and falling over several times. Inside the cathedral, he lay down at the cardinal's feet. He interrupted the reading of the reforms to say he was a poor fishmonger who wanted to go back to work. He burst into tears, and tried to tear off his hated new silver clothes. He ran to embrace Arcos, speaking incoherently and promising gifts as the viceroy swore on the Bible and the majestic *Te deum* began. At the end, he fought to clear a way for Arcos, yelling, *Make way for his excellency, you scum*. Back on his horse outside he told the crowd lucidly enough, *You're done with me now. Here is your master. Be faithful to the king.* On his way back to the palace, the viceroy ordered his coach to pass by the Market. The coach stopped for a moment outside Masaniello's hovel and Bernardina, appearing at the window, was granted a gracious little viceregal wave.

On Sunday morning, as the people's militias were disarmed and the barricades dismantled in the streets, Masaniello personally took the viceroy a present of fresh fish from the early catch. Arcos in return graciously offered him a boat loaded with food and drink for a pleasure outing to Posillipo. He had too much sun that day, and too much of the viceroy's wine. The wine may have been poisoned, like the perfume inhaled from a viceregal bouquet two days before. Masaniello was wild and incoherent when he got back home. On Monday, after a night of sweat and delirium, he resumed command at the Market in the morning, ordering the summary execution of a further series of rapidly identified enemies of the people. He followed with a manic series of orders for expropriations and punishments for the aristocrats and high appointments for Market youths, breaking off deliberations at one point to dive into the sea and cool off in the stifling summer heat. But the food crisis was past, relief seemed to have been won. Arcos had sworn and signed. Masaniello's radicalism now threatened the business interests backing Genoino. The people of the Market were suddenly exhausted by the hot days and nights of conflict, crisis, death, danger. Even disoriented, Masaniello was too astute an interpreter of the Market's mood not to realize that his influence was draining into the dirt, and that in the old, old way of the Italian South the vacuum was being created around him that portended his end. What else could he do but carry on?

In the afternoon he went boating again to Posillipo and again he came back incoherent. While he was offstage, some local business people now looked for a piece of the new regime. Several planned to corner grain and bread supplies. They worked to win over those young militants alienated by Masaniello's erratic and arbitrary turn. Arcos quietly reinforced the garrisons of the city forts and distributed five thousand arquebuses and other weaponry to citizens disposed to maintain order. When Masaniello staggered home he was held prisoner in his tiny house on the corner of Broken Alley while new plans for his physical elimination were finalized. But he summoned Cosimo Fanzago that evening, the best sculptor and architect in Naples, to give him further instructions for the design of the *Epitaph* to be built in the middle of the Market square. This was the monument of the people's revolution in Naples. It would bear engraved on its marble sides the statement of the rights of self-government that had been granted to Naples by the emperor Charles V, permanent and immutable evidence of the city's privilege. Fanzago, a distinguished professional used to working with very different clients, understood that declining the commission was not an option.

Masaniello had sent Marco Vitale, his student friend from jail and now his secretary, to the Castelnuovo with a message for Arcos. The viceroy detained Vitale on some pretext and had the drawbridge raised, thinking to have him seized and hanged. It got late, the plan changed and Vitale stayed overnight at the castle. On his way out next morning he was shot down from behind by arquebus blasts. His body was dragged away behind a horse and dumped by an open sewer.

Tuesday the sixteenth was the Feast of the Madonna of the Carmine. That morning Masaniello escaped from his house guards and—while Arcos issued a proclamation that the viceroy was once again the sole supreme authority and Genoino the viceroy's delegate in citizens' affairs—went into the church of the Carmine. The church was packed as the cardinal celebrated the festival mass and among the crowd the agents of Masaniello's elimination waited. Masaniello took the pulpit and spoke one more time to his people. He reminded them of the hard times now over, and reproached them for ingratitude. He told them he would soon be dead. More than once he announced he was about to be killed. He was as compelling a speaker as ever, and the Market people were moved to tears. Then he spoilt it all again. He tore at his clothes as if he were still wearing the hated silver lamé shirt. He stripped his clothes off entirely and stood naked in the pulpit exclaiming incoherently. Tears turned to jeers as he broke down and was hurried out of the church and into a cell at the convent next door to rest.

He slept for hours and was woken by a knocking at the locked door. Recognizing the voice of a friend, he jumped up barefoot in his shirt to let him in. As he opened the door he was gunned down by arquebus blasts. One of the killers was a wealthy baker, another a grain merchant. A friend hacked off his head and the group rushed off to show it to the viceroy and claim their payment. *Long live the king*, shouted people along the way. Masaniello's head was dumped in the grain store. His body was dragged through the Market and abandoned among the market filth and the jetsam on the beach.

City of the sun

The City of the Sun was imagined in a prison cell in the Castelnuovo in 1602. Tommaso Campanella had lately recovered from near death by torture to convince his judges he was mad. The *dank trench of stinking water* helped him by force of contrast to imagine an ideal society and describe it in luminously simple language as if it were a real place found in a returning traveller's tale, like Thomas More's *Utopia* of eighty-five years before.

Campanella's city drew on his mind's image of the republic he had wildly hoped to set up in Calabria. It was also an ideal contrary of the city of Naples. He knew Naples well, had known it as a free lay citizen. Coming to Naples in his twenties, he had soon slipped away from the convent discipline of San Domenico Maggiore to a place in the household of the marquis del Tufo, who treated him as a social equal and made him a major figure in the lay intellectual life of Naples. A year of enjoyment and busy writing and the marquis's haute cuisine took him to a thermal cure at Pozzuoli. He travelled in style with del Tufo to the stud farm in Apulia where the marquis bred horses. The hunger riots of 1591 had abruptly made him see what a burden the

Spanish excise was on the Neapolitan poor, and what a force the poor were when roused. Then his published work—his Telesian naturalism—got him confined in the convent and ordered back to Calabria.

It all fed into *The City of the Sun* and its images of a city governed by shared rational values, solidarity among people, productive working adults and healthy educated children. Even the horse breeding resurfaced in the detailed attention paid to the ideal society's sexual arrangements. The sun of the little book's title and the healthy outdoor life of its vision stamped every page with reminders of the confinement out of which it was written. *The City of the Sun* also showed that Campanella knew very well how most Neapolitans lived, housed in dank and lightless prison-like homes or sleeping in the filthy narrow streets, ignorant, powerless and desperately poor, bled dry by foreign rulers and exploited by local nobles. It was a visionary antithesis at once of Campanella's own dire condition and of the Neapolitan people's, the more compelling because the means of realizing it were there too in the actual Naples—the sun itself, the climate, the fertility of its earth and sea, the splendour of nature that made the misery so grotesque. Even the shape of Naples, rising around the bay like a gentle amphitheatre, underlay the book's image of a city built in rising terraced circles.

The winding walls that girded the city of Campanella's imagination were lined with paintings representing the known natural world and language, mathematics, science and mechanics, the systems of knowledge. The paintings were for children, to let them learn spontaneously and joyfully as their curiosity and their sense of beauty were aroused when they moved around the city. It was the book's happiest touch and one of the subtlest. Painting was what most people saw in the city's innumerable churches. The hierarchy knew as well as Campanella the powerful effect images might have on young minds, especially the minds of those who were not learning to read. Nobody cared more about the art of images than the church of Rome. Which was why the counter-reformed church policed the images it used to convey its teachings, to make sure a viewer wasn't distracted by eroticism, humour, pagan joyousness, or even the simple pleasures that came from recognizing people, places, things from daily life. Anything mixed, superfluous, conflicted, ambiguous, contemporary, sexy or funny—anything complexly human—was out. Fear and pain, which tended to exclude other feelings, were promoted through an instructive emphasis on early Christian martyrdoms. It was codified in 1584 by cardinal Paleotti in his book of rules for sacred and profane painting. When Campanella was imprisoned fifteen years later, Paleotti's new system was working quite effectively. Campanella's notion of a painterly abundance that could arouse young minds through joy and detail—through being like life—was entirely notional. It was an intuition of genius, learnt from the dire reality of the late sixteenth century.

At one point the Genoese sailor's report on the distant city slipped into a testy comparison with the real Naples of mass unemployment and the decadent wealth of a few.

In Naples there are three hundred thousand people. Fifty thousand of them have no work and struggle and suffer because of it. And the ones with no need to work are ruined too, by sloth and greed and lust and acquisitiveness. They ruin a lot of people by keeping them in service and poor, or making them share their own vices. Meanwhile there are no public services and work in the fields, the army and the trades is done badly with great effort if it's done at all.

Ramming home the message, he goes on to report that *They say*, the people in the city of the sun,

that being desperately poor makes people low, cunning, dishonest, sneaky, criminal, liars and perjurers. And that being rich turns them proud, insolent, ignorant, treacherous, unloving and makes them take advantage of other people who know no better.

People's social behaviour was determined by their social circumstances, and even the rich and powerful paid a price of personal corruption for their place in an unjust order. Psychic health and happiness derived from physical health from childhood on. Adult happiness came from exercise, diet, good sex. When material needs were filled, the mind's activity was rewarding in itself. When everyone's essential needs were met, society flourished. When everyone worked and no work was despised, four hours' work a day was enough. When everything was shared, nobody lacked. Campanella wrote these thoughts three or four hundred years before they became commonplaces of socialist and liberal democratic thinking. He was writing about himself when at the very end he wrote of the people of the sun, *Know this, that they maintain freedom of opinion*. Remembering his own near death under torture, he added, *And they say that if in forty hours of torment a man will not speak when he has resolved to keep silent, not even the stars and their distant influence can force him.*

The sun was modernity, light on the real world in the time after religion.

Duchess of sardines

The only person who tried to recover Masaniello's body and bury it decently was his old godfather Cimino, who days before had urged him to break with Spain when he had the power. Bernardina, whose new clothes and viceregal socializing had been resented, was now jeered at and jostled in the streets, her clothes mostly ripped off. People yelled, *Make way for the duchess of sardines.* Masaniello's mother, his sister and Marco Vitale's mother were pushed and humiliated too. Meanwhile Arcos dispatched a courier to Madrid with the good news. He told the cardinal, the diplomatic corps and other leading citizens who had hurried to the palace with their congratulations, that the administration could recover its lost income in Naples, and then he rode in procession through the city to give thanks at the cathedral. That evening Naples ran out of bread. An aristocrat told a group of anxious, hungry people gathered near the Market that they could eat dirt. *Or hang*, he added as he rode off. Bread was soon on sale again, but the loaf was smaller by a third.

Too late, people saw Masaniello's murder and their own savaging of his body was a wrong done to themselves. His impulse to self-harm had become their own. The surge of impatience at Masaniello's arbitrary acts and delirious behaviour vanished when bread went short. The mood turned within hours. The alarbi retrieved his body, washed it and wrapped it in a sheet. They retrieved his head from one of his killers, the grain dealer Ardizzone, who was renting it out for portraits and death masks, hugely in demand. They sewed it back to his body, washed him in wine and myrrh and laid him out in the Carmine toward the end of the afternoon. *Unbelievable how many people came . . . especially women and others of the lowest sort.* In the flickering candlelight and intensifying emotion around the catafalque, many in the press of people believed they saw Masaniello move, weep, sweat, live, as they reached to touch him and pluck a hair as a relic.

The funeral procession left the church at ten in the evening and moved through Naples to the dead beat of muffled drums and the sound of tens of thousands of people beating their chest. Masaniello's body, head and hands uncovered, was preceded by a long column of orphan children and followed by his horse and his men with arms reversed and banners trailed. Thousands carried torches and candles and the houses along the way hung lamps in their windows and Naples that night *shone like day.* The crowds chanted litanies that mixed Latin and Neapolitan, ending *Sancte Masaniè, ora pro nobis.*

Masaniello's funeral, which involved nearly everyone in western Europe's largest city, was at once an act of reparation and a show of strength. The church recognized this immediately and released all members of all orders and institutions to take part, which they did on the cardinal's orders. The viceroy was careful to show great respect when the huge procession came down Toledo to the royal palace and Castelnuovo, and he sent a squad of pages with torches to accompany Masaniello back along the waterfront to the Carmine. The Spanish soldiery reversed arms as he passed. The Venetian resident saw the funeral procession as a kind of triumph, and heard cries of *Viva Masaniello* along the way. When they got back to the Carmine it was three in the morning. There was a collective crisis when the moment came to bury Masaniello in the church. Burial meant the definitive separation and many of the people present tried to stop it happening.

The movement went on long after Masaniello's murder. It became more radical under newer leaders, and grew from a fight for local justice into a frank struggle to free Naples from Spanish rule. The French under the duke of Guise brought in a fleet of warships and secured several toeholds along the coast close to Naples. Spain came close to defeat. It was more than a year before don Juan the young bastard sailed in, routed the French and crushed the revolution in Naples by force of arms in the summer of 1648. Arcos was sent packing and even young don Juan was felt by Madrid to be too impulsive. Naples needed a professional.

Parthenope restored

In June 1649, the viceroy of Naples, Íñigo Vélez de Guevara, count of Oñate and Villamediana, who had been in office little more than a year, put on a show in the royal palace. It was a dramatized musical entertainment of a kind lately fashionable in Venice, and the viceroy was assisting at the birth of lyric opera in the city where it would be so splendidly at home. Unlike many of his forerunners, the viceroy Oñate was not known as a great lover or patron of the arts. His political importance, however, could hardly be overstated. He was *one of the last high-level politicians operating in the service of the Spanish Habsburgs.*

On this occasion the arts were useful to him. The entertainment was a way of taking minds off a search and destroy operation currently under way against those members of the Neapolitan aristocracy who had supported a failed move by France against Spanish power in Naples. *The flower of the nobility*—those who were not being hunted down—joined the viceroy and the archbishop, still the astute and powerful cardinal Filomarino, in the royal palace for a performance of *The Triumph of Parthenope.* A report from that year described a magnificently engineered scenography, offering a view of Naples and a familiar river, where *on the bank of the rippling Sebeto lay Parthenope deep in sleep, until roused by the clamorous sound of martial and musical instruments accompanied by warrior voices.* Awake, Parthenope launched into a lament in *recitativo* on the recent travails of Naples. The threatened French invasion had merely been a consequence of these more serious troubles. Then, it was reported, in the upper part of the scenery *a Heaven opened* and the audience saw Jupiter appear, surrounded by the other gods, and decide with them to send help to Parthenope in the form of *a sublime and worthy hero / A lord wise and just.* Some among the distinguished audience thought this might have been an allusion to the viceroy, count Oñate himself.

The Neapolitan élite were not the only ones enjoying themselves that June. People outside the palace were being catered for too, by the *Land of Cockaigne*. All over Europe the Tree of Cockaigne was part of the carnival festivities that preceded the austerities of Lent. It was basically a greasy pole with a couple of sausages tied to the top and whoever reached them first won the sausages. In Naples the Land of Cockaigne was always more elaborate, Naples having more poor people than anywhere else in Europe. The rewards were greater and so was the violence of the contest. The Land of Cockaigne involved painted scenery and an ersatz forest of trees, a complex construction usually described as *the Cockaigne machine*, bearing cheeses, hams, sausages and other delights in their upper branches. The mass assault on the food was a brawl that always ended in shed blood, broken bones and quite often deaths. It was an entertaining and reassuring sight for those who were not themselves hungry, and choreographed for laughs.

On this occasion in the summer of 1649 the viceroy, or his events managers and food stylists, opted for something a little more formal, a little more early baroque, in their offering to the poor of Naples. The court artists confected an artificial mountain modelled on the nearby Vesuvius,

at the summit of which a great cauldron could be seen boiling over with maccheroni and trickling down the mountain, at whose base were trees full of toffees, cheeses and hams, fountains of wine and ovens for pasta inhabited by dancing hunchbacks.

Deploying spectacle, drama and music, the viceroy's events people had the dispossessed of Naples process under a long pergola from which were hanging *cheeses made from cow's milk and sheep's milk, sucking pigs, hams and sides of bacon and different kinds of salame and sausage, all quite stunning to the mind.* Finally they arrived at another theatrical construction

> representing Hell, where Tantalus appeared . . . in torments of hunger and thirst. The whole thing was represented in music and when His Excellency passed it was transformed into a Paradise and Parthenope appeared singing many praises of His Excellency.

Whether the rich and abundant foods on display actually reached the Neapolitans who were led past them was not reported, though presumably something was doled out at the end of the lesson. There were no further plaints from Parthenope during the rest of Oñate's five year posting, and he returned to Spain heaped with imperial honours to continue a busy and successful political career into extreme old age. One of the things the viceroy may have been intending to take back to Spain, a little career trophy among many, a sentimental souvenir, was a splendid painting of the seething and prosperous *Market Place in Naples* by Domenico Gargiulo.

Oñate was an unsentimental man, no more interested in painting than he was in elaborately staged musical allegories, but he had a feel for the concrete and he understood image. He knew that in the long run a delightful and compelling representation of popular life in the capital he had administered would do far more for his standing in Madrid than a single performance of a pompous masque before a tiny hand-picked audience of his closest supporters. The viceroy, gazing with his functionaries at this pleasing scene, would have reflected that Micco Spadaro's painting projected a deeply reassuring image of his administration into other times or places. It showed the Spanish empire's Mediterranean capital as clearly busy, prosperous, stunningly beautiful and endlessly entertaining.

Oñate would have been gratified—and anyone knowing the Market would have been struck—by a detail close to the centre of the canvas and the eye's journey over the panorama, from the still life of root vegetables in the lower foreground to the volcano's blue cone in the distance. A graceful fountain, almost grand and oddly formal in a place where only the church was not utilitarian, commercial and temporary. It was unlike a larger and more practical fountain at the back, which offered people a place to drink and wash during a hot morning's work, and animals a place to drink. From a high and dainty central spout, the ornamental fountain's water spilled over a couple of shallow dishes into a pool at ground level, whose mythological figures in stone were hard to distinguish in the painting from the proletarians washing and wallowing at its edges. Oñate had personally commissioned both the service fountain at the back and the display spout in the centre and knew the *witty inscriptions* in praise of himself displayed on a sheet of marble in the middle of the prosperous bustle, and would have liked being reminded of them when he looked at the painting. He commissioned the fountain in 1653 from Cosimo Fanzago, and likely saw it inaugurated before returning to Spain at the end of that year. Gargiulo's painting was probably intended more as a souvenir of the fountain than of the trafficking going on all around it.

The viceroy's dainty fountain was a more portentous creation than it seemed. Fanzago had recycled marble from an earlier structure built on the same spot the year before Oñate arrived in Naples, also designed by Fanzago but never finished. Fanzago had abruptly left Naples in fear of his life and the new fountain commission showed that Oñate understood Fanzago had been caught in a difficult moment and that both viceroy and sculptor were now ready to move on. The fountain and its splashing marble gods represented closure. The unfinished earlier structure had not been a fountain. Its base had been a cuboid block about four meters high, three meters long and two meters deep. People had called it the *Epitaph* and it was the monument to people's rights in Naples that Masaniello had called Fanzago to discuss the night before he was murdered.

It survived in a painting of the Market from the same perspective as Gargiulo's *Market Place* and also painted by Gargiulo. Like the sculptor, the painter had worked at two distinct moments a few years apart. The painter's commission for the *Market Place*, like the sculptor's commission for the fountain it showed, let the painter, too, know that the viceroy understood how artists could be caught up in difficult moments, make wrong choices under pressure, and yet be forgiven by a benign and unmovable secular power. Gargiulo's painting of *Masaniello's Revolt* showed that just below the top of the completed part of Fanzago's *Epitaph*, a base for its never-made statues, ran a narrow ledge. On its two visible sides was a neatly aligned row of a dozen freshly severed heads.

The ledge looked almost designed to accommodate them. Nobody in the piazza was paying any particular attention to the row of heads, and hardly anyone to the naked corpse of a headless man hanging by his foot from a high pole planted in the dirt by the base of the *Epitaph*—Peppe Carafa of the most powerful family in Naples, caught and executed after the failed assassination of Masaniello. The people's stand against the feudal nobility had been even more of a shock to the system in Naples than their rising against the Spanish occupiers. It challenged a much older and more deeply rooted order. *I'm Giuseppe Carafa*, he'd said with uncomprehending arrogance when a nameless man cornered him in the street. *And I'm your executioner*, replied the other as he readied his knife. Fascinated by the moment of portentous violence, Gargiulo did a whiplash capriccio of it too, an image with Carafa's body at three different moments, dragged by shirtless Market boys, being decapitated, lying naked. And Carafa's head, with its aristocrat's long hair and moustache, waved on the end of a pike while Masaniello in his red cap spoke to the crowd from a platform not far off. Unlike Gargiulo's panorama of the pacified *Market Place*, neither *Masaniello's Revolt* nor the sketch of Carafa's severed head was taken to Spain.

The lost painters

In late 1991 an exhibition opened in the depths of the Castel Sant'Elmo, *Battistello Caracciolo and Early Naturalism in Naples*. The vast and splendid show afforded an incomparable look at the work of the elusive Caracciolo. At the time, all I noticed was the sheep.

The *Announcement* from Capodimonte was there. Right next to it was another *Announcement* by the same painter. This was a vertical treatment, and under the hovering children were essentially two figures, the half-dressed shepherd fully awake on the left and the fully dressed sleeper on the right. A third figure was in the shadows behind them, and the outlined head of a barely visible fourth. If the human presence was slightly diminished, the sheep's was radically increased. Here were not two but five plump herbivores, and they had pushed their way to the centre of the picture, all intent on eating. If the human had overtaken the sacred in one painting, here the human was displaced and almost marginalized by the thrusting, busy sheep whose pulsing grey backs compelled your gaze. Nearby was a *Wedding Feast of Jacob and Rachel*—or perhaps *Jacob Asking Laban for Rachel to Be His Wife*—in which several of the guests were recognizable from the other paintings. It was an austere and intimate open-air pastoral gathering, and as if to make this clear, three large sheep, who also seemed familiar, were pushing their way into view from the right, in front of the wedding guests, noses to the ground.

There were some sheepless paintings too by this artist, individual half-figures of the working people from his larger canvases, or others like them. The unknown Master was working what had been Ribera's vein, with no less intensity: country people displaced to the city, gaunt, bearded, sometimes wild-eyed or toothless, given an inalienable dignity. They didn't need the names of philosophers or saints to have the painter project their inner life. There was a mousy, wistful

Girl Sniffing a Rose, perhaps part of this Master's go at the *Five Senses*. The painter laid on the paint with dour brilliance, as if it were sun, sweat, rain, grease, dirt, blood on the skin of the people who lived around sheep. Not on show that night were an *Announcement* stored in Munich (three smaller and more hesitant sheep at the centre), an *Announcement* in New Jersey which later visited Australia (three alert and curious sheep at the centre), an *Announcement* in New York (three large and hungry sheep at the centre) which I only saw in photographs, but all these *Announcements* were the work of the same unknown Master of the *Announcements*.

And they were only the beginning. There was a whole series of images from *Genesis*, like the one from Aix-en-Provence in the show that night. Some years later, from across a vast space in the regional gallery at Palermo, I recognized the Master's unmistakeable hand in a painting of *Jacob and Laban's Flock*, from the same Jacob group and featuring no fewer than six highly individualized sheep at the centre, one lazily resting its head on another's back, with the half-dressed shepherd from the Naples painting and most of the others. The pony was from Naples and Rachel was the mousy girl with the rose. In photographs I found another *Jacob and Laban's Flock* from Rome (two boys, one man, and five sheep who filled nearly half the canvas), a lost *Joseph and His Brothers* (thirteen closely packed men and boys plus four sheep who took up a third of the space). The daylight Old Testament scenes in the open air did not all have sheep. It was a strange kind of open air, different from the gilded blue luminosity of Ribera's late ventures outdoors. Gatherings of muddy farmers and their families—always the communal group, never the individual protagonists, sometimes with their animals, sometimes not—were seen darkly from low down, looming against a livid wintry sky. The paintings transposed the pastoral life of ancient Palestine to the not so different pastoral life of seventeenth century southern Italy. They too showed a life that required no imported sense of value or meaning. They were great paintings on their own account.

The man who painted sheep also did smaller and sheepless paintings. His philosophers and saints, like Ribera's, took old men deeply marked by work, weather and life to embody the life of the mind. There were a lot more philosophers than saints, and some everyday figures like a *Schoolmaster* and a *Lute Player*, who looked no different. Beside these—scabby cracked skin on the back of a hand, the clotted clumps of unbrushed hair and untrimmed beard, the dirt-filled wrinkles of a scaly neck, a face's blotchy skin, complexions made puffy and livid by sickness—Ribera's skeletal oldies seemed polished and generic. The Master's paint was applied like layers of hard experience blasted on to the bodies. There was none of that sense you sometimes found in Ribera—in a subject's uncomprehending stare, an old man's open mouth—that people were being transformed to visual phenomena, into forms and textures outside their own being. These people seemed open and unguarded, living and not facing the painter, as if unaware of his presence.

The human potential of these postures and these averted looks showed when the painter extended this intimate art into smallish horizontal easel paintings of several half-figures. Certain biblical moments—the *Prodigal Son's Return, Jesus*

338

among the Doctors—he did over and over, not like assembly-line martyrdoms but like Cézanne's apples, trying to render something that was eluding him. He did at least four closely similar versions of the *Prodigal Son's Return*, paintings of three half-figures, variously reduced by life but not diminished, the old father and the son bending down to kiss his hand, watched by a third person close behind them. In an overwhelming version, the third figure was the mother, her face convulsed in a laugh of joy changing into a howl. It was another painting that made you think of a moment in *King Lear*, father and daughter reconciled before they died.

> . . . Do not laugh at me,
> For (as I am a man) I thinke this Lady
> To be my child *Cordelia*
> And ſo I am: I am.

Everything else in *Lear* was forgotten in the moment of recognition and forgiveness. In the *Prodigal Son*, the three poorly dressed people seen close up against a blank wall would move anyone with no idea of its subject. *Jesus among the Doctors* always showed aggressive and not very bright religious academics bunched on the side of the canvas and facing off against a Christ in early adolescence, neither child nor man and in no way ideal, a graceless unformed teenager holding his own against the lumpy-faced oldies. They looked like family quarrels. These paintings were so stripped down, so nakedly close and unrelenting that they made the shepherds' floating babies and their modest flurry of fabric look like high baroque artifice.

In 1622 a painter from Apulia moved to Naples with his family from their home near Bari. The painter was nearly sixty and making the move for the sake of his two sons, who were twenty and ten, the elder already a painter like his father and the younger almost ready to begin an apprenticeship. Within a few years both brothers were working in Ribera's studio and the younger, whose name was Francesco Fracanzano, had real and original talent. At twenty he married Salvator Rosa's sister Giovanna and three years later he won a major commission for an important church in Naples, for a group of scenes from the life of the man for which San Gregorio Armeno was named.

When Fracanzano was seventeen, another boy arrived from Apulia to learn painting in Naples. Bartolomeo Passante was eleven years old and came from Brindisi. He went to live in the house on Via Toledo of Pietro Beato, the painter he was apprenticed to. In 1636, when he was eighteen, Passante married the painter's niece, and the moment of setting up his own household was probably when Passante went to work in Ribera's busy studio. He was the man who painted sheep.

It was the year after Fracanzano did his stunningly mature first work at San Gregorio Armeno. Fracanzano was perhaps still working for Ribera when Passante arrived. Whether or not the twenty-four-year-old and the eighteen-year-old from Apulia made friends, the *Gregorio Armeno* paintings burnt themselves into the younger man's mind. The dark, hulking groups Fracanzano painted of the killers, who were seen from low down and silhouetted against lowering stormy skies, so that some of their faces were completely and frighteningly obscured as they looked down at the viewer, were the visual model Passante worked from when he drew on childhood memories of sheep-farming and transhumance in Apulia—as he must have—to paint Old Testament pastoral life. If people thought Passante's painting looked like Fracanzano's—as they still do—they thought it looked even more like Ribera's. From a hundred years later and another world, Bernardo De Dominici groped back to distinguish the student's work from the master's.

> He is so like Ribera that anyone who wants to recognize him has to be very familiar with their styles. His composition and gestures are very like his master's, and even more so is the tremendously thick texture of his paint.

Ribera thought Passante *turned out so well under his guidance that he got Passante to paint many of the works people ordered from other parts of Italy and abroad.*

Which was why so few of his paintings stayed in Naples. Passante, one of the great visionary painters of the seventeenth century, died when he was thirty, when Naples was still in revolt against the Spanish. He did a great many paintings in his short time: about fifty survived to the present, maybe more, done in little over a decade. But Bartolomeo Passante came from the sticks, died young and his paintings were elsewhere, and after death his identity in Naples was blurred. His work got confused with Ribera's and with his slightly older contemporaries', Fracanzano's and Dò's. Years passed and his name was confused in the inventories with a very minor painter's called Bassante. He nearly vanished altogether.

Toward the end of the twentieth century a painting turned up from somewhere, done about three hundred and fifty years before. It was sold by Sotheby's in Monaco and apparently went to Paris, its final destination thereafter as obscure as its origins. It showed a painter at work, who despite thick white hair and beard was not really old but strongly built and vigorous. Seated bare-legged and barefoot and wearing a short old work tunic, he was beginning work on a large still life of a metaphysical kind, like the haunting images of dusty musical instruments that Evaristo Baschenis was starting to paint in Lombardy at this time. Disposed in front of him on a small table covered with a richly patterned rug were a lute lying upside-down on a violin, some sheet music propped open behind the instruments, and heaped behind and above these a trumpet, a big closed folio, an antique bust of a child, a candlestick, a laurel wreath and a skull.

The painter, grasping a palette and touching the canvas with his brush, was looking at neither the objects he was painting nor at his unfinished image of them, but very fixedly at another and smaller figure sitting on the floor and almost lost in the shadow of the canvas's bottom left corner. This was a boy of about fifteen, dressed in black and wearing a black skull cap, with a sheet of paper and a board on his knees, making a red chalk drawing of the painter at work. A warm light from the left invested the painter, played delicately over the heaped objects and barely delineated the boy. The two intent motionless figures were the picture's diagonal poles. A near-smile played on the absorbed boy's face as he worked

342

in the shadow, the distracted painter's downward gaze was almost a glare. The muted subversive presence of the boy shot an electric tension across the image. Yet there was still room for the beauty of the still life, and of the still life of the still life, and for the comedy of the unexpected.

A signature was abraded and illegible except for its first letter, *B*, and the canvas was apparently painted in *the early 1630s* or *a few years after* 1632. In 1632 Bartolomeo Passante was fourteen and apprenticed to Pietro Beato in Via Toledo, who was perhaps a still-life man. The tension between people and things in the painting, as subjects of art, showed in the white-haired man's baffled frown at finding himself painter and painted at once. Was he Pietro Beato, master as model, or a model representing Passante's former master? The same white-haired man appeared as *The Schoolmaster* and in a painting of *Alexis*, a teacher and a father, and he was the forerunner of the whole school of tough and weatherbeaten grey-bearded men who were Passante's philosophers and shepherds.

The Painter's Studio was a meditation on the painter as a man poised between life and art, full of that seventeenth century dramatized imaginative intelligence that culminated twenty years later in Velázquez's *Meninas* and his *Spinners*. It was also a polite and gently teasing declaration of independence by a boy who was going to paint real life and not still life. On a folded sheet of paper lying on the floor by the painter's foot were the words *ANCORA IMPARO*. The old painter was *still learning* because the smiling boy in the corner had a thing or two to teach him. And Ribera too. Passante the painter really began with Ribera and he became *in my view greater than the master*. Roberto Longhi ventured this in 1935 and took care to repeat his daring opinion thirty-four years later. But the tragic realist Bartolomeo Passante announced himself with a smiling polemic.

Overdoing it as usual, Bernardo De Dominici had it that painters in Naples, *excellent in their fields, but lacking judgement*, went around carrying out revenge killings against the occupying Spanish military. A couple of Spanish soldiers had killed a relative of Falcone's in a street skirmish and Falcone, a *swordsman and street fighter* in his younger days, went out with his art students to avenge the killing. The fight left two young painters dead. After that, the painters picked off Spanish soldiers in hit and run attacks. The group's leaders were Falcone, Rosa and Gargiulo. In 1647 these three were forty, thirty-two and thirty-eight, perhaps a bit past the age of street fighting. The younger Fracanzano was thirty-five and close to this group. De Dominici claimed that after Spain's normalization Fracanzano *broke down completely* and, *out of his mind*, tried to incite a new rising against the Spanish, nearly ten years after the first. Oñate sentenced both brothers to hang for sedition. Francesco, *as a mark of professional respect and also to put an end to the tiresome pleas of people begging for his release*, was poisoned in the Castelnuovo.

Under the rhetorical crust of his overdetermined detail, De Dominici convinces. Aniello Falcone drew—with a little help from Leonardo and Michelangelo—a portrait sketch of *Masaniello* shouting in a call to arms, the most thrillingly real of all the visual records of Masaniello, in no way incompatible with Onofrio Palumbo's careful naive full-length rendering of *Masaniello* seen from below, gracefully standing like a barefoot dancer in his fisherman's canvas trousers and red stocking cap, against a low dreamlike panorama of Naples that might have been done by one Monsù Desiderio or the other. Salvator Rosa exalted Masaniello's achievement in his satire on *War. Today a low fisherman lays down the law to kings.* Domenico Gargiulo painted vivid and truthful images of the events at the Market in the days of Masaniello. What Passante did or might have done nobody knew. A few months after Masaniello, he too was dead. Only Ribera, prisoner of *Hispanidad*, lived through the revolution as a hostage in the royal palace.

X

Coda

Greek city

Streets in Naples are not a good place to run. Some of them were laid out nearly three thousand years ago. They can deal with more traffic than they were built for—a few Greeks, a few slaves, a few sheep and goats and a few mules—but with difficulty. The foot traffic and the traffic on wheels in the ancient centre are hard to avoid even if you get out early. The streets themselves are very narrow. This was fine for a couple of thousand years, until motor transport did for them, the motor scooters and the three-wheeled delivery vans that can go anywhere. But returning to Naples a few years ago I had an impulse to run there, as I had every day many years before, though I now had to take a shorter route along some inconvenient streets.

The old streets of Naples are paved in big blocks of black *piperno*, the hardened lava of Vesuvius. They glisten like molten tar when it rains. The blocks are irregular, worn and rounded and so are the larger shifting planes of the street. Your foot always touches ground at a different angle, there's always a curved surface to turn your ankle as the foot takes your weight. It is murder to run here, even in early morning, even when the stones aren't wet with rain or slippery underfoot with sudden smears of fruit or vegetable or worse. But this is where I had to go. The narrow street ran straight as a die over sharp hills and ridges. It was laid out by the Greeks along with a parallel decumano a hundred yards or so south and another to the north, and all are in daily use. These fine straight lines defined the grid of ancient and modern Naples. The street ran downhill to the huge and massively buttressed Castel Capuano at the eastern edge of the old city, where the law courts were which gave Via Tribunali its name. And which housed, until not so long before, the city jail.

I was starting out from a little piazza halfway along, small and easy to miss, though at its centre was Cosimo Fanzago's ornate phallic *guglia* with a statue of Gennaro at the top of the obelisk, erected after Gennaro saved Naples from Vesuvius in 1631. It took six years to start work on it and nearly thirty years of disputes and unpleasantness to finish, but everyone loved what they saw when it was uncovered. At the back of the piazza was a wall of tufo with clumps of weeds growing out of it and steps behind a pair of high iron gates held shut by a rusty chain and padlock, which were the back way in to the chapel of Gennaro's treasure. Opposite the piazzetta on its only open side a dark porch fronted the home of Merisi's *Seven Works*. I turned right into Via Tribunali and headed uphill past church after church on the narrow street. It opened out a bit where the forum had been thousands of years ago, at the great medieval church of San Lorenzo Maggiore, where Boccaccio met Fiammetta, and San Paolo Maggiore, built in the sixteenth century using the eight great pillars of a Roman temple which had preceded it. Hidden down a narrow alley leading to the lower Greek decumano was San Gregorio Armeno, and just ahead San Pietro a Majella and the music conservatory.

At half past six on a May morning the air was bright with sun in Naples, but even in dankest winter people would be moving silently in the dark. Hot breaths of new bread and pastries were exhaled from half-shuttered doorways. Vans arrived, shop shutters rattled up and the first fresh mozzarellas were carried into *salumerie*. Out of side lanes small old people headed purposefully on foot to some inscrutable destination, each with a plastic bag in hand. Always a large full plastic bag well tied at the top. Food? Clothes? The old women seemed headed for the little church just ahead on the right, Santa Maria of the Souls in Purgatory, a place where they could feel at home, small and intimate, with four bronze skulls and thigh bones on stone pillars waist-high in front of the church, in front of the grate with the wilting flowers and the glimmering candles inside. The skulls were polished to a high sheen by the caress of passing hands. One had split and caved in after centuries of touch, and the cavity was reinforced with some rough filler whose greasy sheen looked like brains inside the crumpled cranium. The souls in purgatory substitute the actual skulls and bones in deep crypts elsewhere, that old women with more time could polish and talk to.

349

The street widened at another great medieval church. San Pietro a Majella surged at the road's real end, where traffic took a kink and narrowed into a dim alley of bookshops and music shops. The conservatory at San Pietro a Majella was silent as I passed, but soon the sound of baroque instruments would be bouncing and echoing around the stone walls outside. In the fifteenth century it was Europe's first music school, born out of orphanages and the need to train the orphans in some skill. A narrow passage on the right led to a narrow garden with a statue of Bellini near some musical instrument shops. In a pit were mossy blocks of stone from the Greek city walls. A few feet ahead was a wall of buildings. A street of more music shops fell away sharply and narrowly to the left and rose more grandly on the right as Via Costantinopoli, lined with old bookstores and leading to the eighteenth century cavalry stables where the antiquities were housed. Beyond the archeological museum were the famous and violent quarters of the Sanità and Stella, the ancient Christian catacombs, the palace and the wood and the paintings at Capodimonte and the hills beyond the city.

There was an archway in the wall of houses opposite. Port'Alba led into a kind of tunnel through the buildings above it and into the vast and sunny semicircle of a strangely bleak piazza. When the viceroy Alba built this last of the city gates in 1625, this space was a market place outside the walls and in 1656 they brought the dead and dying here in their tens of thousands when Naples was emptied by the plague. Nearly all the painters died. Gargiulo survived to paint the heaped bodies. In the eighteenth century it was given a splendid neoclassical makeover by Vanvitelli and in the nineteenth it was dedicated to Dante. From the city gate it was downhill all the way. I sped across the glittering surface of the piazza, among the scattered and dazzled figures making random tracks across its new postmodern emptiness. The people with plastic bags were younger here and going to work. Now I pounded down Toledo. Down from Piazza Carità, past the serried banks and the shops, scattering the council workers standing around with brooms, down past San Carlo and the endless royal palace and the vast now empty space in front of it. Then out of the urban darkness, the intoxicating vastness of blue sky, bluer sea, the bay sweeping to the mountain cone and jagged Capri out on the edge of the water. My heart leapt yet again at the rush of blue.

To the water. I was now running past Santa Lucia—fishermen and contrabbandieri all gone—and around the base of Pizzofalcone, the hollow promontory of Mount Echia where the Greeks had first landed their boats, and past the tiny island of Megaris, now joined to the mainland and covered by the Castel dell'Ovo. I would round the *Broken Column* and turn away from the sea up Via Chiaia, along the inland side of Pizzofalcone's base. The Broken Column—broken I think in ancient times—stood above the water by the eighteenth century sewer outlet. This handsome construction, after long neglect, had lately collapsed in a winter storm and its great stone blocks now lay in an abandoned jumble. Rounding the point, I was in shadow again. The sun had come over the shoulder of Vesuvius but Pizzofalcone obscured it here.

As I ran along the water's edge toward the Broken Column I noticed a lady of a certain age moving in the shadow on a large flat rock below, beside the ruined sewer mouth. She was

A chronology

of some events mentioned in this book

1300 BC circa

Bronze Age inhabitants of the island of Ischia in the bay of Naples trade with Mycenaean Greeks.

750 BC circa

Greek colonists from Euboea settle on Ischia and on the mainland at Cuma.

700 BC circa

Homer writes the *Odyssey*.

Greek settlers from Cuma establish the settlement of Parthenope at Mount Echia on the water's edge of modern Santa Lucia in Naples.

530 BC circa

Pozzuoli is founded by Greek settlers from Samos.

470 BC circa

The Cuman settlers found the *new city* of Neapolis alongside Palepolis—the *old city* of Parthenope—and combine the two into a single walled city.

326 BC

The Romans take Naples, which becomes a Greek-speaking ally of Rome.

194 BC

The Romans refound Pozzuoli.

90 BC *circa*

The Romans grant full citizenship to the people of Naples and Campania, and develop the bay area; Pozzuoli becomes the major port for Roman grain supplies, diminishing Naples.

73 BC

The Thracian slave gladiator Spartacus leads a group of followers in a break for freedom at Capua; it grows into a mass revolt against Rome of slaves and serfs in Campania and Italy.

71 BC

Spartacus is killed in battle and his slave rebellion defeated.

45 BC

Virgil moves to Naples for the rest of his life.

31 BC

The thirteen years of civil war in Italy that follow the murder of Julius Caesar in 44 BC end in victory for Octavian, who four years later becomes the emperor Augustus.

19 BC

Virgil dies at Brindisi and is buried in Naples: the *Aeneid* is published.

20 AD *circa*

Tiberius, successor to Augustus as emperor, builds a huge villa on Capri and spends much time there.

50 AD *circa*

Naples grows to a city of thirty thousand people.

59 AD

Nero follows up an unsuccessful attempt to drown his mother in the bay of Naples with a successful murder at home.

64

Nero builds his Golden House in Rome on several hundred acres cleared by fire and makes his lyric début in Naples.

65 circa

Petronius writes his *Satyricon*, of which the surviving fragment is set in southern Italy and mostly in Pozzuoli or Naples.

66

Facing death from Nero, Petronius kills himself in a leisurely manner.

79

Vesuvius erupts catastrophically, burying Pompeii and Herculaneum near its base.

86

Martial publishes his first epigrams in Rome: after twelve years and twelve books he goes home to Spain.

150 circa

Lucius Apuleius, a Berber born in the Roman colony of today's Algeria, writes his *Metamorphoses*, also known as *The Golden Ass*, the one wholly surviving Latin novel of the ancient Mediterranean and source, model or inspiration for—among those mentioned in this book—Boccaccio, Cervantes and Basile.

180 circa

Jewish and other Middle Eastern trading communities move from Pozzuoli to Naples, whose economy flourishes.

250

The Romans begin systematic repression of Christians.

305 circa

The early Christian activist Gennaro is beheaded outside Pozzuoli.

Romulus Augustulus, last Roman emperor in the West, is exiled to Naples by the Goths and dies on Megaris.

553

The Byzantines defeat the Goths in war and gain control of Naples, which becomes an independent dukedom allied to Byzantium and heavily pressed by Lombards on land and raiders from Turkey and North Africa at sea.

1139

The Normans under Roger II in Sicily conquer Naples and end its autonomy as a dukedom.

1224

The emperor Frederick II founds Europe's first lay university in Naples.

1250

Frederick II dies.

1266

The Angevins from southern France occupy southern Italy and make Naples their capital, transforming it from one of many southern coastal cities to a major centre of power in Italy.

1268

Conradin, last of the Hohenstaufen, is beheaded in the Market Place in Naples at fifteen.

1272

Thomas Aquinas teaches in Naples for two years.

1279

The Angevins start building the Castelnuovo as the king's residence in Naples, and finish five years later; they also build San Lorenzo Maggiore.

1283

Work begins on the church and convent of San Domenico Maggiore, completed forty years later.

1306

Dante begins writing his *Comedy*, in which Virgil guides him through the underworlds of Hell and Purgatory.

1325

Giovanni Boccaccio arrives in Naples, now a city of forty thousand people, at the age of twelve; he lives in the city for fifteen years, until financial crisis forces his return to Florence in 1340.

1348

Boccaccio begins to write the *Decameron* in Florence's plague year and completes it three or five years later.

1362

Hoping to find a position at the Angevin court, Boccaccio returns to Naples in a humiliating and disastrous revisiting of the places of his youth; he will describe the experience in a savage book-length letter to a friend the following year.

1380 circa

The anonymous *Chronicle of Parthenope* is written.

1389

Gennaro's blood liquefies for the first time.

1442

The Aragonese of north-eastern Spain supplant the Angevins in Naples and their king Alfonso V sets up his court there.

Naples is now a city of a hundred thousand people.

1443

Alfonso becomes king of the Two Sicilies and rebuilds the Castelnuovo.

1458

Alfonso dies and is succeeded as king of Naples by his son Ferdinando I, known in Naples as don Ferrante.

1480

Gennaro's lost remains are accidentally rediscovered and sent to Naples.

1486

After the failure of the barons' plot against Ferrante, he invites the principals to a dynastic wedding in the Castelnuovo, seizes and executes them.

1493

Columbus sees three mermaids on his Atlantic crossing.

1494

Ferrante dies and his successors follow in rapid sequence as the Aragonese dynasty disintegrates.

1495

French armies invade Italy and temporarily occupy Naples; defeated in battle by the Spanish they withdraw from Italy.

1503

Naples is occupied by the Spanish military under Gonzalo Fernández de Córdoba, and will remain a Spanish possession for over two hundred years.

1504

The Barbarossa brothers launch naval war against Catholic power in Italy and the central Mediterranean.

1505

Neapolitans riot over food prices.

1508

Neapolitans riot over food prices.

1510

Giovanna duchess of Amalfi and her bourgeois lover Antonio Bologna leave Amalfi for the North, where they and their children are both later murdered by her brothers.

1520

Dragut joins the Barbarossas' fleet.

1527

Rome is sacked by Charles V's Spanish and German mercenaries.

Neapolitans promise Gennaro a chapel for his remains, in thanks for his ending an epidemic.

The painter Polidoro Caldara moves from Rome to Naples.

1534

Hayreddin Barbarossa takes Capri and threatens Rome.

1535

The emperor Charles V visits Naples; his remembered promise of autonomy will be at issue in the insurrection of 1647.

1536

The Spanish viceroy Pedro de Toledo has a major new road built in Naples and named after himself; it is part of a new system of reinforced fortifications for Naples as the centre of Spain's war against Turkey in the Mediterranean.

The mulberry plantations of the Neapolitan silk industry on the hill above Via Toledo are replaced by a housing development to quarter the occupation troops; the Spanish Quarters become the centre of prostitution in Naples, and will remain so for nearly five hundred years.

1543

Polidoro Caldara is robbed and murdered in Messina.

1547

Naples revolts against the threatened introduction of the Spanish Inquisition.

Dragut sacks Malta.

1548

Giordano Bruno is born in Nola near Naples.

1551

Galeazzo Caracciolo becomes a Protestant and abandons Naples for Geneva.

1552

Dragut several times defeats Catholic fleets in the bay of Naples.

1553

Pedro de Toledo dies.

Calvin orders the dissident Spanish intellectual Miguel Serveto burnt in Geneva.

1557

The Spanish state is bankrupt.

1558

Giovambattista Della Porta publishes the first edition of his book *Natural Magic*.

1560

The Spanish state is bankrupt.

1561

Dragut's fleet blockades Naples.

Spanish forces massacre thousands of men, women and children in Calabria as heretics.

1562

Bruno is sent to Naples to study at fourteen.

1564

Gian Francesco Alois, Protestant friend of Galeazzo Caracciolo, is beheaded and burnt with another dissident at the Market in Naples.

Calvin dies in Geneva.

1565

Dragut is killed in the long siege of Malta.

Bruno becomes a Dominican novice in Naples at seventeen.

1566

Michele Ghislieri marks his election as pope Pius V by burning fifteen heretics in Rome.

Giovambattista Della Porta publishes *The Art of Remembering* in Naples.

1568

Tommaso Campanella is born in Stilo in Calabria.

Luigi Tansillo, author of the *Grape Harvester*, dies.

Bruno is taken to Rome to demonstrate the art of memory to pope Ghislieri.

1570 *circa*

Belisario Corenzio arrives in Naples from Greece at twelve.

Miguel de Cervantes begins five years' service as a marine in the Spanish armed forces based in Naples.

1571

Catholic navies destroy the Islamic navies at Lepanto in the Gulf of Corinth. Cervantes loses the use of his left hand in the battle.

Michelangelo Merisi is born in Milan to parents from Caravaggio.

1575

Giambattista Basile is born at Posillipo.

Bruno graduates in theology with a thesis on Thomas Aquinas.

Returning to Spain from Naples, Cervantes is captured by Islamic corsairs and spends five years as a slave in Algiers.

The Spanish state is bankrupt.

1576

Facing arrest by the Inquisition, Bruno flees Naples and Rome.

1578

Giovan Battista Caracciolo is born in Naples.

1579

Bruno arrives in Geneva and is imprisoned for libel; released some weeks later, he immediately leaves for France.

Della Porta is investigated by the Inquisition in Naples for his studies of natural phenomena.

1581

After two years teaching in Toulouse, Bruno is forced by religious conflict to move to Paris.

1582

Cardinal Paleotti lays down the law on what may and what may not be painted in sacred and profane art, and on how what may be painted may and may not be painted.

1583

In Paris, Bruno teaches the art of memory to king Henri III and publishes his play *Candleman* and several works in Latin on memory and philosophy; then he moves to London, writes other works in Latin and lectures at Oxford.

1585

Neapolitans protest against bread prices and kill and castrate city administrator Starace for speculating in wheat; mass reprisals follow: dozens are sentenced to torture and death, hundreds imprisoned or banished; twelve thousand others flee Naples in fear of arrest.

After publishing in London five philosophical dialogues in Italian Bruno returns to Paris.

1586

Authorities try and fail to evict the Dominicans by force from one of their convents in Naples.

Bruno antagonizes Paris intellectuals with a lecture on Aristotle and in a politically dangerous moment leaves for Germany.

Galeazzo Caracciolo dies in Geneva.

Della Porta publishes his book *On Human Physiognomy*.

1587

Bruno teaches for two years at the University of Wittenberg.

1588

Spain's *Invincible Armada*—including four galleys and ten companies of infantry drummed up from Naples—is wrecked off the English coast in a failed invasion attempt.

Bruno moves to Prague but fails to find a post there.

The naturalist philosopher Bernardino Telesio dies at Cosenza in Calabria.

1589

In Helmstadt, Bruno publishes several works on magic.

Campanella arrives in Naples at twenty-one and meets Della Porta among other scientific thinkers.

1590

Bruno moves to Frankfurt and writes three philosophical works.

Della Porta publishes a second and much amplified edition of *Natural Magic*, containing new discussions of optics and physics, including the telescope, the camera obscura and magnetism.

1591

Bruno publishes several philosophical works, writes others, is expelled from Frankfurt and moves to Zurich, where he teaches philosophy; in autumn he accepts an invitation to teach the art of memory in Venice.

Hunger riots break out in Naples at the end of summer.

1592

Bruno is reported to the Inquisition by his private student and arrested in Venice.

Campanella is confined in San Domenico Maggiore for defending Telesio's materialist philosophy; ordered to return to Calabria, he heads north to Rome and Florence and beyond.

1593

Bruno is extradited to Rome.

Campanella meets Galileo in Padua and Della Porta in Venice.

1594

Luigi Rodriguez arrives from Palermo in Sicily to paint in Naples at the age of fourteen.

Campanella is arrested by the Inquisition and after attempting to escape is extradited to Rome.

1595

A siege of San Domenico Maggiore in Naples by papal and Spanish forces fails to expel the monks and is abandoned.

1596

The Spanish state is bankrupt.

1597

Campanella is released and ordered back to Calabria; he makes a lengthy stop in Naples on the way.

1599

Campanella leads a failed revolution in Calabria.

After seven years as prisoner of the Inquisition in Rome Bruno definitively refuses to abjure his heretical beliefs.

1600

Bruno is burnt alive in Rome.

Michelangelo Merisi da Caravaggio makes his public début in Rome with his *Matthew* paintings.

Naples reaches a population of around three hundred thousand.

1601

Campanella is tried for sedition in Naples, tortured, found mad and imprisoned indefinitely.

1602

Campanella writes *The City of the Sun* in a dungeon of the Castelnuovo.

1605

Cervantes publishes the first part of *Don Quixote* in Madrid.

1606

Merisi arrives in Naples in the autumn after fleeing a murder charge in Rome, and completes his *Seven Works of Mercy* in January 1607.

1607

The Spanish state is bankrupt.

Merisi moves to Malta and later Sicily.

1608

Work begins on Gennaro's chapel in Naples.

Basile resigns his military commission in Venice and returns to Naples.

1609

Merisi returns to Naples and is attacked and nearly killed on arrival.

The painter Luigi Rodriguez dies at thirty.

1610

Merisi leaves Naples for Rome and disappears.

1611

The painter Artemisia Gentileschi is raped at eighteen in Rome by her father's colleague, the painter Agostino Tassi.

1613

Cervantes publishes his *Exemplary Stories*, including *Corner Boy and Little Cutter*.

1614

Battistello Caracciolo visits Orazio Gentileschi in Rome.

1615

Cervantes publishes the second part of *Don Quixote*.

1616

The Spanish painter Jusepe de Ribera arrives in Naples at twenty-five and will stay until his death in 1652.

Galileo is investigated by the Inquisition; Campanella writes a *Defence of Galileo* from prison.

Cervantes dies in Madrid at sixty-nine.

1618

Bartolomeo Passante is born in Brindisi in Apulia.

1619

The Spanish viceroy Osuña, seeking alliance with the bourgeoisie in his struggle against the local barons, appoints the lawyer Giulio Genoino people's representative in the city administration.

1620

Madrid recalls the viceroy Osuña from Naples.

Wanted for treason, Genoino flees Naples by sea, is overtaken, arrested and tried in Madrid.

Tommaso Aniello d'Amalfi, known as Masaniello, is born at the Market in Naples.

1622

Guido Reni arrives in Naples on commission to decorate Gennaro's chapel, and leaves immediately after his servant is attacked.

Belisario Corenzio is arrested for ordering an attack on Reni's servant but released for lack of evidence.

After time in prison in Madrid and Naples, Genoino is sentenced to life imprisonment in a Spanish fortress on the coast of Morocco.

1626

After twenty-six years in prison, Campanella is released from the Castelnuovo by the Spanish; almost immediately he is seized by the Inquisition and transferred to their prison in Rome for another three years.

Ribera and Caracciolo are witnesses at the wedding in Naples of Juan Do.

1627

The Spanish state is bankrupt.

1629

Bartolomeo Passante arrives in Naples at eleven to become an apprentice painter with the otherwise unknown Pietro Beato.

1630

Artemisia Gentileschi moves to Naples.

1631

The viceroy Alcalá commissions Ribera to paint the bearded lady of the Abruzzi, Magdalena Venturi, with her husband and her youngest child.

Domenico Zampieri arrives in Naples on commission to decorate Gennaro's chapel.

Vesuvius erupts, killing three thousand people and threatening Naples.

1632

The painter Francesco Fracanzano marries the painter Salvator Rosa's sister.
Giambattista Basile dies in an epidemic.

1633

Galileo is found guilty of heresy and his works are placed on the Index.

1634

Campanella moves to Paris and is received by cardinal Richelieu and Louis XIII.

Adriana Basile begins publishing her brother's *Story of Stories*.

1635

Battistello Caracciolo dies at fifty-seven.

Jacques Callot dies in Nancy at forty-three.

Genoino is reprieved and released from prison.

1636

The last volume of Basile's *Story of Stories* is published in Naples by his sister Adriana.

The painter Bartolomeo Passante marries at eighteen and joins Ribera's studio.

1637

Work is completed on Gennaro's chapel.

1638

Artemisia Gentileschi visits her father Orazio in England and helps him work on his royal commissions.

1639

Genoino, now in his seventies, is allowed to return to Naples.

The viceroy Medina begins raising revenue for Spain through the Neapolitan financier Bartolomeo Aquino.

Campanella dies in Paris.

1640 circa

Ribera's health breaks down around the time he turns fifty.

1641

Zampieri dies in Naples, perhaps poisoned, his work on Gennaro's chapel unfinished.

At twenty-one Masaniello marries the sixteen-year-old Market girl Bernardina Pisa.

1642

Civil war begins in England and Artemisia returns to Naples.

Cosimo Fanzago designs the vast Palazzo Donn'Anna on the water at Posillipo for Anna Carafa, the viceroy Medina's Neapolitan wife: it will be left uncompleted.

Galileo dies.

1644

The viceroy Medina is recalled to Madrid.

1646

Unable to raise the revenue demanded by Madrid, the admiral of Castille resigns as viceroy of Naples in February and is replaced by the duke of Arcos.

Gennaro's Chapel of the Treasure is opened.

Belisario Corenzio dies at eighty-eight.

1647

Arcos reimposes on fruit, staple food of the Neapolitan poor, a sales tax which had been abolished twenty-five years before.

Genoino makes contact with Masaniello in the spring to discuss action against the new tax.

In the other Spanish vicerealm of Sicily, Palermo revolts against Spanish taxes and spurs preparations for protest in Naples.

Masaniello leads a popular uprising against Spanish misgovernment in Naples and is murdered after eight days.

Peppe Carafa, of the powerful baronial family, is killed and beheaded in the Market Place.

Ribera and his family take refuge in the royal palace.

After Masaniello's death the movement radicalizes into a struggle against Spanish rule and spreads to the provinces of the vicerealm.

1648

The painter Bartolomeo Passante dies at thirty.

French forces led by the duke of Guise land along the coast around Naples and are routed at the end of summer by Spanish forces under the king's son don Juan, who also crushes the insurrection in Naples, more than a year after its beginning.

1649

Charles I of England is beheaded.

1650

The population of Naples is around half a million.

1652

Ribera dies.

1653

Artemisia dies.

1656

A plague epidemic kills most of the people in Naples, including the painters Juan Do, Aniello Falcone, Massimo Stanzione, Bernardo Cavallino, Pacecco De Rosa and perhaps Francesco Fracanzano; Domenico Gargiulo survives and paints the heaps of corpses.

1674

Gaspare Roomer, financier and art collector, dies.

1692

Carlo Celano publishes his *Information on the Beautiful, the Ancient and the Curious in the City of Naples*.

1725

Bernardo De Dominici begins writing his *Lives of Neapolitan Painters, Sculptors and Architects*.

1745

De Dominici finishes publishing the three volumes of his *Lives*.

1799

The Parthenopean Republic is declared and crushed by the Bourbon monarchy a few months later with the help of Nelson and the Royal Navy; over a hundred leaders and intellectuals of the Neapolitan bourgeoisie are executed at the Market and many hundreds more imprisoned for life or exiled.

Masaniello's remains are stolen by the Bourbons from the church of the Carmine and disappear forever.

1817

Stendhal arrives in Naples.

1860

The Bourbon king flees as Garibaldi and his forces reach Naples; in the interregnum, order is maintained in Naples by the camorra.

1890 *circa*

After a major cholera epidemic in 1883, most of the old medieval quarters along the waterfront of Naples, largely unchanged since the times of Boccaccio and Masaniello, are razed and rebuilt along the axis of a new main road from the railway station to the Castelnuovo; the coast at Santa Lucia is transformed by reclamation work.

1943

Naples rises against its German occupiers and the Wehrmacht abandons the city.

American and British forces arrive and occupy Naples.

1944

Vesuvius erupts.

1949

Fernand Braudel publishes the first version of *The Mediterranean and the Mediterranean World in the Age of Philip II*; a revised and amplified edition will follow in 1966.

1980

An earthquake devastates Irpinia and damages Naples: two thousand die.

1982

Hundreds die in gang wars in Naples.

Notes

page vi
> *Mendicus exul*   Petronius, *Satyricon* 81
> *Vvuie che facite*   Anonimo napoletano, *Santa Lucia*

Preface

page xvii
> *The Case*   John T. Spike, 'The Case of the Master of the Annunciation to the
> Shepherds, alias Bartolomeo Passante', in *Studi di Storia dell'Arte* 3, 1992,
> pp203–12
>
> *academic debates*   John T. Spike in *Darkness and Light. Caravaggio and his World*,
> exhibition catalogue, Sydney and Melbourne 2003 p152

page xviii
> *pignatta maritata*   *pignatta maritata* or *minestra maritata*, the original Neapolitan
> dish, a soup in which a small amount of pork is married with a large
> amount of the many kinds of green leaf vegetable that along with fruit were
> the diet in the times before pasta, when Neapolitans were known to other
> Italians as *mangiafoglie*, or *leaf eaters*.

I   Canopus

page 2
> *grabbed*   *pigliato dai Turchi*

page 5

Little Ferrante Ferrantino

page 6

they serve cit Antonio Ghirelli, *Storia di Napoli* [1973], rev ed Torino 1992 p19

Those people C.P. Cavafy, 'Waiting for the barbarians', in *Collected Poems* tr
    Keeley & Sherrard ed Savidis, Princeton 1975 p18

page 16

the most crowded Stendhal, *Rome, Naples et Florence (1826)* in Stendhal, *Voyages*
    en Italie ed De Litto, Paris 1973 p511

the patter John Horne Burns, *The Gallery* [1947], New York 2004 p208

page 17

amari bitters and all very sweet

page 20

Tower of Babel Wien, Kunsthistorisches Museum

page 23

Tavola Strozzi Napoli, S Martino

page 24

from there Carlo Celano, *Notizie del bello dell'antico e del curioso della città di Napoli*
    [1692] ed Chiarini [1856–1860], facsimile reprint Napoli 2000, Vol V
    Tomo I p734

page 27

'a finanz' guardia di finanza, customs and excise police

page 28

wild Celano 1856 Vol IV p636

the Neapolitans Celano 1856 Vol IV p636

Are we up Celano 1856 Vol IV p636

page 29

Spanish Quarters Quartieri spagnoli

page 30

full of Celano 1856 Vol IV p544

fights Celano 1856 Vol IV p544

page 33

housing Luigi Firpo, 'Campanella, Tommaso' in *Dizionario Biografico degli*
    Italiani Vol XVII, Roma 1974 p375

page 34

I've burnt cit Firpo 1974 p375

Natural Magic Giovambattista Della Porta, *Magia naturalis*, Napoli 1589, *De*
    rifractione 1593

page 35

the devouring Tommaso Campanella, 'Al carcere', in *Opere di Giordano Bruno e*
    di Tommaso Campanella ed Guzzo & Amerio, Milano & Napoli 1956 pp853f

page 38

make new law contemporary report cit Germana Ernst in Tommaso
    Campanella, *La città del sole* ed Ernst, Milano 1996 p10

tortured Campanella 1996 p9

II   Quarters

the richest   Miguel de Cervantes, *Don Quixote de La Mancha*, Primera parte, Capítulo LI [1605], *Obras Completas*, Madrid 1993 Vol I p520

page 68

the Spanish   cit Benedetto Croce, 'Scene della vita dei soldati spagnuoli a Napoli' [1926] in Croce, *Un paradiso abitato da diavoli* ed Galasso, Milano 2006 p51

III   Wings

page 79

the bearded woman   Giovambattista Della Porta, *Della fisionomia dell'huomo*, Napoli 1610 p246, cit James Clifton '"Ad vivum mire depinxit". Toward a Reconstruction of Ribera's Art Theory' in *Storia dell'arte* 83, 1995 p127 n7

she has   11 February 1631, cit Clifton 1995 pp126f: from G. De Vito, 'Ribera e la "svolta" degli anni trenta' in *Ricerche sul '600 napoletano*, Milano 1983 p43

The Bearded Lady   Toledo, Museo Fundación Duque de Lerma

page 80

painted [her]   ad vivum mire depinxit cit Clifton 1995 p112

miracle of nature   magnum natura miraculum cit Clifton 1995 p112

page 81

Creatures   Cristoforo Colombo cit Gwen Benwell & Arthur Waugh, *Sea Enchantress. The Tale of the Mermaid and her Kin*, London 1961 p81

page 82

their high   Homer, *The Odyssey* tr Fagles, New York 1996, XII l199 p277

leaving us   James George Frazer in Apollodorus, *The Library*, ed & tr Frazer [1921], Cambridge Mass & London 1996, Vol II p291 n2

from the thighs   Apollodorus 1996 Vol II p291

page 84

meadow   Homer 1996 XII l51 p273

lying face down   Gabriel García Márquez, 'A Very Old Man with Enormous Wings. A Tale for Children' [1968], in *Collected Stories* tr Rabassa, New York &c 1984 p205

page 85

too calm   Federico Fellini, 'La dolce vita' in *Quattro film*, Torino 1974 p278

something between   Fellini 1974 pp278f

throw it back   Fellini 1974 p279

familiar   García Márquez 1984 p205

page 86

no longer   García Márquez 1984 p210

this was   Vladimir Nabokov, *Lolita* [1955] in *Novels 1955–1962*, New York 1996 p11

page 88

millennial adolescence   Giuseppe Tomasi di Lampedusa, 'La sirena' [1957] in *Opere* ed Polo, Milano 1995 p426

sailors and fishermen   Tomasi di Lampedusa 1995 p426

She only ate   Tomasi di Lampedusa 1995 pp426f

page 90

mud and ashes   Adolf Hitler 1943 cit Ghirelli 1992 p508

finding [Naples]   Fabrizia Ramondino *Althénopis* [1983], Torino 1995 p10

expressed a preference   Norman Lewis, *Naples '44. An Intelligence Officer in the Italian Labyrinth* [1978] New York 1994 p61

boiled and served   Lewis 1994 p61

all Neapolitans   Lewis 1994 p61

A faint cry   Curzio Malaparte, *La pelle* [1949], Firenze 1966 p175

A little girl   Malaparte 1966 pp175f

page 91

weare Both feete   Ovid, *Shakespeare's Ovid being Arthur Golding's translation of the Metamorphoses* [1567], ed Rouse, London 1904, V ll686f p115

page 93

the little Spaniard   *lo spagnoletto*

during the first   Jusepe de Ribera 1625, cit Jonathan Brown, *Painting in Spain 1500–1700. Yale University Press Pelican History of Art*, New Haven & London 1998 p4

page 94

a loving mother   Ribera 1625, cit Brown 1998 p4

page 95

Seven Works of Mercy   Napoli, Pio Monte della Misericordia

visit the sick   Giulio Cesare Capaccio, *Il forastiero* [1634 but 1630], facsimile reprint ed Strazzullo, Napoli 1993 p921

Matthew   Roma, S Luigi dei Francesi

page 96

I was   *The Gospel according to St Matthew* tr 1611, 25 35f

page 99

people's representative   *eletto del popolo*

got rich   Venetian resident in dispatches 16 May 1585, cit Rosario Villari, *La rivolta antispagnola a Napoli. Le origini (1585–1647)* [1967], Roma & Bari 1994 p42 n25

over 400,000 tomoli   G.A. Summonte, *Historia della Città e Regno di Napoli* 1643 cit Villari 1994 p38 n17

he would make   Venetian resident 16 May 1585, cit Villari 1994 p42 n25

page 100

Everyone seems   cit Villari 1994 p42 n25

All the rich   Tomaso Costo 1585 cit Villari 1994 p44

page 101

The mob   Capaccio 1630 p489

Now you've got   Anon, *Il tumulto napoletano dell'anno 1585* cit Villari 1994 p52

they say   Anon, *Il tumulto . . . 1585* cit Villari 1994 p52

you couldn't   Anon, *Il tumulto . . . 1585* cit Villari 1994 p52 n55

page 102

    The loaves   Anon cit Giuseppe Galasso, *Alla periferia dell'impero. Il regno di Napoli nel periodo spagnolo (secoli XVI–XVII)*, Torino 1994 p345

    the famine   Fabrizio Barnaba 23 April 1607 cit Galasso 1994 p345

    would be abandoned   Duke of Urbino's agent 5 December 1615, cit Galasso 1994 pp345f

page 103

    Whipping   Napoli, Capodimonte

    Resurrection   lost

page 104

    the house   census 1616 cit Brown 1998 p148

    The Sense of Taste   Hartford, Wadsworth Atheneum

    Bean Eater   *Il Mangiafagioli*: Roma, Galleria Colonna

    Sight   Ciudad Mexico, Museo Franz Mayer

page 105

    tainted / His brush   George Gordon, Lord Byron 1823, *Don Juan* Canto XIII 71 ll7f

    Philip   Madrid, Prado

    Lawrence   Melbourne, National Gallery of Victoria

page 107

    standard martyrdom   Brown 1998 p151

    In the foreground   Brown 1998 p151

    Peter Killed   Roma, S Maria del Popolo

    Pray you   William Shakespeare 1605, *The Tragedy of King Lear*, V 3 l311

page 108

    Jeromes   Montserrat, Museo del Monasterio de Santa Maria & Roma, Galleria Borghese

    Drunken Silenus   Napoli, Capodimonte

page 109

    Apollo Skinning Marsyas   Napoli, Capodimonte & Bruxelles, Beaux-arts

    Ixion   *Ixion*: Madrid, Prado

page 110

    a Neapolitan   Giordano Bruno 1584, *La cena de le ceneri*, Dialogo quarto, in Bruno, *Dialoghi filosofici italiani* ed Ciliberto, Milano 2000 p101

    Clubfoot Boy   Paris, Louvre

IV   Waterfront

page 113

    extremely beautiful   Giovanni Boccaccio circa 1350, *Decameron*, ed Branca, Milano 1985 II 5 p120

    Bad Hole   *Malpertugio*

page 114

    to die   Boccaccio 1985 p133

    Prostitution in Naples   Salvatore Di Giacomo, *La prostituzione in Napoli nei secoli XV, XVI e XVII. Documenti inediti* [1899], Napoli 1968

Littlehole Lane   Vico Pertusillo

or being so   Di Giacomo 1968 pp45f

page 115

looked like   Boccaccio 1985 p129

a left-hand turn   Boccaccio 1985 p129

loyal familiar   Robert of Anjou 1328 cit Branca in Boccaccio 1985 pL

raised in Naples   Boccaccio 1363, 'Epistola a Francesco Nelli' in Giovanni
   Boccaccio, *Opere in versi. Corbaccio. Trattatello in laude di Dante. Prose latine.*
   Epistole ed Ricci, Milano & Napoli 1965 p1160

The brilliant   Vittore Branca in Boccaccio 1985 pL

page 117

living in   Benedetto Croce, *Storie e leggende napoletane* [1919] ed Galasso, Milano
   1990 pp86f

page 119

the first   Vittore Branca in Boccaccio 1985 pLII

when he makes   Domenico Rea, 'Boccaccio a Napoli' in *Opere* ed Durante,
   Milano 2005 pp1405f

I not only   Giovanni Boccaccio 1344, 'L'Elegia di Madonna Fiammetta', in
   Boccaccio, *Decameron. Filocolo. Ameto. Fiammetta* ed Salinari & Sapegno,
   Milano & Napoli 1952 VI pp1197f

page 120

Boccaccio   Rea 2005 p1406

Crow   Corbaccio circa 1365

page 122

a wretched   'Epistola a Francesco Nelli' 1363, in Boccaccio 1965 pp1154f

page 123

greedy and hungry   Boccaccio 1965 pp1155f

The chief   Boccaccio 1965 p1156

The food   Boccaccio 1965 pp1157f

page 124

All I wanted   Boccaccio 1965 pp1159f

in case   Boccaccio 1965 p1160

page 125

the totality   Erich Auerbach, *Mimesis. The Representation of Reality in Western
   Literature* [1946] tr Trask [1953], Princeton & Oxford 2003 p259

page 126

lovely   Boccaccio, *Decameron* VII 2 in Boccaccio 1985 p567

good-looking   Boccaccio 1985 p567

page 127

What's the story   Boccaccio 1985 p568

some really   Boccaccio 1985 p568

not that kind   Boccaccio 1985 p568

longue durée   very long term in Fernand Braudel, *The Mediterranean and the
   Mediterranean World in the Age of Philip II* [1949 & 1966] tr Reynolds [1971],
   Berkeley Los Angeles & London 1995, Vol I p23

page 128

blinded   Rea 2005 p1402

just as   Boccaccio 1985 p570

page 132

come from   Camillo Porzio, *La Conguira de' Baroni del Regno di Napoli contra Il Re Ferdinando I* [1565], ed D'Aloe, Napoli 1859 p16

such wealth   Porzio 1859 p15

page 133

He was   Porzio 1859 p175

his sons   Porzio 1859 p176

page 134

the king   Porzio 1859 p176

waiting   Porzio 1859 p175

they began   Porzio 1859 p176

Amazement   Porzio 1859 p176

the people   Porzio 1859 p177

The king   Porzio 1859 p176

Everything   Porzio 1859 p175

page 135

and when the king's   Porzio 1859 p177

147 pieces   Porzio 1859 p178 & n

They were shut   Porzio 1859 pp178f

most disappeared   Alan Ryder, 'The papal states and the kingdom of Naples' in *The New Cambridge Medieval History Volume VII c.1415–c.1500* [1998] ed Allmand, Cambridge 2006 p585

even his women   Porzio 1859 pp175f

as if he wanted   Porzio 1859 p177

was dragged   Porzio 1859 p182

page 136

high enough   Porzio 1859 p184

often behave   Niccolò Machiavelli circa 1513 in *Discorsi sopra la prima deca di Tito Livio* [1513–1517], in Niccolò Machiavelli, *Opere I* ed Vivanti, Torino 1997 Libro primo capitolo 40, p288

had attained   Machiavelli 1997 Libro terzo, capitolo 6 pp429f

museum of mummies   Jacob Burckhardt, *The Civilization of the Renaissance in Italy* [1860] tr Middleton [1878], London 1995 p25

the end   Burckhardt 1995 p26

page 137

men utterly hostile   Machiavelli 1997 p311

page 138

honestly rich   Matteo Bandello, *Novelle* [1554], Vol 1 ed Brognoligo, Bari & Roma 1910 XXVI p346

their marriage   Bandello 1910 p350

You know   Bandello 1910 p351

pregnant   Bandello 1910 p351

page 139

astonished   Bandello 1910 p353

I'd rather live   Bandello 1910 p353

they would do   Bandello 1910 p351

made so many   Bandello 1910 p354

knew that   Bandello 1910 p354

page 140

not seeing   Bandello 1910 p354

Bologna was riding   Bandello 1910 pp354f

Bologna and   Bandello 1910 p355

a very gallant   Bandello 1910 p347

page 141

not wanting   Bandello 1910 p356

page 142

My lord   Bandello 1910 p355

there were people   Bandello 1910 p357

he wanted   Bandello 1910 p357

page 143

proportional   Bernardo De Dominici, *Vite de' pittori, scultori ed architetti napoletani*, Napoli 1742–1745 & facsimile reprint Sala Bolognese 1979 Vol II p295

he never finished   De Dominici 1742–1745 Vol II p298

page 144

Matthew   Roma, S Luigi dei Francesi

page 145

Immaculate Conception   Napoli, S Maria della Stella

page 146

the completely   Michael Stoughton in *Civiltà del Seicento a Napoli* [1984] exhibition catalogue, Napoli 1998 Vol I p200

Rosary Madonna   Wien, Kunsthistorisches Museum

Mary Dead   Paris, Louvre

Pilgrims' Madonna   Roma, S Agostino

page 147

Madonna and Child in Glory   Catanzaro, Museo Provinciale

Crucifixion   Napoli, Museo Civico di Castelnuovo

Andrew   Cleveland, Ohio, Cleveland Museum of Art

page 148

Salome with John the Baptist's Head   Firenze, Corridoio Vasariano

Christ Baptized by John   Napoli, Quadreria dei Girolamini

Ursula Transfixed   Napoli, Banca Commerciale Italiana

Signor Damiano   Lanfranco Massa 1610 in Vincenzo Pacelli, *L'ultimo Caravaggio. Dalla Maddalena a mezza figura ai due san Giovanni (1606–1610)*, II ed Todi 1995 pp104f

as for Caracciolo   Massa 1610 in Pacelli 1995 p104

V Shadow

page 154

he liked women Giordano Bruno cit Mocenigo 1592 in Bruno, *Un'autobiografia*
 ed Ciliberto, Napoli 1994 p44 & in Luigi Firpo, *Il processo di Giordano Bruno*
 ed Quaglioni, Roma 1993 p158

the church Giordano Bruno cit Mocenigo 1592 in Bruno 1994 p45 & Firpo
 1993 pp158f

They've discovered Giordano Bruno, *La cena de le ceneri* 1584 in Bruno, *Dialoghi
 filosofici italiani* ed Ciliberto Milano 2000 p27

page 155

wise, beautiful Giordano Bruno 1582, 'Alla Signora Morgana B.' in Bruno,
 Opere Complete Œuvres complètes I *Candelaio* ed Aquilecchia, II ed Paris 2003
 p11

page 156

to learn Giordano Bruno 1592 in Bruno 1994 p41 & Firpo 1993 p156

Naples and Rome Bruno 2003 V 18 p355

when he Francesco Graziani 1592, cit Luigi Firpo, *Il processo di Giordano Bruno*
 ed Quaglioni, Roma 1993 p251

page 157

After hearing Graziani 1592, cit Firpo 1993 p251

declamation cit Vincenzo Spampanato, *Vita di Giordano Bruno con documenti editi
 ed inediti*, Messina 1921 & facsimile reprint Paris 2000 pp131f n3

Then he discovered Graziani 1592 cit Firpo 1993 p251

page 158

David with Goliath's Head Roma, Galleria Borghese

David Roma, Galleria Borghese

page 159

Salome with John the Baptist's Head Sevilla, Museo de Bellas Artes

personal L. Bortolotti, 'Lomi (Gentileschi), Orazio' in *Dizionario Biografico degli
 Italiani*, Roma & online at www.treccani.it

page 160

[Caracciolo] Lanfranco Massa 1624, cit Stefano Causa, 'Battistello' in *Battistello
 Caracciolo e il primo naturalismo a Napoli* ed Bologna, exhibition catalogue,
 Napoli 1991 p188

repeatedly asked Pio Monte della Misericordia, *Libro delle conclusioni* 27 August
 1613, cit Vincenzo Pacelli, *Caravaggio. Le Sette Opere di Misericordia* [1984], II
 ed Napoli 1993 p68

page 161

may not Pio Monte della Misericordia 1613 cit Pacelli 1993 p68

that said painting Pio Monte della Misericordia 1613 cit Pacelli 1993 p69

no person Pio Monte della Misericordia *Libro delle conclusioni* 1 June 1621 cit
 Pacelli 1993 p69

Peter Freed Napoli, Pio Monte della Misericordia

page 162

a thin man   Charles-Nicolas Cochin, *Voyage d'Italie*, Paris 1763 cit Roberto
  Longhi, 'Antologia della critica caravaggesca' *Paragone* 21, 1951 p49

not in the air   Cochin 1763 cit Longhi 1951 p49

page 164

having highly   Cosimo II of Tuscany 1618, cit Stefano Causa, 'Battistello' in
  Battistello Caracciolo . . . 1991 p192

page 165

Spaccanapoli   Splitnaples

in their cells   cit Spampanato 1921 p183 n1

page 166

trouble   1556 & 1558 proclamations cit Spampanato 1921 p107

page 167

a lookout   Lagarde cit Spampanato pp123f & n1

many times   Archivio di Stato di Napoli, *Monasteri soppressi* [v Spampanato 1921
  pp601ff] 1568 cit Spampanato 1921 p137 & n4

spoiled   Monasteri soppressi 1570 cit Spampanato 1921 p138 & n4

incorrigible   Monasteri soppressi 1570 cit Spampanato 1921 p138 & nn

page 168

excommunication   Monasteri soppressi 1571 cit Spampanato 1921 p135 n4

repeated   Monasteri soppressi 1572 cit Spampanato 1921 p197 & n1

armed   Monasteri soppressi 1571 cit Spampanato 1921 p196

deeply   Monasteri soppressi 1571 cit Spampanato 1921 p196

life   Monasteri soppressi 1572 cit Spampanato 1921 p197 & n2

witnessed   Monasteri soppressi 1574 cit Spampanato 1921 p199

many scandals   Monasteri soppressi 1568 cit Spampanato 1921 p139 & n3

lapses   Monasteri soppressi 1568 cit Spampanato 1921 p139 n5

especially serious   Villari 1994 p75 n117

page 169

a delicately   cit Villari 1994 p75 n117

knights   cit Villari 1994 p75 n117

gravely pained   Santori cit Spampanato 1921 p136 & n2

heretics   cit Villari 1994 pp71f

page 170

carrying pistols   cit Spampanato 1921 p202

page 171

ready   Spampanato 1921 p202

happy   cit Spampanato 1921 p203

all of Naples   cit Spampanato 1921 p203

My master   Giordano Bruno 1592 in Bruno 1994 p89 & Firpo 1993 pp190f

page 172

for making   cit Spampanato 1921 p231

the evil   cit Spampanato 1921 p232

made secret use   Giordano Bruno 1592 in Bruno 1994 p90 & Firpo 1993 p191

page 173

in a coach   Guillaume Cotin 1585, 'Documenti parigini' cit Spampanato 1921 pp654f

jump   Giordano Bruno 1592 in Bruno 1994 p90 & Firpo 1993 p191

page 174

I received   Giordano Bruno 1592 in Bruno 1994 p90 & Firpo 1993 p191

page 175

the crude   De Dominici 1742–1745 Vol II p276

Christ   De Dominici 1742–1745 Vol II p277

using the same   De Dominici 1742–1745 Vol II p277

page 176

Christ Washing the Feet   Napoli, S Martino

Joseph and Potiphar's Wife   Zürich, Fondation Rau

Judgement of Solomon   Firenze, private coll

Lot and His Daughters   Milano, private coll

Noli Mi Tangere   Don't touch me: Prato, Museo Civico

page 177

Joseph and the Child Jesus   Venezia, private coll

Earthly Trinity   Napoli, Pietà dei Turchini

page 178

scugnizzi   street kids

page 179

Whipping   Napoli, Capodimonte

Lucy's Burial   Siracusa, Palazzo Bellomo

Lazarus Raised   Messina, Museo Regionale

Cosmas and Damian   Berlin, Staatliche Museen Gemäldegalerie

bronze light   Vincenzo Pacelli, La pittura napoletana da Caravaggio a Luca
    Giordano, Napoli 1996 p55

grave bronze   Roberto Longhi, Battistello 1915, cit Causa in Battistello
    Caracciolo . . . 1991 p181

Child Jesus   Napoli, private coll

page 180

an Italian   cit Benedetto Croce, Vite di avventure di fede e di passione [1935] ed
    Galasso, Milano 2002 p231

page 181

gentleman   Croce 2002 p206

a naturally severe   Croce 2002 p209

page 182

to live   Croce 2002 p220

page 184

son of a   Paul VI Carafa 1557 cit Bernardo Navagero cit Croce 2002 p239

holy and perfect   Adriano Prosperi, Tribunali della coscienza. Inquisitori, confessori,
    missionari, Torino 1996 p206

if our own   Paul VI Carafa 1557 cit Navagero cit Croce 2002 p239

page 185

long grown used   Jean Calvin 1558 cit Croce 2002 p244

loves him   Calvin 1558 cit Croce 2002 p244 n2

page 186

a magnanimous   cit Croce 2002 p282

page 187

seemed more   Scipione Ammirato cit Croce 2002 p285

telling everyone   Ammirato cit Croce 2002 p285

page 188

Physician   Delio Cantimori, *Eretici italiani del Cinquecento* [1939] ed Prosperi,
  Torino 1992 p49

this daring Spaniard   Cantimori 1992 p59

VI   Underground

page 190

candleman   candelaio

insipid   'Argomento ed ordine della commedia' in Bruno 2003 p17

A man   Bruno 2003 IV 4 p225

spent all night   Bruno 2003 IV 9 p249

leg on   Bruno 2003 IV 9 p249

page 191

the world   Bruno 2003 II 3 p139

page 193

He never   Antonio Persio [1542–1612] cit Vincenzo Spampanato in
  'Introduzione', Giordano Bruno, *Opere italiane III, Candelaio* ed
  Spampanato, Bari 1909 pXXVIII

Ladies   Giambattista Del Tufo cit Spampanato in Bruno 1909 pXXVII

whose art   Romeo De Maio, *Pittura e Controriforma a Napoli*, Roma & Bari 1983
  p13

a great friend   De Dominici 1742–1745 Vol II p120

quite extraordinary   De Dominici 1742–1745 Vol II p119

page 194

Polidoro   Giorgio Vasari 1550 & 1568, 'Pulidoro da Caravaggio e Maturino
  Fiorentino' in *Le vite de' piu eccellenti pittori scultori ed architettori scritte da
  Giorgio Vasari pittore aretino*, ed Milanesi Firenze 1906 facsimile reprint
  Firenze 1998, Vol V p150

They set   Vasari 1906 Vol V p151

in weaponry   Pietro Summonte 1524, cit Pierluigi Leone de Castris, 'La pittura
  del Cinquecento', in *Storia e civiltà della Campania. Il Rinascimento e l'Età
  Barocca*, ed Pugliese Caratelli, Napoli 1994 p181

page 200

bring back   Virgil 24 BC, *Aeneid* tr Fagles, New York 2006 VI ll792ff

page 201

Here is   Virgil 2006 VI l791

page 202

antro della Sibilla   Sibyl's cave

page 205

  great ditches   Plutarch circa 110, *Life of Lucullus* 39 tr North 1579

page 206

  homes of Venus   Martial 88, *Epigrams* IV 44

  the town   *civitas* cit Theodor Kraus, *Pompeii and Herculaneum* [1973] New York
      1975 p13

  apt for   *Cronaca di Partenope* 1382

page 207

  graeca urbs   Petronius circa 65, *Satyricon* 81

page 208

  What I'd like   Petronius, *Satyricon* 48

  dangling   Petronius, *Satyricon* 48

  I want   Petronius, *Satyricon* 48

page 209

  the theatre   Tacitus circa 120, *Annals* XV 34

  practically   Tacitus, *Annals* XV 33

  only   Suetonius 121, *Lives of the Caesars* VI 22

page 210

  snivelled   Martial, *Epigrams* VIII 55 120

page 211

  Arms   Virgil, *Aeneid* I 11

page 212

  dark wood   *selva oscura*: Dante Alighieri circa 1307, *Inferno* I 12

  hard to   P *Vergili Maronis Aeneidos Liber VI*, ed T.E. Page [1888], London 1940
      pxx

page 213

  Sunt lacrimae   Virgil, *Aeneid* I 1462

page 214

  of those   Plutarch circa 110, *Crassus* 8 tr North 1579

page 215

  divers heardmen   Plutarch, *Crassus* 9 tr North

page 217

  In the end   Plutarch, Crassus 11 tr North

  saying   Plutarch, *Crassus* 11 tr North

page 218

  This Spartacus   Plutarch, *Crassus* 8 tr North

page 219

  a huge   Giovan Battista Manso, marchese di Villa 1631, cit Leonardo Di Mauro,
      'L'eruzione del Vesuvio nel 1631' in *Civiltà del Seicento a Napoli* [1984],
      Napoli 1998, Vol II p37

  burnt clothes   Manso 1631 p37

  People went   Manso 1631 p38

page 220

  increased   Manso 1631 p38

  To take   Manso 1631 pp38f

as the holy   Manso 1631 p39

miraculous   Manso 1631 p39

page 221

People   De Maio 1983 p209

page 222

the church   De Maio 1983 p45

monumental   Touring Club Italiano, *Guida d'Italia. Napoli e dintorni*, VI edition,
  Milano 2001 p216

page 223

His reputation   De Dominici 1742–1745 Vol II p296

His commissions   De Dominici 1742–1745 Vol II p298

page 224

no other   De Dominici 1742–1745 Vol II p299

page 225

had just done   Carlo Cesare Malvasia, 'Vita di Guido Reni' in *Felsina pittrice.
  Vite de' pittori bolognesi* [1678] ed Zanotti, Bologna 1841 facsimile reprint
  Sala Bolognese 1967, Vol II p25

mistook   Giambattista Passeri, *Vite de' pittori scultori ed architetti che anno lavorato in
  Roma. Morti dal 1641 fino al 1673* [1679], Roma 1772 facsimile reprint Sala
  Bolognese 1976 p80

page 226

released   Rudolf & Margot Wittkower, *Born under Saturn. The Character and
  Conduct of Artists: A Documented History from Antiquity to the French Revolution*
  [1963], New York & London 1969 p251

VII Market

page 227

Market Place in Naples   Medinaceli, Casa Ducal

page 230

The painting   De Dominici 1742–1745 Vol III p196

The Market   Celano 2000 Vol IV p185

packed   Giovanni Battista Chiarini 1859 in Celano 2000 Vol IV p197

page 231

for years   De Dominici 1742–1745 Vol III p190

Schoolmarm   Napoli, Capodimonte

Lucy Giving to the Poor   Napoli, Capodimonte

oracle of battles   De Dominici 1742–1745 Vol III p80

battle scene   F. Saxl, 'The Battle Scene without a Hero. Aniello Falcone and his
  Patrons', *Journal of the Warburg and Courtauld Institutes* III, 1939 p70

showed   G. Scavizzi, 'Falcone, Aniello', *Dizionario Biografico degli Italiani*

page 232

part of   G. Scavizzi, 'Falcone, Aniello', *Dizionario Biografico degli Italiani*

Concert   Madrid, Prado

Self-portrait   London, National Gallery

His main   De Dominici 1742–1745 Vol III p192
page 234
his greener   De Dominici 1742–1745 Vol III p192
page 235
move[d] viewers   De Dominici 1742–1745 Vol III p192
Women Washing Laundry   Napoli, private coll
Fishermen Attacked   Napoli, private coll
Criminals Punished   Napoli, S Martino
Riding Lesson   Napoli, private coll
page 236
The workaday   Malvasia 1841 p237
with his whole   Passeri 1772 p33
page 237
the only   Passeri 1772 p33
hated him   Passeri 1772 p42
page 238
was no painter   Passeri cit Clifton 1995 p129 n46
didn't even   Giovanni Pietro Bellori, *Le vite de' pittori scultori e architetti moderni*
    [1672], ed Borea, Torino 1976 p353 & Passeri 1772 p38
overworking   Bellori 1976 p353
uncouth   Passeri 1772 p44
turned   Malvasia 1841 p238
since nothing   Malvasia 1841 p238
Gennaro Leaves the Furnace Unharmed   Napoli, Cappella del Tesoro di S
    Gennaro
page 239
the compositional   Alfonso E. Pérez-Sánchez, 'Ribera, Jusepe de', *Dictionary of
    Art*, ed Turner, London & New York 1996 Vol 26 p311
Domenichino's Revenge   Jonathan Brown, *Painting in Spain 1500–1700*, Yale
    University Press, Pelican History of Art, New Haven & London 1998 p161
page 240
the counterfeiter   Benedetto Croce 1892, 'Il falsario', *Napoli nobilissima* I, cit
    Thomas Willette, 'Bernardo De Dominici . . . contributo alla riabilitazione
    di una fonte' in *Ricerche sul '600 napoletano*, Milano 1986 p256
shameless lies   *spudorate menzogne*: Ulisse Prota-Giurleo, *Pittori napoletani del
    Seicento*, Napoli 1953 p97
shameless mystification   *spudorata mistificazione*: Prota-Giurleo 1953 p123
his saints   De Dominici 1742–1745 Vol II p298
certainly invented   F. Abbate, 'Corenzio, Belisario' in *Dizionario Biografico degli
    Italiani*
page 241
our Luigi   Carlo Celano, *Notizie del bello dell'antico e del curioso della città di Napoli*
    [1692], ed Chiarini Napoli 1856–1860, facsimile reprint Napoli 2000, Vol
    IV p190

page 242

Luigi was   Celano 1856–1860 Vol IV p191

he had   Celano 1856–1860 Vol IV p191

page 243

a Flemish   Capaccio 1634 p863

Roomer   De Dominici 1742–1745 Vol III p343

a lover   De Dominici 1742–1745 Vol III p343

His ships   Francis Haskell, *Patrons and painters. A Study in the Relations between Italian Art and Society in the Age of the Baroque* [1963], New Haven & London 1980 p205

page 244

a series   Capaccio 1634 p863

page 245

a very poor   Michelangelo Schipa, *Masaniello*, Bari 1925 p68

the most audacious   Villari 1994 p138

page 247

mothers   17 March 1642 cit Villari 1994 p148

page 248

stunted   Francesco Capecelatro c1650, *Annali della città di Napoli*, cit Villari 1994 p139

This marriage   Bartolomeo d'Aquino 1640 cit Villari 1994 pp178f

page 249

fierce   Viceroy Medina 1640 cit Villari 1994 p179

a class solidarity   Villari 1994 p178

page 250

No longer   Anon ms 1647 cit Silvana D'Alessio, *Masaniello. La sua vita e il mito in Europa*, Roma 2007 p66

married women   Bartolommeo Capasso, *La casa e la famiglia di Masaniello. Ricordi della storia & della vita napoletana nel secolo XVII* [1875 & 1905], Napoli 1919, facsimile reprint as *Masaniello. Ricordi della storia & della vita napoletana nel secolo XVII* Napoli 1987 p80

grain   Capasso 1919 p42

bad government   mal governo

page 252

fetch a hiding   cit Schipa 1925 p73

page 253

handsome   D'Alessio 2007 p68

a youth   Buraña, *Relaciones . . .* Madrid 1650, cit Giuseppe Campolieti, *Masaniello*, Novara 1989 p44

mad homosexual   Buraña 1650 cit Campolieti 1989 p42

page 254

Marco   *se ne servì il Marco per creato dentro le carcere* Capecelatro 1647 cit D'Alessio 2007 p132

a witty   Giraffi 1647 cit D'Alessio 2007 p62

page 256

with payment   Braudel 1995 Vol I p89

page 257

before the riches   John A. Marino, *Pastoral Economics in the Kingdom of Naples*,
    Baltimore & London 1988 p17

green lanes   M.L. Ryder, *Sheep and Man* [1983], London 2007 p373

White dogs   Ryder 2007 pp373f

page 258

and except   Ryder 2007 pp374f

driven by   Ryder 2007 p374

Transhumance   Braudel 1995, Vol I p94

page 259

shepherd organization   Ryder 2007 p375

VIII Palace

page 270

Speedy Luke   Luca Fa'presto

Self-portrait   Napoli, Pio Monte della Misericordia

page 272

The Story of Stories   Lo cunto de li cunti

page 273

Mary Dead   Paris, Louvre

left undying   Ferdinando Gonzaga 26 June 1610, cit L. Pannella, 'Basile,
    Andreana (Andriana), detta la bella Adriana' in *Dizionario Biografico degli
    Italiani*

page 275

the oldest   Benedetto Croce, 'Giambattista Basile e l'elaborazione artistica delle
    fiabe popolari' [1925] in Croce, *Storia dell'età barocca in Italia* [1929], Milano
    1993 p539

kitchen fire cat   gatta cenerentola

I wish   Giambattista Basile, 'La gatta Cenerentola' in *Lo cunto de li cunti overo Lo
    trattenemiento de peccerille* [1634–1636], tr & ed Rak, Milano 1986 I 6 pp124f

page 277

flew to   Basile 1986 I 6 pp136f

But an old   Basile 1986 I 10 pp208f

page 278

I had myself   Basile 1986 I 10 pp214f

I'm the shade   Basile 1986 II 7 pp390f

monster   orco, female orca

page 281

One day   Capasso 1919 p70

page 283

followed by   E. Di Rienzo, 'Genoino, Giulio' in *Dizionario Biografico degli Italiani*
    Vol LIII, Roma 1999 p140

page 284

The widespread   Villari 1994 p199

page 286

He persuaded Giordano Bruno 1592, in Bruno 1994 p48 & in Firpo 1993 p160

page 287

in order Bruno 1592, in Bruno 1994 p47 & in Firpo 1993 p160

I had no Bruno 1592, in Bruno 1994 p47 & in Firpo 1993 p160

a habit Bruno 1592, in Bruno 1994 p47 & in Firpo 1993 p160

page 288

arrested for 'Documenti ginevrini' I 1579 cit Spampanato 1921 p632

the monk 'Documenti ginevrini' II 1579 cit Spampanato 1921 p633

claimed 'Documenti ginevrini' IV 1579 cit Spampanato 1921 p634

for having made 'Documenti ginevrini' V 1579 cit Spampanato 1921 pp634f

page 289

not to tolerate 'Documenti ginevrini' IV 1579 cit Spampanato 1921 p634

freedom Bruno 1592 in Bruno 1994 p47 & in Firpo 1993 p160

I became Bruno 1592 in Bruno 1994 p49 & in Firpo 1993 pp161f

page 290

that Italian George Abbott 1604 cit Frances A. Yates, *Giordano Bruno and the Hermetic Tradition* [1964], Chicago 1991 pp208f

hart George Abbott 1604 cit Yates 1991 p208

page 291

[I] was born Giordano Bruno, *La cena de le ceneri* [1584], ed Guzzo Milano 1995 p85

a constellation Bruno 1995 p84

the most disrespectful Bruno 1995 p43

a most pleasant Jacopo Corbinelli 1586, cit Ciliberto 1990 p204

page 292

more things William Shakespeare 1600, *The Tragedie of Hamlet, Prince of Denmark*, I 5 ll184f

Though I was Bruno, *Oratio valedictoria* 1588, in *Opere di Giordano Bruno e Tommaso Campanella* ed Augusto Guzzo & Romano Amerio, Milano & Napoli 1956 pp686ff

I was Gospel according to St Matthew tr 1611 25.35f

page 293

My profession Bruno 1592 in Bruno 1994 p40 & in Firpo 1993 p156

He said that Zuane Mocenigo 1592 in Bruno 1994 pp23f & in Firpo 1993 pp143f

page 294

He said he Mocenigo 1592 in Bruno 1994 pp26f & in Firpo 1993 pp145f

page 295

I told him Mocenigo 1592 in Bruno 1994 pp44f & in Firpo 1993 pp158f

I heard Bruno Mocenigo 1592 in Bruno 1994 pp23f & in Firpo 1993 pp143f

I heard him Mocenigo 1592 in Bruno 1994 pp43f & in Firpo 1993 p158

page 296

no duty Inquisition 1599 cit Ricci p537

return to Inquisition 1600 cit Ricci p537

in a threatening   Kaspar Schoppe 1600 in Firpo 1993 pp348ff & cit Ricci p543

You're more   Bruno 1600 cit Schoppe in Firpo 1993 pp348ff & cit Ricci p543

page 297

tavern workers   Anon 1647 cit D'Alessio p66

When he was   Anon *Vita di Masaniello* circa 1647 cit D'Alessio p70

page 298

friends   Schipa 1925 p73

he had nothing   Anon *Vita di Masaniello* c 1647 cit D'Alessio p69

spies   T. Simonetta 1647 cit D'Alessio p37

page 299

Go and   *Gospel according to St Luke* tr 1611 10.37

page 301

One day   Lord Alexander Giraffi, *An exact history of the late revolutions in Naples and of their monstrous successes, not to be parallel'd by any antient or modern history,* London 1664 p10 [English translation by James Howell of Alessandro Giraffi, *Le rivolutioni di Napoli,* Venezia 1647]

ragged   Schipa 1925 p78

A little after   Giraffi 1664 p10

page 302

God gives   Schipa 1925 p79

I'm an honourable   Schipa 1925 p79

page 303

You're the one   T. Della Moneca, *Istoria delle revoluzioni di Napoli dell'anno 1647* . . . unpublished ms c 1647 cit D'Alessio 2007 p54

page 304

Let me   cit Schipa 1925 p82

IX   Sheep

page 306

weakness   *flaqueza en el seso* Ribera 1650 cit Walker . . . as in Vincenzo Pacelli, 'Processo tra Ribera e un committente', *Napoli Nobilissima* 1979, Vol XVII p34 n20

Don Juan José de Austria on Horseback   Madrid, Palacio Real

page 307

Adoration of the Shepherds   Escorial, San Lorenzo

Adoration   Paris, Louvre

page 308

signed by   *the two Adorations from the early 1640s in the Escorial . . . are signed by Ribera and . . . after recent restoration, can clearly be assigned to the artist,* Nicola Spinosa, 'Ribera and Neapolitan Painting' in Alfonso E. Pérez Sánchez and Nicola Spinosa, *Jusepe de Ribera 1591–1652* exhibition catalogue, New York 1992 p32 n14

Adoration   Messina, Museo Regionale

Adoration   ex Palermo, Oratorio di S Lorenzo, whereabouts unknown

page 309

Announcement to the Shepherds   Napoli, Capodimonte

page 311

shepherds   *The Gospel according to St Luke*, tr 1611 2 8ff

page 312

a ricotta   De Dominici 1742–1745 Vol III p22

page 313

Shepherds   London, National Gallery

with broomsticks, chairlegs   Schipa 1925 p83

page 314

Having burnt   Emilio Bonaventura Altieri to papal secretary of state Panciroli
    1647 cit Aurelio Musi, *La rivolta di Masaniello nella scena politica barocca* [1989]
    II ed, Napoli 2002 p94

page 315

made Naples   Marino Verde cit Schipa 1925 p86

Get back   Giuseppe Donzelli, *Partenope liberata overo Racconto dell'Heroica
    risolutione fatta dal Popolo di Napoli per sottrarsi con tutto il Regno
    dall'Insupportabil Giogo degli Sgagnuoli*, Napoli 1648 cit D'Alessio 2007 p60

a low   Maiolino Bisaccioni, *Historia delle guerre civili*, Venezia 1655 cit Musi 2002
    pp96f

page 316

this Masaniello   Ascanio Filomarino 1647 cit Musi 2002 p96

page 317

with a thousand   Masaniello 1647 cit Ghirelli 1992 p57

page 318

I ask   Masaniello 1647 cit Schipa 1925 p102

page 319

It's all done   Masaniello 1647 cit Schipa 1925 p103

page 320

Make way   Masaniello 1647 cit Schipa 1925 p106

You're done   Masaniello 1647 cit Schipa 1925 p107

page 323

dank trench   Tommaso Campanella cit Franco Mollia in Tommaso Campanella,
    La città del sole e altri scritti, ed Mollia, Milano 1991 p27

page 325

In Naples   Campanella 1996 p65

page 326

They say   Campanella 1996 pp65f

Know this   Campanella 1996 p94

page 327

Make way   Ottaviano Sauli 1647 cit D'Alessio 2007 p169

page 328

Unbelievable   Francesco Capecelatro cit Campolieti 1989 p204 *one of the* Rosario Villari, *Elogio della dissimulazione. La lotta politica nel Seicento* [1987], Roma & Bari 2003 p106

The flower Racconto . . . 1649, cit Franco Mancini, 'L'immaginario di regime. Apparati e scenografie alla corte del viceré', in *Civiltà del Seicento a Napoli* [1985] exhibition catalogue, Napoli 1998, Vol II p27

on the bank Racconto . . . 1649, cit Mancini 1998 p27

a Heaven Racconto . . . 1649, cit Mancini 1998 p27

a sublime Racconto . . . 1649, cit Mancini 1998 p27

page 331

the Cockaigne Mancini 1998 p31

at the summit Relazione . . . 1649, cit Mancini 1998 p32

page 332

cheeses Relazione . . . 1649, cit Mancini 1998 p32

representing Hell Relazione . . . 1649, cit Mancini 1998 p32

page 333

witty inscriptions Celano 2000 Vol IV p186

page 334

Masaniello's Revolt Napoli, S Martino

page 335

I'm Giuseppe cit Ottaviano Sauli 1647 cit D'Alessio 2007 p105

page 336

Announcement Birmingham, City Art Gallery

Wedding Feast of Jacob and Rachel Aix-en-Provence, Musée Granet

page 337

Girl Sniffing a Rose Milano, private coll

Announcement München, Alte Pinakothek

Announcement New Jersey, Johnson Collection

Announcement New York, ex Brooklyn Museum

Jacob and Laban's Flock Palermo, Galleria Regionale

Jacob and Laban's Flock Roma, Palazzo Braschi

Joseph and His Brothers whereabouts unknown

page 338

Schoolmaster whereabouts unknown

Lute Player whereabouts unknown

Prodigal Son's Return Napoli, Capodimonte [two] & Dulwich, Dulwich College & Bristol, City Museum

Jesus among the Doctors Napoli, Gesù Nuovo & Dublin, National Gallery & Nantes, Musée des Beaux-arts

page 339

Do not laugh William Shakespeare 1605, *The Tragedy of King Lear*, IV 7 ll68ff

page 340

Gregorio Armeno Napoli, S Gregorio Armeno

page 341

He is so De Dominici 1742–1745 Vol III pp23f

turned out   De Dominici 1742–1745 Vol III p23

page 343

the early 1630s   Unsigned entry, 'Master of the Annunciation to the Shepherds', *The Dictionary of Art* ed Turner, London & New York 1996 Vol 20 p617

a few years   Nicola Spinosa, 'La pittura del Seicento nell'Italia meridionale' in *La pittura in Italia. Il Seicento*, ed Gregori & Schleier [1988], Milano 2001 Vol II p474

Alexis   Czech Republic, Opočno Castle

The Painter's Studio   whereabouts unknown

Meninas   Madrid, Prado

Spinners   Las Hilanderas: Madrid, Prado

ANCORA   I'm still learning

in my view   Roberto Longhi 1935, 'I pittori della realtà in Francia' reprinted in *Paragone* 269, 1972 p17: & v Longhi, 'G.B. Spinelli e i naturalisti napoletani del Seicento', *Paragone* 227, 1969 p50

page 344

excellent   De Dominici 1742–1745 Vol III p84

swordsman   come solito di quei che maneggian le spade, faceva anch'egli il bizzarro e il bravo, De Dominici 1742–1745 Vol III p74

broke down   venne in umor tanto fantastico e cadde in tale stravolgimento di cervello che . . . De Dominici 1742–1745 Vol III p86

as a mark   De Dominici 1742–1745 Vol III p86

Masaniello   New York, Pierpont Morgan Library

page 345

Masaniello   Genova, Collezione Martino Oberto

Today a low fisherman   Salvator Rosa, 'La Guerra', *Satire* [. . .], cit Capasso 1919 p139

An index

of writers and artists

ALSO AVAILABLE BY PETER ROBB

M
THE CARAVAGGIO ENIGMA

M is the name of an enigma. In his short and violent life, Michelangelo Merisi, from Caravaggio, changed art forever. In the process he laid bare his own sexual longing and the brutal realities of his life with shocking frankness. Like no painter before him and few since, M the man appears in his art. Causing a huge controversy on publication, M is strikingly different from the usual painter's life. As a book about art and life and how they connect, there has never been anything quite like it.

'A great read: it grabs, it kicks, it lives'
GUARDIAN

'A terrific book ... Robb makes the work come alive, the man come alive,
and the life come alive'
TONY PARSONS

'It is a work that speaks: Peter Robb makes us listen'
THE TIMES

B L O O M S B U R Y

A DEATH IN BRAZIL

Brazil is one of the most beautiful, seductive and joyous places on earth. And a place of almost unimaginable distance between its wealthy and its poor, a place of extraordinary levels of crime, violence and corruption, whose dark past of slavery and exploitation still shows in waves of daily killings.

Peter Robb's book describes the recent rise of a boy from the bottom of the heap to become the country's first working-class president. Lula's eight years in office reversed effects of centuries of injustice, and Brazil was a world presence when Lula left office in 2011 with stratospheric levels of popular approval.

A Death in Brazil delves into Brazil's past, Baroque and beyond, to the magical first moment of Europe's New World. It explores food, art, history – the work of Brazil's great nineteenth-century novelist Machado de Assis, grandson of slaves, and the TV soaps watched nightly by tens of millions – in the recreation of a twenty-year personal encounter with The Marvellous Country.

'Robb is a superb stylist, and this brilliant dissection of modern Brazil is unputdownable'
THE SUNDAY TIMES

'Outstanding … a heady and fascinating picture of an extraordinary country'
DAILY TELEGRAPH

'Fascinating and revealing … It is the Brazil that Robb sees beyond the sensations that gives his book its great travelling dimension'
NEW YORK TIMES

ORDER YOUR COPY: BY PHONE 01256 302 699; BY EMAIL: DIRECT@MACMILLAN.CO.UK
DELIVERY IS USUALLY 3–5 WORKING DAYS. FREE POSTAGE AND PACKAGING FOR ORDERS OVER £20.
ONLINE: WWW.BLOOMSBURY.COM/BOOKSHOP
PRICES AND AVAILABILITY SUBJECT TO CHANGE WITHOUT NOTICE.

WWW.BLOOMSBURY.COM/PETERROBB

B L O O M S B U R Y